Praise for *Becoming the Witch*

"Inspiringly full to the brim with folklore, techniques, and information to connect to nature, the natural world, the night sky, and --- f... By inviting us on her journey, Danae N ;htful, refreshingly open, honest and joyful ta cour- aging us to look with awe at ourselves a asure that will ease the soul and fill the heart. / begin or add to your magical bookshelf."

—Anna Pignataro, illustrator and author

"From the opening of *Becoming the Witch*, the reader is initiated into an enchanted world of arcane arts; richly informed and poetically rendered. This work is the product of the author's lifelong education and dedicated practice of witchcraft—from her calling to live the path of the witch; which is all about self-knowledge, harmony with nature, working with the elements, and spellcraft. The prose is spellbinding and authentic, and the author's wealth of knowledge is exhaustive. I felt lucky to have access to both the theory and history, which is delivered in a comprehensive but accessible manner for beginners to advanced practitioners or the witchy-curious."

—Ruth McIver, author of *I Shot the Devil*

"There are no usual ways to describe this exquisitely rendered book, filled with the spirit of the witch. It is a wonder: mesmerizing, poetic, familiar, and wise. It is as if the most ancient, clear, and powerful part of yourself found a voice and began to guide you along the path, pointing out the magickal detail you may have overlooked if you had not had this companion. It is a beautiful, resonant, iconic and clever work, uncluttered, thoughtful, and imaginative—yet grounded in the complex weaving of occult history."

—Lucy Cavendish, author of many oracle and affirmation decks, including *Secrets of the Witch*

"This beautiful book is a work of inspiration and wonder. Whether you are a novice witch looking for initiation or the crone well versed in the art the witch within you will awaken. An excellent resource for traditional and creative spell casting, it carries you deep into the heart of magick."

—Jayne Stevenson, writer and dreamworker

BECOMING *the*
WITCH

About the Author

Danae Moon Thorp (Melbourne, Australia) is a witch, psychic reader, and founder of SpellBox, a popular metaphysical store. She is also the creator of the *Spellbox Witch's Calendar*, and she has been a guest on many Melbourne radio stations.

BECOMING *the*
WITCH
The ART *of* MAGICK

DANAE MOON THORP

Llewellyn Publications | Woodbury, Minnesota

FIRST EDITION
First Printing, 2021

Cover design by Kevin R. Brown
Interior art by Llewellyn Art Department

Llewellyn Publications is a registered trademark of Llewellyn Worldwide Ltd.

Library of Congress Cataloging-in-Publication Data
Names: Thorp, Danae Moon, author.
Title: Becoming the witch : the art of magick / Danae Moon Thorp.
Description: First edition. | Woodbury, Minnesota : Llewellyn Publications,
    2021. | Includes bibliographical references.
Identifiers: LCCN 2021022386 (print) | LCCN 2021022387 (ebook) | ISBN
    9780738769189 (paperback) | ISBN 9780738769417 (ebook)
Subjects: LCSH: Witchcraft. | Witches. | Magic.
Classification: LCC BF1566 .T4675 2021 (print) | LCC BF1566 (ebook) | DDC
    133.4/3—dc23
LC record available at https://lccn.loc.gov/2021022386
LC ebook record available at https://lccn.loc.gov/2021022387

Llewellyn Publications
A Division of Llewellyn Worldwide Ltd.
2143 Wooddale Drive
Woodbury, MN 55125-2989
www.llewellyn.com

Printed in the United States of America

For my husband, Jeff—true love.

Contents

Spells

Chapter Ten

Introduction

I learnt about magick while looking for mushrooms under tall gum trees when I was too young for school. The colours of the land, the scent from the silent trees and the mist spoke to me of a mystical energy that was not seen with the eyes, it was felt in the heart. Within this world, life was rich and mysterious, perfect and exciting.

This is where I initiated myself into the Old Craft, where I first experienced the magickal lifeforce. No person had ever spoken to me of this energy. This knowledge was given to me by the whispering wind, the spying rabbits, and the Earth beneath my feet.

This is when I felt truly alive and I knew I was a witch.

Invisible threads connect every tree, creature, stone, ocean, person, heart, mind, thought, and action in this world. You can weave these threads from moon and stars, to courage and hope, from your spirit to a tree, from your heart to the ocean, your mind to the wind. When you become the witch, you will weave these threads.

The word *witch* comes from the old English names *wicca*, a male practitioner of magick, and *wicce*, the name for a female witch. Both originate from the Old English word *wiccian*.[1]

There are many other names used to describe a person who has magickal power and the knowledge to heal. The Greeks referred to the witch as pharmakis aligning her with medicine.[2] In Italy she was referred to as strega, her religion La Vecchia meaning "the ways."[3] To the early Greeks the witch was the priestess to Hecate, goddess of the crossroads, so became associated with the wisdom of age and the power of the hag.[4] In Latin she was called saga and malefica.[5]

The witch has always been thought of as someone different, mysterious, independent, and powerful, someone who inspires fascination as well as fear. The witch is vulnerable as well. She has fears and doubts. She needs to heal and renew. She creates wonder and also mistakes. The witch sees herself and all around her as a play of light and shadow. Through her spells she connects with the shadow, as well as the light within her. She must know both aspects of herself and own them. This is the witch's power.

Becoming the witch is an intriguing path, both simple and complex. There is no doctrine involved, no one tells you what to believe in. It is a way of seeing life, yourself, and others in a magickal way. It is imaginative, creative, practical, and powerful. It is a way to find meaning and to meet every beautiful and strange aspect of yourself. It is a way to transform.

In this book the word witch is "every witch" and includes you, the person reading these words. I call the witch "she," but gender is not important. Witches are all genders and anyone who loves the idea of being a witch most likely is. The

---

1. Jeffrey B. Russell and Alexander Brooks, *A History of Witchcraft: Sorcerers, Heretics, and Pagans* (London: Thames & Hudson Ltd, 2007), 12.

2. "Pharmakis," Online Etymology Dictionary, accessed August 21, 2020, https://www.etymonline.com/word/pharmacy.

3. Raven Grimassi, *Italian Witchcraft: The Old Religion of Southern Europe* (St. Paul, MN: Llewellyn Publications, 2012), 4.

4. Raymond Buckland, *The Witch Book: The Encyclopedia of Witchcraft, Wicca, and Neopaganism* (Canton, MI: Visible Ink Press, 2002), 330.

5. English–Latin translation of "Witch," Glosbe.com, accessed August 21, 2020, https://glosbe.com/en/la/witch.

God and the Goddess are energies that exist in everyone. They are forces of light and shadow. They tell our stories.

The spells in this book include ingredients, symbols, actions, words, and charms to craft. Please read Ethics and Care on page 356 before choosing ingredients. Always feel free to change any of these spells to suit and substitute any ingredients. You can always read through the spells and while imagining them, you will create magick. They can be used for meditation. Some of the spells are very simple, others are elaborate. I hope you find them inspiring, a collection of imaginative worlds within hallowed circles.

Every part of the spell creates an energy that manifests within yourself and also outside of yourself. Through your imagination you will manifest this energy as a form of some kind: an image, colour, or movement. While creating the spells in this book you need to connect with the meaning of what you are saying and doing, because every part of the spell is sacred.

Your imagination is immensely compelling and is the portal to spells and the invisible world. When an action, a word, or an object in a spell is aligned with a divine thought or image in your mind, a thread is woven to create magick. When a word is spoken with truth and courage it becomes hallowed. Every action, word, and ingredient in a spell is to be imbued with a divine purpose. To do this you will weave divine threads that connect your heart and mind to a higher energy and you will see your life in an extraordinary way.

During a spell your imagination needs to align with everything you say and do. You are creating something to be in awe of, and from the moment the spell begins, a change takes place within you as well as in the world around you. During each spell you will create a sacred story of your life, just like painting a picture, and when you do this, you will become sacred.

You can create spells with others or in a group or coven. A coven is a group of witches who share values and beliefs and who has practiced spells together over time. To be effective everyone involved needs to be kindred and to hold the same intent. For very personal spells it is sometimes harder to contain a level of intimacy in a large group. A deep level of respect and sacredness needs to be created always. However, when a spell is created with like-minded others it can be healing and transformative. Spells that celebrate occasions, the seasons, and life can be a wild, fun experience with a large group of witches or with others who see the value in ritual and ceremony.

On your journey to becoming the witch, you will become a divine weaver of life, wanting to create, to invent, and discover yourself and the world. Prepare to have wild notions, to meet a sage in a dream, hear a voice when the leaves rustle in the wind, and to be bewitched by the moon.

While the imagination is the key to creating spells, knowledge takes you to a deeper understanding. It gives you a structure in becoming a witch, an understanding of practices used in witchcraft, telling you the origins, the studies, and inspirations that birthed the witch today. Through this learning you will begin to understand symbols, the language of the witch, and you will express meaning through them. Mixing paints to create different colours is knowledge, how you choose the ingredients and hues is imagination. Knowledge is of the mind. It inspires ways to think. The imagination is purely of the heart and is the way to feel.

Through this book I write about myths, occult knowledge, folklore, herbalism, and magick symbolism so you understand that the roots of witchcraft are ancient, universal, and intriguing. This knowledge is immense. I have included some inspiration hoping to awaken your intrigue.

With imagination and knowledge, you will become the witch and create powerful energy that will help you grow, to find fulfillment and meaning.

The twenty-first century witch is everywhere: in the realms of nature, in the suburbs, and in the city. She is beyond the stereotypes of history, yet all these archetypes live within her. She is all ages and faces and is not defined by culture, race, or gender. The witch depicts liberation from the mundane and defiance of oppressive religion. Rebellious, imaginative, clever, and kind, the witch is a complexity of every emotion and embodies the energies light and dark, illumination and shadow.

She is the divine feminine, seeker, magician, enchanter, weaver of magick, and oracle. She is the voice in everyone who speaks of the sacred energy found in Nature and the heart in everyone calling to the rise of the Goddess.

Her voice has always been heard in the whispering wind...

Become the witch by using the power of your voice. Say aloud the incantation to follow as you "see" a story in your mind. In your imagination, picture the moon, an eye opening on your brow, whispering secrets to the faeries, then go within yourself...

Incantation

"The moon, bewitch my thoughts from now.
Eye to open on my brow.
To weave my truth in every spell,
My secrets to the faeries tell.
I travel to the world within,
The light, the dark,
The change,
Begin!"

ONE
The Story

When the first human prayed to the moon, made offerings to a sacred tree, and celebrated the dawn, the spirit of the witch was there.

You stand on the same ancient earth as your ancestors; feel the same wind, the sun's warmth, and hear the ocean waves crashing down. Like your ancestors, you yearn to meet the spirit in all these things. You yearn for wonder and meaning.

Your home, Earth, is a spinning sphere within a galaxy. Your home also tilts and wobbles. By day your sun brings light, by night your moon reflects this light or sleeps in shadow in a starry bed.

Imagine a time when the planets, the creatures, the plants, and the rivers were a part of you, living within you as your world, connected deeply to your soul. Imagine the awe in your heart of their power. Once there was a natural world, a place that was in constant change, embraced in the mystery of beginnings and endings, of birth and of death. Find the memory of this world within you and you will become the witch. This world was home, food, drink, fear, elation, and mystery. The moon and Earth, Goddess. The sun, the God's own eye.

From a feeling within an ancient heart, from a thought that birthed in an ancient mind, rose this belief that a spirit, a magickal entity, lived within everything.

Nature was once deemed hallowed and auspicious. Spirits, gods, and goddesses were born from the mountains, the lakes, the winds, and the trees. This was your ancestor's natural relationship with Earth, a mystical, imaginative, sacred relationship.

They heard the whispering of the wind as it moved through the trees, watched the birds carrying messages to the heavens. The future came to them in dreams. The seasons held them in a mystical embrace and everything in Nature, the stones, the creatures, the oceans, and mountains, had a spirit.

Once long ago, the great mysteries of birth and death, the skies, the break of day, the fall of night, and the rise of the moon were imbued with divine meaning. Animals were brothers and sisters who gave your ancestors life. The caves gave them shelter, the rivers quenched thirst, and the forests gave food. Everything in Nature was inspiring, humbling, and omniscient.

Myths of ethereal beings rose from plants and mountains, stories told of hallowed places, of magickal lands, of animals who were gods, of gods who were stars. Then, the river had a soul, the ocean was goddess, ghosts haunted the forests, and the wind pointed the way. Divine beings called out from every rock and burrow, giving a voice, an expression to the energy of the natural world, to the elements, the seasons, and the creatures.

These long-ago beliefs speak of the intimate relationship your ancient family had with the world. They speak of a time when the planets, the stars, the Earth, the trees, the rivers, and the wind were deemed to have absolute influence over them. And they still do over you.

The witch's story is born from this sacred relationship to Nature. It is told in myths, in the bubbling cauldrons of ancient goddesses, and the flying broomsticks of faery tales. She moved in circles under the moonlight with ancient spirits, with the women who healed with herbs and with dancers of the fire festivals. She talked with divine animals and became them in magick rite, and with the shaman of the forest she entered the world of dream and ghosts. She was the traveller, the merchant of charms, and the reader of cards. Her thoughts were born from her desire to be free, to seek truth and fulfillment. The witch has always lived outside the walls of society yet those within it have been drawn to her wisdom and knowledge. Her beliefs are her own and her temple has always been Nature.

You are the witch, one with Nature's heartbeat, connected to all things, to others, to the creatures and life of the Earth, the beauty of the Heavens, and to the shadow and unknown of the Underworld.

The Birth of Wonder

There are many creation stories that speak of the how Earth came to be. The African god, Amma, created the Universal Egg. When the Egg cracked open life was brought to the world, activating the seasons, the plants, and the skies. The Egg also birthed structure as well as its opposing force, chaos.[6] An ancient Māori story tells that creation was activated when Papa, the female Earth, and Rangi, the male sky, broke their steadfast embrace.[7] The Greek goddess Gaia was the Earth itself. She was born from chaos before time began. All creatures and plants came into existence through her.[8] Nammu, the Sumerian goddess of the waters, brought forth the Universe. She was also the great abyss, unfathomable, infinite.[9] All these stories speak of a beginning-creation through the union of opposites. When opposites meet a remarkable force is activated. This occurs with the meeting of light and dark, structure and chaos, female and male, beginnings and endings, life and death. Hold this thought, for it will bring to you a deep understanding of witchcraft as we travel together through this book.

The Goddess Above

So, from the spark of creation the stories told that life was birthed from the Earth in the form of creatures, plants, ocean, mountains, deserts, and volcanos. Life was seen to also come from woman and when a woman birthed new life something always happened: her water broke. This same water moved on the Earth as rivers, lakes, streams, and the vast seas. Earth and water became one

---

6. Roy Willis, ed. *World Mythology: The Illustrated Guide* (London: Duncan Baird Publishers, 1996), 267.

7. Janet Farrar and Stewart Farrar, *The Witches' God* (Blaine, WA: Phoenix Publishing Inc., 2008), 222, 223.

8. Patricia Monaghan, *The New Book of Goddesses and Heroines* (St. Paul, MN: Llewellyn Publications, 1997), 131.

9. Monaghan, *The New Book of Goddesses and Heroines*, 226.

with the power to create life. So Earth, the mountains, the hills, forests, deserts, lava, the dirt itself, became Great Mother and so did the waters of this world. Both elements gave life, a divine and mysterious act. Water and Earth became Goddess.

The Goddess Below

With the creation of life comes the creation of the unknown, chaos, death itself. A divine giver of life is also able to take life away; the opposing force is always in a steadfast embrace. So, the Goddess merged with death itself and the passages of initiation. She became ruler of a place known as the Underworld. Here she presided over the realms of transformation as well as the afterlife. This goddess spoke of fear, hardship, and mortality. She shadowed the world with everything humankind hoped to avoid.

The Underworld Goddess embodied the opposing force to the light of life, so she became commander over darkness. Her knowledge of darkness, of hardship, and of fear deemed her also champion of endurance. So, as well as bringer of dread, she was also seen as victor of battles, by the force of her will and unrelenting self-belief.

The God

The Goddess's divine partner was the God. His divinity was seen in the sky, the sun, lightning, the force of fire, and the speed of the wind.

Like the Goddess, the God was found in other elements as well, for there are countless stories from all places and cultures. Within the myths, both goddess and god are depicted in a myriad of roles, expressions of nature, reflections of the human psyche, both glorious and flawed. They both have been given the character of hunter, warrior, lover, shape-shifter, oracle, healer, and ruler of all the realms. But it was the Goddess who was the ultimate life-giver.

Gods and goddesses were born in all lands from the soul of Nature and their names are countless. These divine beings breathed through all life on Earth and were found in the endless sky, in the darkness and the void. They created and ended life, rising and retreating through the wheel of seasons, in a world made of fire, air, water, earth, and spirit. You are made from these same forces, at one with something truly divine.

Myth of the Witch

The myth of the witch began in these ancient memories and stories. When a clay goddess was formed in human hands and the dance of a shaman was created in ochre, the witch was there. She was there when ancestors called to the spirit of the eagle and the future was seen in the pattern of scattered bones. When life and death held hands, when beginnings and endings were initiations, the seeds of witchcraft broke open.

You still hear the same thunder that clapped in ancient Sumer where the sky god, Anu, was born. You still look to the morning star, Venus, that birthed the goddess Ishtar in the faraway land of Babylon.

These stories speak of creation, of the three realms of Sky, Earth, and the Underworld. They tell of a continuous dance of change, a marriage of light and dark, of initiations and trials and passages of transformation. Bring these stories into your heart and mind and you will begin to understand yourself and the world around you.

As a witch you will write your words of power with Thoth, the Egyptian god of writing. You will light your candle the same way as the ancient priestess lit the tallow. You will enter the world of the ancient Norse and cross the rainbow bridge, the Bifrost, to the realm of the gods where you will sleep on a branch of the World Tree. As a witch you will see the bow of the goddess Diana in the crescent moon and feel the power of Apollo, god of light, in the warmth of the sun. You will see Kali, the Hindu goddess of destruction, in your own experience of fury and fear.

Ignite your imagination to see the tribes of the fae rising from the hilltops of the Celts. Meet the wee folk at the wells. Feel the trunk of Ganesha, the Hindu elephant god, and smell the sulphur of the Underworld. Open your listening to hear ancient bells calling to the divine, bringing the heavens to Earth. Journey beyond the ordinary, beyond your identity in the mundane world, and allow your imagination to thrive.

Your Story

Around you, and within you, the cycle of birth, death, and rebirth is forever in motion. Trees grow, you grow, trees fall, and sometimes so do you. And then you grow again. This is the thread that binds all things, and within this pattern the experience of meaning and purpose is discovered.

Weave this thread and make your own sacred tapestry. Create your story, the story you want to live. Hear the trees whisper, "Be at one with everything."

Recite this incantation aloud and as you do allow a story to unfold in your mind. These words create an initiation and will open a doorway in your psyche to becoming the witch.

Incantation

"Spirit of the Witch, take my hand.
Call to ancestors,
Their spirits are the flames.
In the ocean, in my dreams,
I am a bird's song,
Flying through the dark,
To find the path of the moon.
My heart one with Mother Earth."

TWO

The Divine Realms

You have a vast world within you as well as around you. The world around you includes the visible and the invisible. You see the physical world but not beneath the surface. The world within you also harbours the known and the unknown. This is the conscious, what you are aware of about yourself, and the unconscious, what you are unaware of. Both worlds are extraordinary, limitless, and mysterious. Both your inner world and external world are ever changing and are reflections of each other. Both are aligned to an energy calling you to meaning, to connection and purpose. The more you discover the unknown within yourself and the unseen around you, the greater your vision of life will become. To find this, travel within and get to know the darkness, the shadow-self, your fears and pain. Discover also the light within you to claim courage, truth, creation, and love.

In myth, the Cosmic Tree is the Axis Mundi or world pillar.[10] The branches reach to the Sky, the trunk is of the Earth and roots are anchored in the Underworld. The tree is a symbolic depiction of the co-existence of all things; the divine, the Earthly, and the unknown. The three realms contain the planets, the stars, the trees, the ocean, and the inferno in Earth's core. They also house your purpose, physical needs, and your mysteries, dreams, and fears. When you see your life from above and aspire to sacred thinking, you are the cosmic branches reaching into the Sky realm. The truck of the tree, the Earth realm, encapsulates the way you are in this world, what you do, how you connect, and your physical body. The shadow within you, what you are unaware of, is of the Underworld. This is the realm of the unresolved, the waiting and endings.

Through your imagination see your inner world as sacred skies, your connection to earth and transformation through knowledge. In these realms you will meet the Goddess and God of the myth and, through them, you will understand that you are part of everything.

Look at life from above. Connect your thoughts to the moving wind. Find the ocean in your heart and discover truth in the depths. Be of the earth, a part of everything you see, feel, touch, smell, and hear.

The Endless Skies

The skies are a heavenly realm. From above the Goddess and the God look down. Their view is of a divine perception, all-encompassing and limitless. The skies include the planets, the weather, and the wind. All lift the witch's mind and heart to sacred heights as well as spectacular falls. Within the Sky realm, the moon is the most powerful influence and guide for the witch. The moon is the high priestess of the night sky, the witch's Goddess, your Goddess.

Rotating around your home, the Earth, the moon is a mysterious orb in the night sky reflecting the light of the sun. She orbits the spinning Earth in around twenty-seven days, and you will never see the dark side of the moon because it takes the same amount of time to rotate as it does to orbit.

The moon and Earth dance around the sun creating the phases of the moon's reflecting light. As the moon orbits the Earth, parts of her orb are lit by

---

10. Udo Becker, ed. *The Element Encyclopedia of Symbols.* trans. Lance W. Garmer (New York: The Continuum Publishing Company, 1996), 333.

the sun according to her position. When the moon is between the sun and the Earth and the three planets are almost in line, she is in shadow to Earth's eye and is called the new moon.

As the moon moves out of the alignment, the light on her surface gradually increases, or waxes, until she is fully illuminated at the full moon. This is when the Earth is between the sun and the moon. Then the light begins to decrease or wane, as she orbits, until the next new moon.

The allure and mystery of the moon is entwined in the heart of the witch. Her energy calls to the wild, to the raw nature in all creatures, including you. She is the mother of dreams and the light of the imagination, the ever-changing mirror of the heavens. The moon has a mysterious hold on the subconscious, the dream world and the realm of the heart. Her power to mesmerize, unhinge, bewitch, and enchant has led her to be thought of as Goddess of the Witch.

The moon also embodies the shadow, the mystery of our psyche, the unseen, the inward, secrets, hauntings, and incredible yearnings. The moon's metal is silver. Her velvet light; a lantern of the divine.

As goddess of the starry night and keeper of secrets, the moon's reflection of the sun's light calls you to look within. She is the divine mirror of the Oracle, the reflection of truth. The moon's element is water, for the ocean tides move within her magnetic embrace. She is mysterious, sensitive, psychic, and all-powerful. She is the planet that invigorates creativity, the mystical portal taking us to the hidden inner realms of past, present, and future.

The moon's energy also speaks of madness and our shadow self, the part of us that remains unknown. Through her powers the witch shape-shifts into other creatures, connecting with instinct, the psychic, and the untamed. You too will learn how to shape-shift, to awaken and experience dreamlike dimensions of yourself that will enable you to create change under the moon's bewitchment.

The moon beckons you to become one with the ancestors, with those who looked to the night skies in awe. She welcomes you to talk to spirits, to the trees and the invisible. She will journey you away from the expected and the mundane.

As enchantress of mysteries, the moon lights the way and then cloaks your path in shadow. Creatures of the dark and water animals hear her heart and move to its beat. The mystical and the wild rise and fall according to the moon; witches take to their brooms, dark forces stir, and beautiful wishes become real under the spell of her kiss.

Her light waxes and wanes mirroring the phases of life. From the dark, the unknown of the new moon, light appears as a thin sliver in the dark sky. Somewhere in memory this same beginning of light appears at every creature's birth, including yours.

To begin, here is a simple spoken spell to recite under the moon any time. All you need is to have a wish in your mind. Imagine what you are saying, see the threads you weave.

> "I draw down the moon and cast a spell.
> A wish I weave, a story I tell.
> With witch's moon I connect tonight.
> Weaving wind, with sea, with dark and light."

The Three Moon Goddesses

Stories tell of the moon as the embodiment of three Goddesses of different ages, the enchantress, the protective mother, and the ancient sorceress known as the Triple Goddess. Each represents the three stages of life: youth, maturity, and old age. Each Goddess has unique powers, mystical abilities, and spiritual knowledge. All three Goddesses are the one glorious deity. They reside within the witch and also within you.

The spirit of the young Goddess of the waxing moon is enthusiastic and passionate. She is wild, reckless, and wants all life has to offer. The Mother Goddess of the full moon is nurturing, healing, forgiving, and protective. The grandmother of the waning moon embodies mastery of transformation and unfathomable insight. Called crone and hag, she has been the most feared and also the most scorned of the goddesses throughout history. She has been demeaned, portrayed as mad and useless, yet she resides at the closest place to the heavens and is the embodiment of wisdom and authenticity. She is adept and can only be understood through profound experience, truth, and insight, for she sees life from the doorstep of death. She no longer has time for untruths or the trivial and has the power to dispel all that is not aligned with the heavens.

The ancient Greeks called the power of the waxing moon, Artemis. She was the goddess of wild animals and the hunt. The full moon was Selene, the mother who no one could hide from. Hecate, the crone queen of witches, was the waning moon.[11]

The Rising Girl: The Waxing Moon

During the waxing phase, the moon's energy is receptive and embracing. The young Goddess calls out "Let's go!" and always replies "Yes!" to a desire or dream. She is willing, wanting, and wishing. The waxing moon is the wisher, full of hope, expectation, and the love of life.

Imagine telling your deepest yearnings to a young woman who knows no bounds, who is carefree and independent. The young Goddess wields the power of rapture and zeal for everything of beauty and unlimited possibility. Speak to her of your wildest imaginings.

Many young goddesses in the world's stories are at one with the waxing moon. The huntress, Artemis, is the virgin, not in a physical sense but by her choosing of independence and oneness with Nature and animals.[12] She is the personification of freedom, agility, and wilfulness. Her arrow is bringer of swift death, symbolic of youthful energy, for at this stage of life nothing stays the same for long. Artemis helped with the birth of her twin brother, Apollo,[13] so the energy of the waxing moon is aligned to the birthing of all things. Her strength speaks of a deep connection to knowledge. Her lightness of heart is entwined with a profound state of mind that requires a connection to freedom, will, sacrifice, and authenticity.

The waxing moon is energising, attracting, and adventurous. It heralds true beauty, abundance, desire, gaining, new love, freshness, passion, and romance. Imagine running with a girl of the wilds.

Becoming the witch begins with connecting to the phases of the moon. Soon you will learn more about the witch's circle and how spells work; however, for now begin with the experience of a spell. Allow the moon to capture your imagination and liberate your mind from thinking. Accept and go through each step and be very present in the moment. See what comes to you during the spell, for when you allow your thoughts to rest, your intuition will deepen

---

11. Rosemary Ellen Guiley, *The Encyclopedia of Witches and Witchcraft* (New York: Facts on File, Inc., 1989), 102.

12. Guiley, *The Encyclopedia of Witches and Witchcraft.* 103.

13. Guiley, *The Encyclopedia of Witches and Witchcraft.* 103.

and you will be guided. Imagine every action is creating energy. Visualise the words you say. What does the goddess in the spell look like? Does she change? When she "holds your hand," what do you feel? See everything in your mind. In these moon spells you will make an offering. For now, simply know an offering is a gift. The first spell is to the waxing moon.

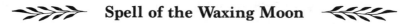 **Spell of the Waxing Moon**

Purpose: To make contact with the Goddess of the waxing moon. To give rise to her within you.

When to cast: During the waxing moon, at night.

Where to cast: Indoors or outside. Use a table or the ground to place items on.

You will need: Find a flower from Nature to use as an offering. A handful of leaves. A bowl of water.

Begin standing, with the bowl and offering before you.

1. With the leaves in your hand, extend your arm and, turning in a circle, allow the leaves to fall.

2. Hold the offering to your heart.

3. Say:

> "Goddess of the waxing moon rise within my heart.
> I call to attract and desire. I am open and willing.
> Girl of the Moon, hold my hand."

4. Place the offering into the water. Say:

> "To wish."

5. When you are finished, imagine your circle of leaves ascending into the night sky.

After the spell: On the following night, take the offering out of the bowl and pour the water over your hands. Refill the bowl with water and place the offering in it. Place the bowl by your bed. Keep for three nights and then pour the contents on the earth.

Mother's Embrace: The Full Moon

When the Earth is almost between the sun and the moon, the sun's light shines fully on the part of the moon facing the Earth and it is a full moon. This phase of the moon has always been considered highly auspicious, potent, and bewitching. It is a time when the goddess Selene drives her chariot out of the ocean and into the night sky.[14] Her myth is one of the many that binds the moon with the seas and therefore to the witch's heart.

Selene is the moon itself, the illuminated orb. She embodies the power of the planet in her form of the charioteer and, like the Crone Goddess Hecate, she holds a torch to light the way. Selene is known as the "eye of the night" for she sees everything. She is the all-knowing mother: pregnant, nurturing, and promising.

Like all good mothers, the full moon brings gifts of fulfilment, protection, and guidance. She wishes the best for her children and wants them to see the best in themselves. She calls you to her mirror, fully illuminated. Here she asks you to "see" your potential. To "see all" is to receive Selene's gift. The full moon shines light on the path of the night taking you home.

Mother Moon wipes away the tears that well under her light. Her oneness with the vast ocean unleashes feelings from the deep inside you. A heart can drown at the full moon through a flood of sadness or fear, for raw feelings surface from the unconscious at this time. Mothers see the truth in their child. The full moon calls you to connect with your heart, completely unguarded, for then you see your truth and begin to know yourself as she does.

This rawness brings you closer to instinct to becoming a creature, a dreamer, a spirit-talker. Stories speak of shape-shifting, becoming spellbound and entranced by the full moon. These stories hold truth at the core. Energy peaks at the full moon, emotions heighten and can become overwhelming. Under the sway of this divine madness, creativity is liberated as the imagination flourishes.

The full moon opens portals to vivid dreaming and other worlds. The third eye opens, bringing vision, insight, and prophetic experience under her bewitching aura.

Mother Moon beckons you to break free of the restraints of the mind and the mundane world. Wildness, deep yearnings, pain, passion, and brilliant

---

14. Guiley, *The Encyclopedia of Witches and Witchcraft.* 314.

vision can be liberated within her embrace. Art is created, dance becomes a spiritual force, songs call in ancestors, and you will see the unseen.

Like all good mothers, the full moon calls us to reveal, release, and fall into her arms. And when you look into the mirror, fall away from what you think you know. Like the spell of the waxing moon, you need to imagine every action and word is creating a powerful energy within and around you.

⟫⟫➤ Spell of the Full Moon ⟪⟪⟪

Purpose: To make contact with the Goddess of the full moon. To give rise to her within you.

When to cast: On the full moon, at night.

Where to cast: Indoors or outside. Use a table or the ground to place items on.

You will need: Find a leaf from nature to use as an offering. A handful of flower petals.

A bowl of water.

Begin standing, with the bowl and offering before you.

1. With the petals in your hand, extend your arm and, turning in a circle, allow them to fall.

2. Hold the offering to your heart.

3. Say:

   "Goddess of the full moon rise within my heart. I call to truth, illumination, and guidance. Mother Moon embrace me."

4. Place the offering into the bowl of water. Say:

   "To reflect."

5. When you are finished, imagine your circle of petals ascending into the night sky.

After the spell: On the following night, take the offering out of the bowl and pour the water over your hands. Refill the bowl with water and place the offering in it. Place the bowl by your bed. Keep for three nights and then pour the contents on the earth.

Grandmother's Shadow: Waning Moon to New Moon

The moon's light begins to decrease after the full moon and the waning phase begins. This is the shadow of the old Goddess's cauldron. Hecate, the Greek goddess of the waning moon, is wisdom embodied. She takes you to a deep level of truth for this Goddess knows the ghosts who haunt the psyche, your fears, pain, and sadness. Hecate is the chthonic aspect of the waning moon, the guide to and from the Underworld. Her power is banishing and purifying. She offers transcendence through hardship and endings.

Grandma Moon takes you to deep change, relinquishing worn-out habits and banishing what drains the spirit. Through her you will become aware of old patterns, ruts, and destructive thinking. As she is the guide to endings, she is also the guide to rebirth and renewal, so holds the promise of light.

She is the bringer of psychic insight, heightening the power of divination. She offers the ability to scry, read cards, understand animal language, and communicate with spirits.

The crone of the moon weaves a tapestry of psychic vision, of battles won and lost, of endings, undying courage, and enlightenment through living authentically. And when you speak to ghosts, know that Grandma Moon is your voice.

 **Spell of the Waning Moon**

Purpose: To make contact with the Goddess of the waning moon. To give rise to her within you.

When to cast: During the waning moon, at night.

Where to cast: Indoors or outside. Use a table or the ground to place items on.

You will need: Find a stone from Nature to use as an offering. A handful of salt. A bowl of water.

Begin standing, with the bowl and offering before you.

1. With the salt in your hand, extend your arm and, turning in a circle, allow the salt to fall.

2. Hold the offering to your heart.

3. Say:

   "Goddess of the waning moon rise within my heart. I call to courage, knowledge, and wisdom. Grandmother Moon, place your hand on my heart."

4. Place the offering into the bowl of water. Say:

   "To dispel."

5. When you are finished, imagine your circle of salt ascending into the night sky.

After the spell: On the following night, take the offering out of the bowl and pour the water over your hands. Refill the bowl with water and place the offering in it. Place the bowl by your bed. Keep for three nights and then pour the contents on the earth.

The Old Goddess also resides over the new moon. The light of the waning moon gradually diminishes until there is no sunlight reflected on the side of the moon seen from Earth, and she is in complete darkness. This is the new moon, the Crone's portal or doorway to the future. This is a time for a new beginning, opportunity, and to start again. Like the full moon, the new moon is a potent lunar phase, the ending and also the beginning of a cycle. While the waning moon releases and banishes, the new moon offers you renewal.

The energy created at the new moon builds through the waxing phase and comes to fruition at the next full moon. Look into the darkness of the night and ask Grandmother to open her door.

For this new moon spell something new is added, a symbol in the form of a key. As you read further into this book, you will come to an understanding of how symbols work. Symbols are the language of spells and their meaning reaches far beyond words. For now, think about the function of a key. This spell also involves some witch's crafting, the tying of knots. What does a knot do? Again imagine Grandmother Moon and her "portal."

 **Spell of the New Moon**

Purpose: To make contact with the Goddess of the new moon. To give rise to her within you.

When to cast: On the new moon, at night.

Where to cast: Indoors or outside. Use a table or the ground to place items on.

You will need: An old key and string (around 18 in. or 44 cm)
Begin at a table.

1. Create a circle with the string. Imagine this circle is a portal to the future.

2. Hold the key to your heart.

3. Say:

   "Goddess of the new moon rise within my heart. I call to change, to transformation, and beginnings. Grandmother Moon open your portal to the future."

4. Place the key into the circle. Say:

   "To begin."

5. When you are finished, leave the key in the circle overnight under the new moon.

After the spell: The following day, thread the string through the key. Tie nine knots along it. The number nine in numerology aligns with truth, wisdom, and unity. Keep the key in a significant place and hold it to connect with the energy of the new moon.

You have met the moon in all her splendid phases and made offerings to her. A sacred relationship has begun with all aspects of the Moon Goddess.

The Sun: God's Own Eye

In the realm of the Sky there are countless stars. One of these stars is the Sun, the Light.

The moon's light is not her own, it is the illumination of the sun reflected on her surface. The sun is therefore the opposite force. It is the source of the light, the fire element, the ruler of the day's skies, the rising and setting eye of the God.

While the moon is reflective, passive, and inward, the sun's energy is fiery, active, decisive, and illuminating. The moon is the domain of the subconscious, of dreams and the shadow. The sun is consciousness and vitality. The sun's metal is gold. The sun has been associated with the gods in most myths, though in some ancient stories the sun was also Goddess.

Amaterasu is the Japanese Sun goddess in the eastern Shinto pantheon.[15] In her myth she retreated into a cave after her brother insulted her and so the Earth became enveloped in darkness. Amaterasu was eventually enticed out of the cave by the sounds of a wild party. When she emerged from the darkness, the other deities who hoped for her return held up a mirror. She looked in the mirror and was captivated by her own dazzling image. While entranced, Amaterasu was bound with ropes to ensure she would never leave the Sky again. This story speaks of the bedazzlement of the sun's glory as well as the moon, symbolized by the mirror reflection.

The sun is pulled across the sky by the chariot of the Greek god, Helios. He is the divine Sun itself, and the brother of the Moon, Selene. Helios later became Apollo, the god of light, who continued to drive the solar chariot through the heavens.[16] Ra, the Egyptian god of the sun, crossed the sky each day in a boat and then entered the Underworld at sunset to be reborn each morning at dawn.[17] The Hindu god of the sun, Surya, is also a charioteer. He is a victor and charismatic warrior. Like many of the world's solar gods, he is the bringer of healing and good fortune.[18]

---

15. C. A. Burland, *Myths of Life and Death* (London: Macmillan, 1974), 48–52.

16. Farrar, *The Witches' God.* 183.

17. Farrar, *The Witches' God.* 135.

18. Arthur Cotterell and Rachel Storm, *The Ultimate Encyclopedia of Mythology* (London: Anness Publishing Ltd, 1999), 406, 407.

The sun's energy is restoring, illuminating; it is happy and brings lucky times, hope, and play. The gods and goddesses of the Norse pantheon adored Baldur, their beautiful god of light. He was the illumination in their realm and in their hearts. Perfect in every way.[19] Like the sun you radiate when happy and feel warm when you are loved.

The sun creates red, orange, and yellow hues as he rises at dawn in the east. Dawn speaks of the possibilities of the new day, of hope and inspiration. The morning birds herald the sun, the Earth wakes and light appears above the horizon. The Australian kookaburra laughs as the sun dawns, a symbolic collaboration of happiness.

The sun tells the time. It breaks through the darkness of clouds, bringing warmth and life. It sets again at dusk in another pool of colours calling us to sleep.

Both moon and sun are dual energies that live within you. Their realms are night and day, light and shadow, mystery and illumination. The moon has secrets. The sun sings the song of life. She is inward, passive, and wears the cloak of the occult. He is open and active. The sun is the source. The moon is the reflection.

When you see beyond your eyes you become the moon, and when you burst with bright energy, you are the sun. Both moon and sun speak of your connection to the Divine and your life is bound to them. They are timeless deities and their story is your story. When you look to the rising sun, know you are witnessing the birth of the future.

You have made offerings to the three goddesses of the moon. Now to connect with the energy of the sun, the source. This spell requires you to find a *wand* in nature. Again, you will learn about the wand later through these pages, but for now know that a wand is a witch's tool used to focus and direct your energy. Tree branches are unique and come in fascinating shapes. Look around in nature or a park and find a branch small enough to hold. When you hold it does it feel like an extension of your arm? What does its shape tell you? What tree does it belong to?

---

19. Daniel McCoy, *The Viking Spirit: An Introduction to Norse Mythology and Religion* (CreateSpace Independent Publishing Platform, 2016), 44.

During this spell, visualise light and warmth. It is an energy but imagine it as a colour or a form. "See" the sun as a guiding father, a happy brother, a loving partner, or a bright happy boy.

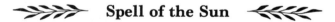

Spell of the Sun

Purpose: To make contact with the God of the sun. To give rise to him within you.

When to cast: During the day.

Where to cast: Outdoors in the light. Use a table or the ground to place items on.

You will need: A branch found in Nature.

Begin standing.

1. Hold the branch outright.

2. Turn as you imagine fire coming out of the end of the branch, forming a circle of light around you.

3. Hold the branch skyward. Say:

   "Sun rise within my mind. I call to brightness, luck, and warmth. Father Sun light my life."

4. Hold the branch to your brow. Say:

   "To shine."

5. When you are finished, imagine your circle of light ascending into the sun.

After the spell: Keep the branch as a sacred tool. You have asked for the sun to live within you and through you. A divine relationship with this God begins.

The Sacred Earth

The goddesses and gods are of the Earth as well as the sky. They embody the creative powers of the planet and the glory of the seasons.

The ancient Greeks named the Earth Gaia. She is the Great Mother who also birthed time. Gaia's sexual union with her son Uranus, god of the Heavens, created the creatures and plants of the world. The Earth Goddess is also embodied in the Anatolian deity, Cybele. Cybele was the mountain goddess, guarded by two lions. They are solar animals aligning her also to the sun. Her emblems of corn symbolically speak of Earth's bounty and the harvest.[20]

The Earth Goddess, as Universal Mother, also rose as Danu in Irish myth. Danu birthed the race of Gaelic deities called the Tuatha Dé Danann. In later legends they became the faery folk. Danu is the embodiment of abundance. She is often associated with Anu, another ancient Irish goddess of prosperity who was aligned with the produce of the Earth.[21]

Earth Mother is also the Hindu fertility deity Parvati. In her myth she conceives her son from sheer desire while holding a piece of cloth to her nipple. Her son is eventually transformed into the beautiful elephant god, Ganesha. Parvati's story tells of the power of the Earth Goddess and her unrelenting yearning to be mother and to create life.[22]

As well as creator, the Earth is also the Goddess in decline and decay. For all plants wither and die in time. Autumn begins with falling leaves. This is when the Slavic witch Baba Yaga rides through the cold skies in a mortar and pestle with her broom sweeping behind her. In her original form, as Baba, she was the old woman of autumn and lived in the last sheaf of grain to be harvested.[23]

The stark landscape of winter calls the Crone Goddesses to stir their cauldrons. This is their time on Earth, a phase of passing and of endings. She is the high priestess of winter, a time of dormancy and stillness. The Earth Crone Goddesses, however, promise renewal after decline. So, in spring, Ostara, the Saxon goddess of the dawn and embodiment of fertility rises to usher in growth from beneath the surface of the Earth.[24]

---

20. Joseph Campbell, ed. Saffron Rossi, *Goddesses: Mysteries of the Feminine Divine* (Novato, California: New World Library, 2013), 26.

21. Monaghan, *The New Book of Goddesses and Heroines*, 49, 97.

22. Monaghan, *The New Book of Goddesses and Heroines*, 249.

23. Monaghan, *The New Book of Goddesses and Heroines*, 65.

24. Edain McCoy, *Sabbats: A Witch's Approach to Living the Old Ways* (St. Paul, MN: Llewellyn Publications, 2003), 109.

Ostara's companion is the hare, a night creature spellbound by the moon. Ostara's powers combine the watery energy of the moon with the fertility of Earth to create new life. The moon's energy and the reproductive powers of Earth come together again in the myth of the Mayan goddess Ixchel. She is another tri-fold deity. She is the young fertile goddess associated again with the rabbit. She is also mother deity of medicine bound to the power of the rainbow and the serpent. In her crone aspect she is goddess of healing, rain, and plants.[25]

Earth is embodied in the Greek triple-goddess, Persephone, Demeter, and Hecate. Each Goddess depicts Earth through the seasons.

Earth as Goddess is depicted in the Greek myth of Persephone's abduction by Hades, god of the Underworld. Persephone is first flower's bloom, bold and adventurous. She is spring itself and was loved deeply by her mother Demeter, goddess of the harvest. Her sudden disappearance caused unbearable pain for Demeter, invoking autumn, the season of wilting. The goddess of witchcraft, Hecate, hears the young goddess's cries in the Underworld and comes to Demeter's assistance. Hecate is a complex goddess, associated with the dark moon. However, in this myth her role has been seen as "the wise crone,"[26] an Earth mother version of the matured Demeter, all-knowing as she nears death. As the crone she is the barren, unfertile winter. After negotiation with the sky god Zeus, Persephone is released and returns to the surface of the Earth and life in the form of spring is birthed. However, Persephone is bound to return to the Underworld every autumn because while she was in the realm, she ate the pomegranate, fruit of the Underworld.[27]

This story not only speaks of the seasons, it also speaks of your inner world and your life's journey. It is a story of sacrifice, initiation, and transformation, the gaining of knowledge through the loss of innocence. When Persephone eats nature in the form of the pomegranate, produce of the Underworld, she liberates a part of her own nature. The eating of the fruit symbolises her choice to lose her innocence, symbolized by her virginity. This is her sacrifice. She knows this act will bind her to her shadow-self and liberate a power that had, until

---

25. Merlin Stone, *Ancient Mirrors of Womanhood: A Treasury of Goddess and Heroine Lore from Around the World* (Boston: Beacon Press, 1990), 92–96.

26. Monaghan, *The New Book of Goddesses and Heroines*, 147.

27. Anne Baring and Jules Cashford, *The Myth of the Goddess: Evolution of an Image* (London: Penguin Books, 1993), 364–367.

then, remained unready within her. Through the gaining of knowledge symbolized by consuming the fruit, transformation occurs, and Persephone is elevated from virginal spring maiden to commanding Queen of the Underworld.

Persephone however still retains the beauty of spring but now has the knowledge of a different beauty, a deep formidable power. This is a story about the integration of light and shadow. As a witch you need to venture into your shadow, the unconscious that harbours everything hard to face, painful experience and destructive thinking. The shadow is what makes you whole and always will. The powerful energy that resides there can be transformed into a spiritual force that enhances life instead of deleting it. Awareness, connection, and will to change is a choice. Go within and tasting the fruit of knowledge, allow it to elevate you to Queen.

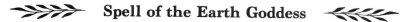

Spell of the Earth Goddess

Purpose: To initiate yourself as Witch. To acknowledge the Goddess of Earth, within and around you. Imagine you weave a picture as you create this spell. Every thought you have is brought into form, so it exists as energy. "See" the circle; know your offerings are an acknowledgement of a sacred relationship. How does each goddess appear to you? Listen to any messages during the spell. Think of this spell as an initiation where you truly begin to think of yourself as a witch.

When to cast: During any phase of the moon. Day or night.

Where to cast: Indoors or outside. Use a table or the ground to place items on.

You will need: Three offering bowls. Flower seeds of any kind for the Young Goddess. Rice for the Mother Goddess. Salt for the Crone Goddess. Place the seeds, rice, and salt in one of the three bowls.
Begin with the offering bowls before you.

1. Take a little of each offering in your hand, extend your arm, and, turning in a circle, allow the seeds, rice, and salt to fall.

2. Place your hands over your heart.

3. Say:

> "I invite the Goddesses of Earth to come into my
> circle. Seeds for new life, rice for fertility, and salt for
> strength. These are my offerings. Sister, mother, and
> grandmother, live within and around me."

4. Place the offerings on the Earth. Say:

> "To rise a witch, to become a witch, to know as a
> witch."

5. When you are finished, imagine your circle of offerings
   descending into the Earth.

After the spell: Bury the seeds in the Earth. Your divine relationship
with the Earth Goddess in all her aspects has begun.

The Divine Underworld

The Underworld is a symbolic realm in universal myths. This realm is imagined
to be beneath the Earth because it is a reflection of what resides beneath the
surface of awareness. It is the subconscious and the hidden.

The Underworld is the realm you enter through the experience of trauma,
heartbreak, grief, disconnection, addiction, and deep regret, as well as fear and
hate. It is the state of dreams lost, profound disappointment, rejection, and
despair. The experience of the Underworld is harrowing, and you are never the
same again after you have been there.

This realm is strange and powerful. It is the place where aspects of the self
are hidden away, where your shadow resides. Being stuck in illusions of endless
bad luck, unworthiness, hopelessness, disconnection, and perpetual dissatisfac-
tion will take you to the Underworld to meet your shadow-self. The shadow is
the part of your inner world that has remained hidden because it is too painful
to face and easier to keep secret. It is the aspect of the self that is untreated,
unhealed, or poisonous. Sometimes it takes a tragedy, a breakdown, or illness
to confront the shadow because a conscious state of hardship often reveals what
lies beneath the surface.

In the Underworld you have a choice to own every part of your being, your fall, your tears, and your loss. And when you ascend from this realm, with knowledge of the world, you, like Persephone, will connect with your power.

This journey of sacrifice and initiation is told in the myth of the ancient Sumerian goddess Inanna and in the almost identical story of the Babylonia goddess Ishtar.[28] Inanna entered the Underworld and faced the Queen of Death, Eriskegal, Inanna's crone aspect as well as sister. At the entry of the Underworld, the goddess had to remove all embellishments and clothing to pass through Eriskegal's gates. The symbolism of nakedness speaks of the need for complete truth, the separation from illusion and distractions, in order to undergo a deep spiritual experience. This theme of nakedness before entering the Underworld is also found in the myth of Isis, the great Egyptian goddess, who cuts off her hair and puts on mourning clothes before embarking on her quest to recover her dead husband Osiris.[29]

Both Inanna and Ishtar endured hardship, captivity, and reckoning while in the Underworld. Their stories are similar to each other, with variations, but both goddesses return to Earth's surface more knowledgeable and powerful. Ishtar rescued her lover, Tammuz, the vegetation god from the realm, and restored balance to the Earth. Inanna, upon returning, discovers the true nature of her lover, also a vegetation deity, and banishes him to Eriskegal's realm.

The Underworld is a state of mind, a time necessary for growth and transformation. It is the realm where compassion arises from hardship, courage from fear, and grace from loss. Everyone needs to go there.

When you feel like this, it is time to knock on Eriskegal's door, willing to face her with courage and truth. When someone you love is gone, if something terrible has happened, if rejection and anguish call, hold on to Inanna's hand and wait for the door to open. When it does, you will experience the power of Eriskegal's mighty embrace.

The Underworld is also the realm of the Afterlife. Underworld Goddesses speak of fear, sickness, and physical death. In Norse myth, Hel presides in a realm of misery, sickness, old age, and madness. The dark concepts embodied in her mythical world mirrors the suffering of these experiences in life. Hel's

---

28. Monica Sjöö and Barbara Mor, *The Great Cosmic Mother: Rediscovering the Religion of the Earth* (New York: HarperCollins Publishers, 1987), 168.

29. Baring and Cashford, *The Myth of the Goddess*. 228.

name actually means the "one who covers up" and her path is called Troublesome Road. Her myth tells you that when fear is hidden and not acknowledged, it flourishes.[30]

Kali is a Hindu deity of destruction. She is also Mother of Creation, an incarnation of opposite energies and their dependence on one another. Kali's physical image, her adornment of dismembered bodies and her blood lust, is a terrifying display. She is the embodiment of fear. Yet she teaches that through facing fear, it will diminish. To look upon Kali is hard, yet the longer you look, the less fearful you become.[31]

In the Underworld be still, listen, and wait. Breathe through the pain, the yearning. Weave your threads to the stars and moon. Surrender. Everything moves without you.

Learn to sway with Mother Kali. She knows of her realm and feels at home.

During the spell that follows, you will acknowledge the shadow within yourself, what is hard to face and also endure. Bring meaning to every action and word. This spell also involves symbols, this time a coin and an apple. What does a coin mean to you? What stories do you know that speak of the potency of apples? What does the Underworld Goddess look like? What messages does she bring you? Surrender to any feelings that arise and connect with the courage and transformation this realm offers.

Spell of the Underworld Goddess

Purpose: To make contact with the Underworld Goddess. To give rise to her within you. To connect with your shadow.

When to cast: On the new moon, at night.

Where to cast: Indoors or outside. Use a table or the ground to place items on.

You will need: A coin and an apple. A handful of salt.
Begin standing with the offerings before you.

---

30. Monaghan, *The New Book of Goddesses and Heroines*, 149.

31. Monaghan, *The New Book of Goddesses and Heroines*, 177.

1. With the salt in your hand, extend your arm and, turning in a circle, allow the salt to fall.

2. Place the apple on your heart and say:

   "I invite the Goddess of the Underworld into my circle. Touch my wounded heart. When I feel broken in life's storm and everything is in pieces."

3. Place the coin on your heart and say:

   "Moonlight to come through the door of tears. Mend me with your kiss."

4. When you are finished, imagine your circle of salt disappearing into the Earth.

After the spell: Keep your coin with your key of the new moon spell. Eat the apple while you allow messages from the Underworld Goddess to come into your mind.

The Goddesses and Gods of the Three Realms are within you, around you, and beyond you. Every deity speaks of an aspect of you and speaks of your story.

Goddess is the moon, the Earth, and the unknown. She is the guiding light, the dark, the longing, the courage, the kiss, the trees, and the lakes. The Goddess is healer, warrior, lover, wish-maker, muse, oracle, high priestess, girl, mother, grandma, and witch.

He is the skies, the sun, lightning, and the wind. He is the brilliance of light and the courage in action. The God is thought, passion, and sacrifice. He is sage, champion, speed, messages, and the word. God is boy, father, grandfather, and wizard.

Stir your bubbling cauldron and your wild, wild dreams. Hear words through rustling leaves, as a guiding voice. See the moon as your divine mirror reflecting your own fantastic story.

The myths of the Skies, the Earth, and the Underworld are the witch's story, your story. They speak of divine threads that connect you to everything. You have begun weaving these divine threads through your reciting of words and the offering spells. These threads are called *magick*. Magick is an energy found within you and in the world around you. It is also found in words, thoughts, dreams, and intentions.

During a spell you create magick.

THREE
The Magick Spell

The word "spell" is Old English, meaning "a saying or story." Also compared with the Old Saxon "Spel."[32]

During a spell you weave a story: the story you want to live. You do this with the threads of an energy called *magick*, a sacred essence.

Magick is both visible and invisible. Listen to the thunder and you will hear it, look to the night sky you will see it, move close to someone you love and you will feel it, choose to be kind and you will activate it. Magick is created when someone cries for a stranger's loss and when someone dies holding another's hand. It is the rapture of falling in love, the purity of innocence, and a moment of profound realization. Magick is the experience of dreams and reading the future in a card. It is when something in you changes, when you dispel fear, embrace compassion, and when you wish for something to happen, and it does. Magick is divine energy and the experience of it is life changing.

---

32. "Spell," Online Etymology Dictionary, accessed August 21, 2020, https://www.etymonline
.com/word/spell.

You can sense magick in your bones, see it the trees, feel it in courage, think it in the mind. You can also create it as an act.

An act of magick takes many forms. What is common to every act of magick is the connection to a divine influence, or energy, to create change. Sometimes an act of magick occurs though mysterious coincidences, through profound dreams, a change in the constellations, or an inspiration out of nowhere and you act because of it. You may feel something change in your heart and then express it, like feeling a friend's pain and then reaching out to them.

Another act of magick starts with a conscious intention. It is holding a thought, a desire or a hope in your mind then showing it through words or actions. Sometimes these actions are symbolic, encapsulating complexity simply. A wish said aloud or written down is an act of magick, as is throwing a coin into a fountain for luck and blowing out birthday candles. For the witch it is the creation of a mystical ceremony called a *spell*. A spell involves actions, words, and objects that have meaning and energetic influence. The witch's spell also encompasses the four elements of *fire, air, water*, and *earth*, for they hold the magick of Nature and with their essence you can create the act of magick and will weave change.

Each element holds and vibrates a powerful energy, a character and otherworldly effect so it is not limited to its own existence. Your world is made of the elements and so are you. The essence of these forces permeates everything. The movement of the wind in one part of the world changes the weather in another part. The movement of your thoughts and actions also influences everything. Everything you say and do affects something else, so know you hold power to make changes in yourself as well as the world. The following words speak of the existence of the elements in everything and their profound sway. "The Elements therefore are the first of all things, and all things are of, and according to them, and they are in all things, and diffuse their virtues through all things." Cornelius Agrippa (1486–1535) German occultist.[33]

The Earth gives birth to the plants and trees, the rain creates rivers, the ocean's tides bow to the moon's ever-changing light. The sunlight germinates Earth's plants, the rain hydrates them, and the air is their breath. Their breath becomes

---

33. Henry Cornelius Agrippa, *Three Books of Occult Philosophy*, Edited and annotated by Donald Tyson, trans. James Freake (St. Paul, MN: Llewellyn Publications, 1998), 24.

your breath, their fruit, your food, the rain your drink, the sun your light. We live in a world where life sustains life, where every creature, plant, river, and wave play a part in the perfection of the Universe.

This world, the world that you see, feel, hear, taste, and smell is made of the four elements: fire, air, water, and earth. The sensory experience of Nature is extraordinary. Swimming in the ocean, climbing a mountain, and looking at a tree have a mysterious effect on the heart and mind. This world holds an essence, an incredible vibration. It is magick and it has the power to transform you, to bring you closer to the Divine and to knowing who you are. The magick of Nature holds within its core the energy of opposites, a hallowed pattern of light and dark, creation and destruction, birth and death. In the pages that follow you will explore this further, within each element as well as yourself.

Travel beyond your eyes to see that in every flower, river, star, and breeze, a spirit resides—a divine being, a god, a goddess. Connect with this magick and weave threads that bind you to the moon, to the birds, and to the deepest ocean.

Your spell is an invitation to change, to imbue your life with meaning. It begins with a willingness to enter the unknown and to surrender to sacred energy. There is nothing ordinary about this, so ordinary thinking has no place during a spell. The experience is otherworldly and healing, for during the spell you will communicate with a hallowed power and will merge with mystery. You will meet an energy that knows you deeply and wishes you well, and you will always want to feel this way. The experience of a spell will bring change to your life because your thinking will change, and when this happens your life changes too.

You can create a spell without ever knowing why it works. Most children never ask why, they simply experience. However, through time, magick has been studied to gain knowledge and bring a deeper understanding by mystics, sages, occultists, and astrologers. These studies were influenced by the culture, thinking, and religion of the time. Many, if not most, of these explorations were from men, not women; were intellectual; and for today's witch, interesting, but not so relatable. However, emerging from history comes the legend of *The Emerald Tablet*, a manuscript that contained a theory of how the act of magick works and, on becoming a witch, you will find it profound. This is what was written.

"What is below is like that which is above, and what is above is similar to that which is below to accomplish the wonders of the one thing."

Hermes Trismegistus, from Madame Blatavsky translation.[34]

Veiled in profound mystery, this document is thought to be one of the earliest alchemical workings. It was thought that the *Tablet* was created by a deity, Hermes Trismegistus, who was an embodiment of Thoth, the Egyptian god of magick and the Greek god Hermes, deity of literature, trade, thieves, messages, and the Underworld. The unknown author encapsulated how magick works—the influence of thought on the greater world.

The mind is seen as the microcosm, the internal world. The external world is the macrocosm. A mystical relationship exists between the two, for according to the *Tablet*, the way you think has a profound effect on the realm of actual experience. Both worlds are reflections. When the mind changes, so does the world around you.

When you see the wonder of Nature, your thoughts align with this power. When you think wondrously you will see the wonder of your life. It works both ways. It is not always easy to think this way because worry and fear are potent and influence how the mind works. This is when you will experience the power of a spell because in this *act of magick* you will change your thinking.

During a spell you will create a setting that you deem to be hallowed. As you create this setting, a change begins within you. In this sacred space you take your intention, your wish, or hope from the realm of thinking, so out of fear and doubt. Instead you give it expression and form in the physical world. This is done through symbolic actions, words, and physical objects. Now your intention is no longer in your head; you hold it, you see it with your eyes, and act it out with gestures, sounds, and voice. What was invisible is now visible. What was unheard is now heard. What was in your mind is now in the world around you. During this enactment you will have sensory contact with the elements so their essence of magick merges with your act, your words, and your symbols. Your spell encapsulates a divine vibration and will therefore attract other divine energies to it.

Through your imagination you will *weave* threads of magick through every aspect of the spell to create a sacred story that is, in fact, a picture of your life.

---

34. Hermes Trismegistus, *The Emerald Tablet of Hermes* (Dublin: Merchant Books, 2013), 19.

Weaving is an imaginative art of the witch and during a spell each thought, word, and action is a stitch. The magick of every thread needs to be imagined as a picture in the mind, a feeling in your bones, just as a story is imagined when heard or read.

Many myths speak of the Goddess as weaver. In Mayan mythology an aspect of the goddess Ixchel was a spider.[35] As a spider deity, she spun the thread of life's web from her own body. Her spindle represented the motion of the Universe. In Navaho myth, Spider Woman, also known as Grandmother Spider, spins her web, connecting all aspects of life.[36] The spinning wheel is one of the emblems of Athena, Greek goddess of wisdom.[37] In Norse myth, the three divine entities, the Norns, weave their fabric of destiny at the base of the World Tree[38] while the Fates, in the Greek pantheon, pull out the threads of our life on their tapestry, until the final thread is cut at death.[39]

The art of weaving in the ancient stories symbolises the patterns that shape life; the loom depicts the unfolding story between Earth and the Heavens, and the spinning wheel is the symbol of the Wheel of Life, forever in motion.

The Huichol people of Central Mexico create magick in a ritual where the skill of a weaver is imbued with the energy of a serpent's skin. To infuse the energy of the snake's wondrous pattern with the art of the weaver, she strokes the creature's back. She then moves her hand over her own brow and then over her eyes to merge the snake into her creation. In this ritual the nature of the creature *rubs off* on to the weaver, giving her the skill to reproduce the snake's pattern.[40]

35. Ami Ronnberg and Kathleen Martin, eds. *The Book of Symbols: Reflections on Archetypal Images* (Cologne, Germany: Taschen GMBH, 2010), 456.

36. Ronnberg and Martin, eds. *The Book of Symbols: Reflections on Archetypal Images*, 220.

37. Farrar, *The Witches' Goddess*, 201.

38. Claude Lecouteux, *Encyclopedia of Norse and Germanic Folklore, Mythology, and Magic,* trans. Jon E. Graham (Rocheter, Vermont: Inner Traditions International, 2016), 209.

39. Farrar, *The Witches' Goddess*, 31.

40. J. G. Frazer, *The Golden Bough: A Study in Magic and Religion* (London: Papermac, 1994), 32.

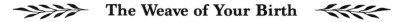 **The Weave of Your Birth**

Purpose: To align your thoughts with magick. To see the invisible threads of magick. To begin to "weave." Imagine everything you say and do is creating a picture. "See" beyond the physical into the invisible world of the witch. During this spell you will create the story of your birth. You will do this symbolically. Even if you know nothing about the events of this time, just imagine and allow everything to unfold. You may like to create this sitting down at a table.

When to cast: On the new moon, at night.

Where to cast: Indoors or outside.

You will need: An egg (if you are vegan, draw or make a symbolic egg). Any items from nature, such as flowers, leaves, twigs, and stones—enough to create a small circle.

Begin with the items before you.

1. Sitting down, hold the egg. Close your eyes. Say:

   "Mother."

2. Imagine a circle of light around you. Say:

   "My thoughts are threads,

   Spun to trees.

   My mind at one with the breeze.

   I weave the story of my birth.

   The day I came to Mother Earth.

   By sun and moon, by ocean deep.

   By threads unseen, I woke from sleep."

3. Now with the items from Nature, create a circle around the egg.

4. Breathe over the circle. Imagine threads of energy connecting your heart and mind to the circle, the sun, the wind, the moon, and the trees.

5. Say the following words and feel their meaning in your heart.

   "Birth, Purpose, Light, Shadow, Create, Love,

   Magick, Rebirth."

6. For a moment be still. Allow your imagination to "speak" of your first moment on Earth.

7. When you are finished, imagine the circle of light disappearing into the egg.

After the spell: Leave the egg and circle for a night. The next day return the items to Nature. Eat the egg in celebration of your birth or crack it onto the Earth. If you made a symbolic egg, keep it in a special place in your home.

A spell is a symbolic act created by you. It is a profound experience. A way you connect with peace, truth, and meaning. It is a way to weave magick around your life. The spell begins with the casting of a *circle*. You have already experienced this, now you will delve deeper into the purpose and power of this powerful symbol. You will bring into this circle the four elements: *fire, air, water, and earth*. This creates your witch's altar. All aspects of the altar will be explored through this book and before each spell there will be a list of what you will need. However, here is a general list of the practical items you will need for your altar and spells. I will refer to these items as "Witch's Utensils," then add the other ingredients for that spell each time.

Witch's Utensils

As a witch you need to be practical and safe while using the elements, so you will require utensils. You will need fireproof holders and containers, made of metal or ceramic, for candles and incense. A metal censer can be used for the burning of charcoal. Take all care burning candles, incense, charcoal, and sealing wax. Never leave a burning candle unattended and cover a hot charcoal with salt when you have finished using it. A spell may not require every element; however, it is good to have utensils for all purposes.

- Candleholders or plates: Sometimes when multiple candles are used, you may position them on a plate. A hint: If the candle isn't self-standing, melt wax onto the plate and stand the candle in it before it sets.

- Incense censer or holders: For burning charcoal, place a bed of salt in the censer or container. This allows some air to move under the charcoal.

- Container for salt.

- Blending vessel for oils. Swirl oils in a small container.

- Bowl for water: Keep nearby when using sealing wax or for burning spells.

- Self-igniting charcoal. To ignite the charcoal, hold it to a flame using tongs. It will begin to spark. Place it on a bed of salt in the censer. Wait for the charcoal to turn ash white, then add resin or incense. Place a pinch of incense to begin and add more if required.

- A candle snuffer and charcoal tongs.

- Matches and taper candles.

FOUR

The Circle, the Elements, and the Witch's Altar

The circle is a powerful symbol. It is the door between the worlds, the portal for the Divine to enter the realm of Earth, a channel to connect the mind to higher thoughts. This symbol provides a mystical boundary between the mundane and the spiritual, the light and the dark, the ordinary and the extraordinary. The circle defines a sacred space where you will weave magick.

Fall into the beauty of the circle, bewitched by the possibilities the magick holds, at one with a better way, at one with everything.

Tribes gather in a circle for ceremony, we dance in circles, and knights sit at a round table to invoke the energy of equality. People of past worlds built stone circles and humans who enter a faery circle may never return home. The following words tell of the invincible power of the circle, so spiritually contained that not even dark entities could enter its enclosure.

"This (the circle) acts as a magical barrier and bars the entry of the spirit or its influence."[41]

The circle has no beginning and no end. It is a symbol of wholeness and eternity. It is a temple where contact with the Divine is made. The circle holds the energy created in a spell. It is a window to a higher realm, a hallowed defined space, your witch's dreamscape. Your energy is protected within the circle and whatever unfolds within it is deemed profound. Spirits, your ancestors, and divine beings come to Earth through the opening, so it is a portal, a place for sacred communication.

Circles represent the Divine and the cosmos. When three circles link, they symbolise the past, present, and future. Wearing a ring is symbolic of an eternal love with another and Eastern Mandalas include the circle to depict the Universe. In Zen Buddhism the circle represents enlightenment.[42] In astrology a circle with a point in the middle is a symbol of the sun.

The circular sun wheel of the Celtic goddess Brigid was placed in homes for protection at the beginning of spring and represented the increasing power of the sun.[43] The seasonal calendar of witchcraft is called the Wheel of the Year to depict life as an ever-turning circle of beginnings and endings. Halos of mystics and saints are often circles. The symbol of the ouroboros, the World Serpent, forms a circle to devour itself, representing life in circular motion. The circle holds energy in a divine embrace and defines a sacred space where witches weave their magick.

Creating the Circle

A circle can be created anywhere, indoors or outside in Nature, during the day or under the night sky. A circle can be still or move as you do. You can cast a circle for protective purposes as well as for spell-making. Casting a circle helps you to centre yourself and contains your energy. The circle creates a barrier between you and negative energy, so when you feel vulnerable or you need to ground yourself you can cast a circle anywhere. All you need to do is imagine

---

41. Agrippa, *Three Books of Occult Philosophy*, Donald Tyson Annotation, 331.

42. J. C. Cooper, *An Illustrated Encyclopaedia of Traditional Symbols* (London: Thames and Hudson, 1978), 36.

43. Anna Franklin, *Working With Fairies: Magick, Spells, Potions, and Recipes to Attract and See Them* (New Jersey: Career Press, 2006), 205.

the symbol and deem it to be sacred. What the circle looks like is up to you. Your circle also needs to be large enough so your arms, when held out, don't extend beyond its boundary. Every part of you needs to be contained within the symbol.

The symbol is profound and when you open your spell with its casting, you will immediately feel magick.

When a circle is cast, a sacred vibration is instantly birthed. Understand that within the circle you will communicate with a spiritual force both within and outside yourself. And although you have created this mystical portal you will also be in awe of it. For within the circle you will forge a magickal pact with divine energy. You will open your life to change, to trust, and also to mystery and surrender.

Like every act of magick, the circle, when cast, needs to be "seen" in the mind, to be imagined while you make it. It is traditional to cast a circle in accordance to the sun's journey across the sky. The name for this action is *deosil*, a clockwise circular movement. Ancient ritual dances and sabbat circles in the Northern Hemisphere were created clockwise by way of their sun. In the Southern Hemisphere, the sun's movement across the sky is counterclockwise, so many witches in this part of the world open a circle in this direction. The old name for this action is *widdershins*.[44] Always allow your heart to guide you; never worry about doing something wrong. Hold your intention strong in your heart, clear your mind, and fall into the magick.

There are countless, creative ways of casting a circle. The symbol can be cast as you turn around with your arm extended and your index finger pointed. It can be cast with the spoken word or symbolically drawn with a magickal object. A circle can also be made with salt, flowers, drawn with chalk, made with string or rope, or anything that creates the shape. When you create a physical circle, you see it with your eyes. This is a powerful way to cast and is present, visual, and "of this world." When you cast an imagined circle, it is invisible. Either way, the circle is always to be seen in your mind as your temple.

When you use the spoken word to cast a circle, powerful energy is created. You speak, you hear, creating an invisible vibration, a spiritual frequency. The sound of your words allows you to visualise what you say and be truly committed to your magickal intention. Always connect with every word, understand its

---

44. Guiley, *The Encyclopedia of Witches and Witchcraft*, 96.

depth of meaning, and believe your voice will resonate with divine purpose. So, speak from the depths of your heart when you call, "I cast a *circle* around me!"

The Circle's Character

Always "see" the circle as a living entity with a profound, mystical character. Then your circle will be powerful and completely your own. The character of your circle will emerge from your imagination. Allow it to come to you. There is a silent knowing, an atmosphere, a presence in every circle and each cast will be different. A spinning circle of daisies may speak of the need to have fun and activate the heart. A circle of purple tears may mourn the loss of a loved one. A watery circle of singing spirits will assist in the invoking of true love and a circle of red warm desert sand will ground and strengthen your energy. Allow the vision of your circle to be born from deep within you.

Magick circles are not always flat surfaces either. They can extend forever like a tunnel to the heavens, or downward like a well to the roots of an imagined tree or the core of the Earth. Through your imagination the circle can be filled with colour, numbers, and other symbols. The "floor" of the circle can be fluid or rock, clouds, or a million angelic hands holding your feet.

Dissolving the Circle

When the spell is complete, the circle is "dissolved" by you. This is done by turning in the opposite direction to which it was cast with the spoken word or through the imagination. Dissolving the circle can also be enacted physically. If your circle is made of salt or flowers, you can scatter the salt or flowers so the circle no longer exists. Like the casting, the dissolving of the circle is imagined in the mind by "seeing" the symbol disappear, fading away, merging into another form, or ascending skyward or descending into the Earth. Like the casting, the dissolving is a sacred act.

Because the vibration of the circle is akin to the Divine, dissolving it into your being, a significant object, or a symbol allows energies to merge and transform.

Sometimes a spell continues over time, say over a few days. Always dissolve the circle each time and recast when the spell continues. If you need to leave the circle during a spell, perhaps for a forgotten item, it is important to not simply walk through the circle whether it is invisible or made from something you can see. There are many creative ways to create a "door" to go in and out of the circle. Each way needs to be imagined and enacted with intent. You can use your index finger to "cut" a door in the circle. When you walk through the "door," close it with a gesture, like moving your hand over it, and "see" it shut. When you return, repeat the same practice. You can "cut a door" into your circle using your witch's tools, such as a wand or an athame. We will look deeper into this later.

Casting Your Circle

This magickal practice will assist you in understanding the character of your circles. Each circle will reflect you and will be an aspect in the creation of your story. Allow your mind to be at ease. When thoughts come into your mind, simply allow them to pass through without engaging with them. You may hear noises around you, but again don't engage with them. Sit in a quiet place either inside or outdoors. The circles you create will speak of your body, heart, mind, and spirit. Deem them to be healing circles. Create the circles in any way you wish. When you surrender to your imagination, something significant will occur. The vision that first appears in your mind is your circle. Sometimes the circle changes, vibrates, and moves. It is important to accept what comes to you. With each circle, simply note the form, colour, and character. Sometimes words, music, and strange symbols may come to you. After the casting, you can contemplate the meaning. See your circle in your mind and imagine what it is made from. If the circle spoke to you, what would it say? What does the symbol's "voice" sound like? What would the circle feel like to touch or what would it taste like? Allow your imagination to create something profound. Bring meaning to every word.

 Practicing the Imagined Circle

1. A circle to heal your body:

Say aloud:

"I cast a circle around me. Within the circle my
body begins to heal."

When you are ready, say:

"I dissolve the circle into my body."

Imagine the circle entering your physical body.

2. A circle to heal your heart:
Say aloud:

"I cast a circle around me. Within the circle my heart begins to heal."

When you are ready, say:

"I dissolve the circle into my heart."

Imagine the circle entering your heart.

3. A circle to heal your mind:
Say aloud:

"I cast a circle around me. Within the circle my mind begins to heal."

When you are ready, say:

"I dissolve the circle into my mind."

Imagine the circle entering your mind.

4. A circle to heal your spirit:
Say aloud:

"I cast a circle around me. Within the circle my spirit begins to heal."

When you are ready, say:

"I dissolve the circle into my spirit."

Imagine the circle filling your being with light.

The Elements in the Circle

Hear the voice of Nature calling you home, taking your spirit beyond the mind to see your world as a magickal place. Then you will become what you see—*magickal.*

During most spells, all the elements are present in the circle, but not always. Sometimes you may only use one element; it is up to you. A candle flame brings the energy of fire; a feather, incense, or your breath brings the power of air; water in a vessel brings the magick of this element into your circle. You may also use a river or ocean stone or perhaps a shell to bring the energy of water to the circle. Salt, sand, stones, or plants bring the energy of earth to your spell.

Everything in Nature emits a mystical vibration. Divine energy emitted by the four elements in your spell gives rise to the same energy within you, for you too are made from fire, air, water, and earth.

When you hold someone's hand, the energetic connection starts with the sensation of flesh and temperature. After a while, the connection deepens and you begin to feel the spirit of the person, the energy beyond the physical. Connecting with the energy of the four elements begins with the five senses. You actually see air rising as incense smoke, hear the sound of water pouring into a bowl, feel the warmth of a flame, taste salt, and smell the scent of herbs. The four elements create atmosphere, mood, shadow, fragrance, sound, vision, and texture. This is your initial experience in the circle, the heightening of the senses. And so, the change begins. Then the energy will call you deeper into the heart of their essence. Each element has a magickal energy of light and shadow. This same energy also resides in you.

In Nature, the power of the four elements is humbling as well as exhilarating, fascinating as well as frightening. Within you the elements also hold opposing forces. Each element can be transformative, creative, and inspiring as well as stagnant, mundane, and destructive. All live in your body, heart, mind, and spirit. All hold power that can liberate or limit, motivate or dull, bring peace or incite chaos. Two opposing forces are found in everything magickal. Fire purifies and can also burn. Water cleanses and can also drown.

Air is breeze as well as a tornado. Earth is stable and also dust.

The flame is the sun and countless stars, the inferno at the core of Earth, the light, and the warmth. Water is the ocean, rivers, streams, lakes, and rain, Life. Air is the wind, breath. Salt, stones, sand, and plants are the Earth, home. With the elements in the circle, you will feel at one with this brilliant force and the transformation from the ordinary to the sacred begins.

Within the circle of a spell, prepare to balance your inner world, bringing growth, wisdom, compassion, insight, and therefore change. Each element within you can move in perfect unison with another. Restore and renew the other within your heart and mind. With the elements you can transform what is stagnant, unkind, and depleted in your life as you weave your own fascinating story.

These elements are the foundation of your witch's altar.

The Witch's Altar

An altar is a shrine, a sanctuary, a hallowed place dedicated to a sacred purpose. Altars occur naturally in Nature, like a circle or grove of trees, an auspicious formation of rocks, a waterfall, or a place inside a cave.

Altars have also been constructed through time and most mystical and religious traditions have them. Hindu altars are abundant with offerings of flowers, fruit, and incense to the deities or ancestors. Many Eastern traditions incorporate altars into places of business, restaurants, as well as the home. Day of the Dead altars in Mexico are decorated with photos of loved ones and saints, candles, offerings, and "bread of the dead." Sweets are placed on the altars for the spirits of children, and painted ceramic skulls and flowers create a vision of colour and splendour. Catholic altars represent the table of the last supper of Christ and include a tabernacle, a small doored box that contains the believed body of Christ. In the temples of the Goddess in India, the priest pours a red powder used to mark women's brows. This Hindu altar is a depiction of a *yoni*,[45] the female sexual organs, representing the goddess Shakti. For the ancient Greeks, a hearth held the sacred flame at their altars, which were also places of sacrifice.[46] Candles, flowers, incense, and offerings decorate most altars everywhere, and the purpose is to emit energy that compels you to connect with other spiritual realms.

Altars are raised to depict oneness with the sacred. They are viewed as the microcosm, a container and focus for hallowed energy, prayer, and connection. Thought also to represent the spiral,[47] as well as a doorway through which spiritual knowledge is acquired. Altars have also been aligned with the symbolism of the mountain and the tree,[48] the connection between the Three Realms.

---

45. Campbell, *Goddesses: Mysteries of the Feminine Divine*, ed. Saffron Rossi, 106.
46. Jason Mankey and Laura Tempest Zakroff, *The Witch's Altar: The Craft, Lore and Magick of Sacred Space* (Woodbury, MN: Llewellyn Publications, 2019), 32.
47. Jean Chevalier and Alain Gheerbrant, *The Penguin Dictionary of Symbols*, trans. John Buchanan-Brown (London: Penguin Press, 1996), 18.
48. Becker, ed. *The Element Encyclopedia of Symbols*, trans. Lance W. Garmer. 333.

Your witch's altar is a place that will resonate a magickal vibration; it is a place for spells, to hold the four elements and your other sacred tools and objects. This witch's shrine may be ever-changing to reflect a dedication, the seasons, and your hopes and dreams. This creates movement and the magick of ending and beginnings, reflecting the movement and phases of your own life. The full moon and new moon are times to add a flower or an offering to the Goddess. The witch's sabbats are a good time to change the energy and embellishments on your altar. If made of wood, you may rub essential oils onto it to purify and add a beautiful scent. Your altar can be elaborate or simple and can borrow elements from any mystical tradition and your own imagination. Your altar always reminds you of magick and will imbue your home with a mystical quality and reverence. The creation of an altar is a spell in itself because you are crafting a story of magick.

Traditionally the four elements are placed in their magickal directions on the altar. This includes the actual element and the witch's tool that belongs to the element. You will learn about the use, symbolism, and power of these tools in a later chapter. Use a compass to locate the direction or use the approximation of the rising and setting sun. In both hemispheres, the sun rises in the east and sets in the west. Even though, between the equinoxes it pivots around the exact directions; the sun will always help you to know the compass points. Always be spontaneous and listen to your intuition when creating your altar for this is a spell in itself. At times you may burn many candles during a spell and don't want to place them all in the same place on the altar, or a spell may require you to position the elements in a circle or another shape.

Traditionally, a candle and tools of the fire element are positioned in the south direction in the Northern Hemisphere and the north direction in the Southern Hemisphere. However, always listen to your own intuition when setting up for a spell. Over time you may use different sized candles and colours and have a collection of holders. Wide candles can be placed on plates and tea lights in containers. Jar candles and floating candles can also be used on your altar. The witch's *wand* is the tool of the fire element and is placed in the same direction.

Air, and therefore incense or a feather, is placed in the east direction. There are many types of incense you can use, including sticks and cones, smudging herbs that are bundled together, and powdered blends of herbs and resin that are burnt on self-igniting charcoal. You will need a metal container, incense holder, or censer for your incense. Place some salt in a container and stand incense sticks in it. A small amount of salt in a censer allows for better burning of the charcoal, as some air moves under it. Some censers have a handle or chain so you can gently create movement to assist igniting charcoal. Gently blowing on the charcoal as it is initially sparking also helps. Found feathers hold the vibration of air and can be used to bring the element to the altar as well as to create movement through the incense smoke. The witch's knife or *athame* is the tool of the air element and is also placed in the east direction.

Water and water element items from Nature are positioned in the west direction. Collect rainwater or water from Nature when you can. However, water from a tap still holds the energy of the element. You may gather a collection of significant containers for the water element; however, the witch's tool of water is the *chalice* and it also holds its element and is placed west. Other tools associated with the water element are the *cauldron* and the *mirror*. Natural items from an ocean, lake, or river can also be positioned in the same direction.

Earth and all that grows and is found in the natural physical world is positioned in the north in the Northern Hemisphere and the south in the Southern Hemisphere. Salt is usually present to represent the earth element as it grounds the witch during spells and is energetically protective. To bring this element's power to your altar, embellish it with flowers, herbs, branches, rocks, and stones. Rice, grains, fruit, and bread are also placed on the altar for seasonal spells and offerings. The witch's pentacle is the tool of the earth element and is also placed in the same direction.

There are other significant objects like the witch's *besom* or *broom*, the *grimoire* or *Book of Shadows*, the *bell*, and *mortar and pestle*. These sacred objects, explained in depth later, may be kept on or near your altar according to your wishes. You may wish to include an altar cloth, statues, or images of the deities, nature spirits, or creatures, both real and mystical. Crystals or divination tools, such as the Tarot, runes, and pendulum, may be included on your altar.

Your altar will change with every spell, and just being close to it will remind you that you are a witch.

Now travel deeper into the magick of the elements...

FIVE
The Element Fire

Imagine the dark, then light. Imagine a spark above your head, a new idea. Imagine the sun bright in your mind. Feel the "flame of love." Picture yourself dancing with fire-spirits, holding a burning torch while entering a cave. Imagine a phoenix rising from hot ashes and see, in your mind's eye, a shield of flames surrounding you.

Fire

Element of Action
The Sun God
The Soul
Spark of Creation
The Energy of Life

Fire is the sun, the stars, and the burning flames of Earth's core. The sun is the wondrous star that illuminates your planet. This same element is found within you in a flush of anger, through the warmth of an embrace, in the pain of a fever, and the rapture of a kiss. Fire rises when you dance. It is the heat in your blood. When there is no warmth in a body there is no life. Fire is the unseen divine spark, the beating of a heart, the fire in your belly when you are excited and wildly enthusiastic. Fire is the burning desire of passion and love within you.

The Egyptians embodied the power of fire in Sekhmet. She is the lioness goddess of the battle and is crowned with a solar disk. Her magick is fire and her fury personifies anger unhinged.[49] In Hawaii, the inferno of the volcano is the goddess Pele. She is the embodiment of the flame and offerings are thrown into her crater to appease her.[50] The ancient Greeks venerated their fire god, Hephaestus, whose element embodied creativity in the forging of weapons for the gods.[51] Fire is also the Roman goddess of the hearth, Vesta. She was seen as the light of the home, the flame itself, and the expression of life.[52]

Fire is the element of action, vitality, and awakening. Fire purifies, invokes power, transmutes, and brings energy. It protects as well as destroys and it also banishes all that is not aligned with its magickal force. Fire is the creative spark, the vital spirit, the bringer of enlightenment, the essence of desire and vitality. It is the element of motivation because it warms things up and gets you going. Fire holds the quality needed in creativity, the ability to transform vision into the physical, and to transcend limitations through the "wildfire" of the imagination. Fire doesn't let ideas rest or remain dormant because by nature it is always moving, providing fuel to awaken.

Fire magick dispels the unwanted and brings illumination through elimination of mundane thinking. It is used to banish dark entities and renders hexes, bad luck, and curses to the Light. Fire's power to destroy can be reckless and out of control, but when in balance its potential is commanding. It protects against depleting and harmful energy and creates energetic boundaries. Symbolically and physically it disintegrates all that comes too close or is harmful.

A connection with the magick of fire is made when a sunrise becomes a new beginning, and when a bonfire excites the heart. When you see the light of fire,

---

49. Manfred Lurker, *An Illustrated Dictionary of the Gods and Symbols of Ancient Egypt*, English Language Edition, (London: Thames and Hudson Ltd, 1995), 106.

50. Stone, *Ancient Mirrors of Womanhood*, 164.

51. Farrar, *The Witches' God*, 28.

52. Farrar, *The Witches' Goddess*, 285.

not only as combustion but a spiritual direction and destination, you understand its magick. When light, the illumination of the physical becomes "Light," you use it to illuminate your heart and mind, to show you the way to be and the way to go.

The divinity of fire is symbolized in Demeter's burning torch. It guided her into the unknown of the Underworld to find her daughter Persephone. At the winter solstice, the Yule log of the Celts burnt bright in the hearth, bringing the magick of fire into the home.[53] Fire was the gift from the Greek god Prometheus to humankind[54] and is also the gentle lights of the will-o'-the-wisps, faery-like creatures that bring illumination to the night.

The Fire Element in a Spell

The magick of fire is present with the flame of a candle during a spell.

The colour associated with the element fire is red and its ruling planet is the Sun. Fire is thought to be masculine in character.[55] It calls in magick from the south in the Northern Hemisphere and from the north in the Southern Hemisphere. This is due to each hemisphere's relationship to the equator, the warmest position on our planet. The mystical salamander is the elemental spirit of fire.

The fire element is of action. It rules the realms of banishment, protection, willpower, illumination, and manifestation. In all spells, the flame "lights" your path to spiritual fulfilment.

Fire magick eliminates fear and doubt through the brightness of Light. It illuminates, showing the way through the darkness of hardship. It connects you to the radiance of the sun, to warmth and brilliance. It is the flame of optimism, hope, and faith. Fire activates the energy of determination, so it is the element of willpower calling you to take charge. It is the force of zeal that pumps through the heart of undying desire, the element of instant attraction and of burning passion. Fire is used for purifying energy, to call on spiritual power, and to make something real, tangible, or effective. Fire brightens the mind's outlook and invokes lion strength. It holds the power to mesmerize and

---

53. McCoy, *Sabbats: A Witch's Approach to Living the Old Ways*, 68, 69.

54. Cotterell and Storm, *The Ultimate Encyclopedia of Mythology*, 77.

55. Chevalier and Gheerbrant, *The Penguin Dictionary of Symbols*, trans. John Buchanan-Brown, 345.

entrance. It transports you to other worlds. The flame is a way to divine and to inspire your psychic abilities. The flame is also used as a divine offering to the spirit world and beckons loved ones closer to brightness.

The candle flame purifies the circle for your sacred enactment.

The Witch's Candle

The candle belongs to the fire element, yet it is the only tool that holds all four elements. The wax and the black soot are earth. The lit candle becomes liquid, so it holds water, and when burning, it transforms to gas, the air element.

Bring the power of the spoken word to the power of the candle. Ignite a candle flame and your imagination to "see" beyond your eyes, as you say:

> "By earth and wind, by rain and sun,
> All elements in the wax are one.
> I see a flame, a sacred light,
> A rising sun, A starlit night."

Candles were once made from rushes and tallow in Egypt and Crete as early as 3000 BC.[56] To the ancient Egyptians, fire represented purification and was the element of banishment. Taweret, their hippopotamus goddess, carries a flaming torch able to destroy demons.[57] Throughout Europe the ancient festivals that marked the seasons all involved the flame. Fire was used to ward off spirits at the witch's sabbat, Samhain. To assist the sun's birth at the winter solstice and to imitate the sun's journey, rolling fiery wheels were sent blazing down hillsides at midsummer.[58]

The candle flame moves, flickers, crackles, and brightens and can be used to communicate with other realms. It is the light that beckons ghosts to come close and can also be the light that keeps unwanted spirits away. Candles are used as offerings to the dead, for they are a symbol of a prayer, a message, or a memory. They are also burnt as petitions and devotions to the deities. The flame voices other worlds and *shows the way* to truth, to the gates of initia-

---

56. "History," National Candle Association, accessed August 20, 2020, https://candles.org /history/.

57. Lurker, *An Illustrated Dictionary of the Gods and Symbols of Ancient Egypt*, 119.

58. McCoy, *Sabbats: A Witch's Approach to Living the Old Ways*, 58.

tion and to ritual. Mystics use the flame to connect with spirit, fortune-tellers read their cards under the glow, and mediums see visions within it. The blacksmith has always been viewed as possessing magickal powers due to the ability to forge with fire.[59] In Britain they were known as "blood charmers," a name for a healer, and were thought to be able to see the future.

Candles are a scrying tool. To scry is to "see" beyond the eyes. The moving flame, the patterns and shapes in the wax, are interpreted in predictions and omens. During scrying you may see an actual shape that depicts something clearly and other times you will intuitively receive a symbolic message through the flame and wax. This message may appear as a picture in your mind's eye, a physical sensation, a sudden emotion, a sound, a voice, or a colour. Use your imaginative powers and insight when scrying because this is your portal to magick thinking and is limitless.

Create a magickal state of mind before any scrying work. As you read the following, visualise every image. Practice each step and your psychic and creative abilities will become powerful. Always relax and allow the energy to flow without trying to make it happen. When you truly connect with your imagination, you step beyond the ordinary world, so allow the magick to come to you naturally.

Start with a question in mind or ask about the past, the present, and the future. You may see an actual picture (like a flying bird). What does this mean to you? Or as you look into the shape, a feeling may come to you, an image in your mind, or a word. Allow the energy to flow. Try not to logically work out what the shape is telling you. The first thing to come to you will be right.

Scrying can be done through all moon phases but is most potent on the full or new moon. On the full moon your intuition is heightened with the rise of emotions and sensitivity. On the new moon, potential to see the unknown and to sense the future will be within your reach. Scrying can be done outdoors or inside at a table or your altar.

The purpose of scrying is to divine, to read the patterns and shapes of the wax or soot when seeking an answer. Scrying is a way to develop your psychic abilities and intuitive powers. This psychic method will also deepen your

---

59. Franklin, *Working With Fairies: Magick, Spells, Potions, and Recipes to Attract and See Them*, 206.

understanding of symbols and the knowledge they hold. Scrying, like spells, communicates in the language of symbols and signs. You will connect deeper and deeper with magick as you learn to read symbols and to "see" as a witch. Scrying also heightens the imagination. It is creative, wonderous, and inventive. Scrying is a creative experience with friends at a gathering too.

Prepare to Scry

Prepare to scry by following these magickal steps. This is a way to free your mind of the mundane and become the witch.

1. Breathe in and out three times. Imagine breathing in light and breathing out worry. Worry can take the form of grey smoke. When a thought comes into your mind, allow it to pass through without engaging with it.

2. Allow your thoughts to become birds or stars or swirling colours. See the image in your mind.

3. Be at one with the sun. Imagine merging with the energy of light and warmth.

4. The sun goddess Amaterasu will shine in your mind. See the beautiful goddess in your imagination.

5. Imagine a flame. It is a magickal doorway. Now "travel" in your mind through its portal.

6. You are ready to scry.

Scrying with Wax and Water

You will need: A candle. You may choose any colour according to your intuition or refer to the colour chart in the Appendix. Wider candles create more wax when burning, so minimum (2 in. or 5 cm) diameter is good. Candle jars can also be used. A burning time of one hour or more is good. You will need to pre-light the candle to allow a pool of melted wax on the top. Bowl of water. Witch's utensils.

Begin with the lit candle and bowl of water before you.

1. Cast a circle around you. Imagine it is formed with candles.

2. Pour the liquid wax from the top of the candle into the bowl of water.

3. The wax forms unique shapes. Allow the answer to come to you.

4. When you are finished, allow the "circle of candles" to fade in your mind.

5. Snuff out the candle.

After scrying: If the candle is not completely burnt, relight it in the future for other magickal purposes. Remove the wax from the water. Dispose of the wax ethically or recycle. Pour water onto the Earth.

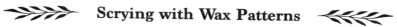

Scrying with Wax Patterns

You will need: A candle. You may choose any colour according to your intuition or refer to the colour chart in the Appendix. This candle can be any size; however, a smaller candle is more practical to flick the wax. Paper, size approximately (12 in. x 8 in; 30 cm x 20 cm). Witch's utensils.

Begin with candle and paper before you.

1. Hold a question in your mind.

2. Cast a circle. Imagine it vibrating with red light.

3. Light the candle.

4. Allow your intuition to guide you as you carefully flick wax over the paper to create a pattern.

5. The answer will come to you in shapes created by the wax.

6. When you are finished, dissolve the "circle of red light" by imagining it ascending to the sun.

7. Snuff out the candle.

After scrying: Write your purpose or question on the paper and include in your psychic journal or grimoire. If the candle is not completely burnt, you can relight it in the future for other magickal purposes.

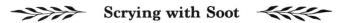 **Scrying with Soot**

You will need: A candle of any size. You may choose any colour according to your intuition or refer to the colour chart in the Appendix. This candle can be any size. Paper of any size. Witch's utensils.

Begin with the candle and paper before you:

1. Hold a question in your mind.

2. Cast a circle. Imagine it's made from flames.

3. Move the paper above the flame, allowing black soot to mark the page.

4. The pattern formed by the soot will speak to you symbolically.

5. When you are finished, imagine the "circle of flames" fading away.

6. Snuff out the candle.

After scrying: Write your purpose or question on the paper and include in your psychic journal or grimoire. If the candle is not completely burnt, you can relight it in the future for other magickal purposes.

Fire is the element of banishment. Banishment is the act of getting rid of unwanted energy within you. Everyone has energy that is depleting, outworn, and destructive. Some people believe they are under a hex or curse and are unable to make things right within them. In some ways hexes and curses are very real because the fear and imbalance is made stronger through not recognising what has created this energy. A state of being hexed is captured in a state of mind that births powerlessness, the inability to change life. If this remains unchecked, it can result in acceptance and sometimes the embracing of a type of half-life where nothing is authentic or magickal. This is heard to the sighs of

"Well, that's just me" and "Nothing will ever change." No doubt, it is hard to change the effects of trauma and other terrible experiences, but combined with the help of counsellors and other therapists, the lighting of a candle in a spell is a way to set your intention and begin to create the magick of illumination.

Sometimes other people's energy can also be absorbed into your own. Being near sadness or anger and other energies can be contagious. It is important to energetically protect yourself and banish depleting energy that comes from someone else. Overly worrying and thinking about someone else can create a situation where you live through them. It is important to be caring but also to be centred and energetically strong. Fear, hurt, and worry can hold on to the heart and mind for a long time. Difficult experiences can live within you and life can become tainted and limited by them. As hard as it is, it is important to shine the "light of fire" on your inner world so you become aware of the shadow, the fear within you. This isn't always easy, and it is often hard to acknowledge. However, when you become aware of your fears, you will be able to transform them and banish them into the *Light*. This may take time, but with each spell you will change, grow, and become wiser. With each spell any unwanted energy will begin to transform into its opposite, so fear becomes trust, disappointment becomes curiosity, and hurt becomes healing. Never be afraid of truth, for with it comes divine inspiration.

Fire Element Banishing Spell

Purpose: To become aware of unwanted energy within you and to give it a magickal form. To transform it into a higher energy; to heal, know, and free yourself.

When to cast: During the waning moon. Day or night.

Where to cast: Indoors at your altar or outside under the sky.

You will need: A purple candle of any size. Bowl of water. Paper approximately 6 in. x 6 in. or 15 cm x 15 cm. A pencil. Take all care with the burning paper. Witch's utensils.

Begin with the ingredients before you.

1. Hold the intention to banish unwanted energy in your mind.

2. Cast a circle. Imagine the circle is made from tall purple candles.

3. Light the candle.

4. Breathe deeply three times.

5. Allow the unwanted energy to "appear" in your heart as a form, symbol, shape, or word.

6. Take a moment to look at it, hear it, smell it, touch it, and even taste it in your imagination.

7. When you know the energy on all these levels, hold the paper to your heart.

8. Imagine the "form," the unwanted energy moving into the paper.

9. Now draw what you imagine on the paper.

10. When you are ready, burn the paper on the candle flame. As the paper burns, imagine the unwanted energy diminishing within you.

11. Place the ash into the bowl of water.

12. When you are finished, imagine the "circle of candles" fading into shadows.

13. Snuff out the candle.

After the spell: Pour the water and ash onto the Earth. If any of the candle remains, relight it in the future with this same intention in mind.

Balancing the Fire Element

Each of the elements exist within you physically as well as energetically.

When the fire element is out of balance within you, you can "burn out" because too much action can be depleting. When you feel this way, you need to stop, ground yourself (earth), and reflect on life through the magick of water. Too much fire can also "burn out" others around you because it can eliminate without discretion. This happens when someone is "shouted down" because of overzealous enthusiasm. Again, the energy of earth is needed for steadfastness and stability. Fiery passion, if left unchecked, can transform into obsession and manifest in foolish action. Desire can be mistaken for love, discussion becomes "heated," and philosophy becomes doctrine. When this occurs, earth's steadfastness can be your anchor and the movement of air can clear your mind. The energy of anger is ruled by fire. Anger and rage have the power to banish what is unjust, but can also go out of control. So, the reason of the mind (air) and the compassion of the heart (water) will restore balance.

In Hindu mythology Kali, the goddess of destruction, dances on the body of the god Shiva, the embodiment of silence and truth. She is the expression of action, found in the fire element. He is divine silence, the air element. Combined, both energies create transcendence.[60]

The element of fire in the circle calls you to act, to create impact on the world around you, and to raise the illumination and warmth of the sun within you. It asks you to nurture the creative spark of an idea and take the next step towards its creation. It is the element of will, so reminds you of your power to be the witch in full command of life.

Hold the flaming torch of the goddess Demeter and illuminate your story with the power of the element fire.

---

60. Cotterell and Storm, *The Ultimate Encyclopedia of Mythology*, 376.

SIX
The Element Air

Hear the echoes of other realms; tree branches move in the wind as the night Goddess weaves your destiny in her tapestry of stars. Imagine walking into a wild wind, one by one each piece of clothing is blown away. The wild wind lifts you from the ground and takes you to a place of flying birds, of which you are now one.

Air
Element of the Mind
Breath of the Gods
Power of Thinking
Intelligence

Air moves as the wind, a breeze, a hurricane, and a whirling tornado. Air carries seeds to new ground and is the ride of the birds. Air can be gentle, furious, or wild. It is the puppet master of the weather. Air blows the clouds, pelts the rain, whips up the ocean, and conjures a dust storm.

The wind brings change and blows cobwebs from the mind. Air calls to freedom with magic-carpet rides through the endless sky. It is the invisible element that moves you in different directions. Air is thoughts in a whirlwind as well as the order of the intellect. It is the breath of fresh air that takes you to a new mindset. This same force moves within you, as your breath, holding you to *life*.

This element can create a vortex of chaos when thinking becomes overwhelming or a vortex clearing when thinking becomes stagnant. Air's power to deconstruct can be destructive, but when in balance its potential is brilliant. Physically it blows away and symbolically it does the same with the mind, so it keeps thinking fresh and ever-changing.

A connection with the magick of air is made when you imagine the wind as a kiss from the heavens and when words in a book create pictures in your mind. When a thought, an inspiration, seems to come out of thin air, you experience this magick, and when a pendulum swings through the air and you divine the future, you have made this connection. Merging your imagination with the element of air happens when you see incense smoke as a divine stairway to the heavens, and on an icy night when your breath creates "frosty ghosts" as it moves from your mouth.

The Greek god Hermes is the embodiment of the air element. He is the bringer of messages from the heavens and guide to the Underworld.[61] The Chinese called their wind goddess Feng Pho Pho. She rode the winds on a tiger's back[62] and in ancient Egypt the arched back of the goddess Nut was the sky itself.[63]

The Element Air in a Spell

Air is present at the spell through your breath, incense smoke, or a feather.

The colour associated with air is yellow and its ruling planet is Mercury. Air calls the magick of the sylph elementals and the energy from the direction east. Air is thought to be masculine in nature.

61. Farrar, *The Witches' God*, 184.

62. Monaghan, *The New Book of Goddesses and Heroines*, 124.

63. Lurker, *An Illustrated Dictionary of the Gods and Symbols of Ancient Egypt*, 90.

The air element is of the mind. It rules the realms of the intellect, knowledge, wisdom, communication, movement, direction, learning, freedom, travel, music, and vision.

Air is the keeper of intelligence, the ruler of thinking. It brings information, expands knowledge, and is the element of learning and discerning. The air element is the force of change, of vision and clarity. Its virtues speak of unlimited thinking. It is the realm of the birds, movement, and the never-ending skies. The ability to master air is rewarded with the symbolic gift of flight, a higher vision of life from the "mountaintop" where the sylphs reside. Hence it is the element of wisdom, fairness, and insight. Air clears the mind of the ordinary and brings heavenly perception. Its magick is used to activate higher thinking and the ability to communicate these thoughts effectively to others. It transforms stagnant energy and calls to freedom.

The quality of air rules humour; it is playful and light as a feather, so it is the opposite of being bogged down, heavy, and void of fun. It is also the element used while working with spirits, smoke scrying, and using tools of divination, like the pendulum.

Air is the ruler of messages, beginnings, and news. Through incense smoke, air moves towards the heavens, taking wishes to other worlds, petitions to the deities, and calls on ancestors for guidance. Divine entities, such as angels and the Greek god Hermes, belong to this element. Their wings speak of their kinship with air and their ability to move between the realms of Earth and the Heavens. They are divine messengers and harbingers of guidance.

The element air inspires movement, flexibility, and change. It inspires the desire to see "which way the wind blows." The energy of air brings knowledge of authenticity, clarity, and cleverness, so through its energy true direction is found and mastery of the mind becomes a journey.

The Magick of the Word and Writing: Air

The air element rules the spoken and written word. To say something aloud, whether in full voice or a whisper, takes the intention from thought to sound. When you speak aloud during a spell, your intention becomes clearer and defined; you hear your words while communicating with a higher force. Words spoken aloud in a spell are called an incantation. Incantations are very powerful as the spoken word is at one with the air. Incantations are often repeated; this reinforces the power and raises the energy of the meaning of the words. Words are a binding force with the Divine.

Writing is aligned with sight and with touch. It is a physical manifestation, so it is potent in the creation of a spell. Anything written or drawn is a contract with the sacred, a binding act of magick. It is a declaration of a quest, made clear. It is a part of the weave that creates your story, symbolically and physically, in the circle. The written word is definite, "set in stone," and absolute.

Var is the Norse goddess of contracts and oaths. Her name comes from the word vow and her role is to ensure promises are honoured and true contracts unbroken.[64]

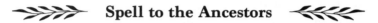

Spell to the Ancestors

Purpose: To connect with long-passed family for guidance and wisdom in all situations. Your ancestors come as a wise, gentle whisper in your mind, an invisible hand pointing the way.

When to cast: During the waxing moon. Day or night.

Where to cast: Indoors at your altar or outside under the sky.

You will need: Paper (3 in. x 3 in. or 7 cm x 7 cm) and a pencil. Begin with the items before you.

1. Cast a "circle of dancing spirits." See them in your imagination.

2. Write the words, "To my ancestors. Guide my way."

3. In your imagination: Hear their footsteps, then their voices.

4. Write down what they say. Allow the words to move through the pencil without your thoughts interrupting them.

5. When you are finished, imagine the "circle of dancing spirits" ascending into the sky.

After the spell: Write your purpose or question on the paper and include in your psychic journal or grimoire.

---

64. Kveldulf Gundarsson, *Teutonic Magic: The Magical and Spiritual Practices of the Germanic Peoples* (St. Paul, MN: Llewellyn Publications Inc., 1990), 232.

Magick of the Name: Air

The ancient Egyptians believed a name was an entity, a living energy.[65] The South American indigenous people in Chiloé keep their names a mystery. They believed mischievous fairies could inflict harm if they had this knowledge.[66] To speak the names of the dead was and still is taboo in many cultures, as this may call the soul back to Earth.[67]

A name brings knowledge and therefore power. Names and naming belong to the element air. To take a secret name or bestow a name is potent magick. The Egyptian goddess, Isis, gained enormous power, for herself and her son Horus, by knowing the secret name of Ra, the Sun God. Ra ruled over all life and the Heavens. His power was beyond any of the other deities. Isis, goddess of magick, desired such power, so fashioned a serpent to poison Ra. When the poison began to diminish the god, he begged Isis to heal him. She agreed, in exchange for knowing his name. His name was passed from his heart to her heart along with his two eyes of the moon and the sun. Isis gifted these to her son Horus the Falcon god.[68]

To know someone by name creates a kinship; to bestow a name creates a bond. Like creating a special name for a friend. It is symbolic of a deep understanding and connection. The ideogram, or unspoken name of Nammu, the Sumerian creation goddess, was the same as the symbol used to denote the ocean, linking her as one with the seas.[69]

Choosing a magickal name is a way for you to step into the mystery and the power of secrecy. Your witch's name defines and strengthens energy inside the circle because the name is known only within this sacred space. A name may also express an alliance with the Divine. You can create a witch's sigil with your name. A sigil is a highly personalised design unique to you. It is your magickal signature.

To create your sigil, arrange the letters of your name in any way, making sure they all connect in some way. The arrangement can be vertical or horizontal, or

---

65. Adele Nozedar, *The Illustrated Signs and Symbols Sourcebook: An A to Z Compendium of Over 1000 Designs* (London: HarperCollins, 2010), 420.

66. Frazer, *The Golden Bough: A Study in Magic and Religion*, 245.

67. Frazer, *The Golden Bough: A Study in Magic and Religion*, 252.

68. Monaghan, *The New Book of Goddesses and Heroines*, 166.

69. Baring and Cashford, *The Myth of the Goddess*, 186.

even back to front, in any order. Each letter can also be drawn in a different size, capital, or small case. Some letters can use other letter shapes to form their own.

The making of the sigil is a powerful tool and, on seeing it, you mysteriously understand a deeper side of yourself.

Scrying a Witch's Name

Purpose: The purpose of this spell is to allow a witch's name to come to you from a divine source.

When to cast: On the new moon. Day or night.

Where to cast: Indoors at your altar or outside under the sky.

You will need: An incense stick of any kind. Witch's Utensils. Begin standing while holding the incense.

1. Light the incense stick. Hold it with your arm extended and turn by way of the sun to create a "circle of clouds" around you.

2. Still holding the incense, say:

   "A witch's name for me to write,
   By light of day and dark of night.
   By moving smoke my name will rise,
   To appear from air, before my eyes."

3. Breathe deeply in and out three times as you wave the incense stick before you.

4. Close your eyes as you move the incense in any way you wish.

5. When you are ready, open your eyes. What name do you see in the smoke? Allow the name to come from your imagination.

6. When you are finished, hold the incense outward again and turn in the opposite direction to dissolve the circle.

After the spell: Record your witch's name and create a sigil with it. It is up to you who you tell. Some witches keep their magickal name secret and others make it known or change their given name to it. It is up to you. Allow the incense to burn completely.

Power of the Breath: Air

Breath is life and breathing onto words or objects connects your lifeforce with the intention represented. When the breath moves from mouth to the written word or object, the act needs to be imagined or "seen" in the mind.

Imagine your breath is a beautiful silver light. This silver light moves into the letters of the name you have created for yourself. With each breath, each letter becomes gold. The light of the letters then becomes the wind and your name becomes one with all things.

The words "breath" and "soul" come together in the name of Psyche, the Greek goddess. Her enrapture with Eros represents everlasting love and devotion.[70] The breath of Sekhmet, the Egyptian lioness goddess, created the vast deserts of Egypt.[71] The goddess Isis moved her wings to create a breath of air and resurrected the god Osiris from the dead.[72]

In the fifteenth century, the occultist Cornelius Agrippa wrote, "... therefore magicians enchanting things are wont to blow and breathe upon."[73] These words express the significance of the breath and its ability to "enchant," and therefore imbue, with a magickal power.

The power of the air element is found in the flight of faeries and the magnificent wings of Pegasus, the flying horse in Greek myth. The power of air is personified in Zeus, Greek god of the skies, and its beauty is embodied in Saraswati, the Hindu goddess of speech, wisdom, and music.[74]

 ## Spell to Enchant Your Witch's Name

Purpose: You have now received your witch's name. In this spell you will enchant it with your lifeforce through the power of breath. You will also imbue your witch's name with meaning and purpose through the written word. Again, this spell asks you to be creative and imaginative.

---

70. Monaghan, *The New Book of Goddesses and Heroines*, 257.

71. Farrar, *The Witches' Goddess*, 269.

72. Monaghan, *The New Book of Goddesses and Heroines*, 165, 166.

73. Agrippa, *Three Books of Occult Philosophy*, 217.

74. Monaghan, *The New Book of Goddesses and Heroines*, 273.

When to cast: On the new moon. Day or night.

Where to cast: Indoors at your altar or outside under the sky.

You will need: Paper (3 in. x 3 in. or 7 cm x 7 cm) and a pencil. Begin sitting with the items before you.

1. Cast your circle by saying:

   "I cast a circle of hallowed words around me."

   What words do you "see" in your mind? Allow them to come from your imagination.

2. Now say:

   "I, (state your witch's name), place my name inside the circle."

3. Using your index finger, write your witch's name in the air. Visualise what it looks like. How does it move around the circle? What colour is it? What does it "feel" like? What does the name "taste" of? What is the scent of your witch's name?

4. Write your witch's name on the paper and draw a circle around it. Inside the circle, add any words that give your name magickal meaning. Words like love, peace...

5. When you are finished, hold the paper, and, from the depth of your heart, say your name and then the other words aloud.

6. Now, breathe slowly onto what has been written. Imagine your breath is a brilliant light that illuminates each word.

7. When you are finished say:

   "I dissolve my 'circle of words' by the power of air."

After the spell: Fold the spell paper and place it under your pillow for three nights. Then keep it in your Book of Shadows.

Power of Sacred Smoke: Air

Incense smoke rises to the heavens and in Eastern tradition it was said to create a stairway to the skies. Incense takes our quests and petitions in its willowy embrace to magickal realms.

The moving smoke creates shapes and visions and has been used to scry, induce trances, and bring insight to the past, present, and future. The perfume of incense creates immediate change to an atmosphere. The fragrance aligns you with nature, the senses, the departed, and the otherworldly. Incense dispels unwanted energy and is used magickally to cleanse and enchant objects, to purify psychic tools like cards and mirrors. Incense transforms the aura and dispels low and mundane energy.

Incense is of the air element and has been used through time to connect with the sacred. The burning of incense is said to have replaced blood sacrifice in Egypt.[75] In many mystical traditions it is a way of communicating with the deities, the departed, and other sacred powers. Australia's First People use the smouldering leaves from the emu, dogwood, and other native plants in purification ceremonies and to welcome others to the country.[76] South American shamans burn the holy wood of their wild tree, palo santo (*Bursera graveolens*), to banish anything spiritually impure. White sage (*Salvia apiana*) is traditional in a First Nations American ceremony used to protect, purify, and heal.[77] Common sage (*Salvia officinalis*) was used for the same purpose in ancient Europe. The Romans dedicated the plant to Jupiter, and it was burnt for purification before harvesting.[78]

During the Mexican Day of the Dead, incense is burnt to guide departed loved ones back home. The smoke creates a mystical road from the spirit world to the realm of Earth.[79] In the Babylonian myth of Ishtar's journey to the

---

75. Marcel De Cleene and Marie Claire Lejeune, *Compendium of Symbolic and Ritual Plants in Europe, Vol 1* (Ghent, Belgium: Man and Culture Publishers, 2003), 345.

76. Frazer, *The Golden Bough: A Study in Magic and Religion*, 197.

77. Scott Cunningham, *Cunningham's Encyclopedia of Magical Herbs* (St. Paul, MN: Llewellyn Publications, 2003) 224.

78. Cunningham, *Cunningham's Encyclopedia of Magical Herbs*, 223.

79. Ronnberg and Martin, eds. *The Book of Symbols: Reflections on Archetypal Images*, 726.

Underworld, burning incense was used to bring her dead lover Tammuz back to life.[80]

There is an immense variety of incenses; however, the two ancient resins of frankincense (*Boswellia carterii*) and myrrh (*Commiphora myrrha*) should be included in every witch's cabinet. These two resins call in sacred opposites, beginnings and endings, life and death. When burnt together, frankincense and myrrh conjure a divine longing, for Heaven and Earth to come closer. Both are offerings to the dead and transport the imagination and the soul to beauty and peace. Both speak of the spirit lands, the magnificence of the unknown, and the passage of initiation.

Both purify and invoke the presence of the sacred and call thoughts to prayer. They were the gifts of the Magi in the story of Christ's birth, considered so sacred they were gifted to acknowledge the arrival of the Divine on Earth. Frankincense was symbolic of Christ's divinity and the myrrh foretold of his eventual death.[81]

Myrrh is the perfume of the Egyptian deity Anubis, god of the Afterlife, and was used for embalming and during ceremonies for the dead.[82] The Egyptians also used the golden sap of frankincense to honour the Sun God Ra as he rose to bring the morning light. In Greek myth, Myrrha, the mother of Adonis, was transformed into the myrrh tree from which her son, the most beautiful of Greek gods, was born.[83] In the story of the rising phoenix, the mythical bird creates a nest of frankincense, myrrh, and other spices. When the time of resurrection has come, the rising sun ignites the funeral pyre and the phoenix both dies and is reborn in its combustion.

---

80. Ronnberg and Martin, eds. *The Book of Symbols: Reflections on Archetypal Images*, 726.

81. Ronnberg and Martin, eds. *The Book of Symbols: Reflections on Archetypal Images*, 726.

82. Paul Beyerl, *The Master Book of Herbalism* (Washington: Phoenix Publishing Inc., 1984), 237.

83. Monaghan, *The New Book of Goddesses and Heroines*, 224.

Spell to Purify the Aura and Home

Purpose: To clear mundane and unwanted energy. This spell is to purify the energy around you and your home. It will raise the spiritual vibration around you and bring lightness and balance. The energy created by the incense is also protective.

When to cast: You may wish to create this spell every new moon or whenever you feel the need. Day or night.

Where to cast: Indoors at your altar, then through every room of your home.

You will need: An incense blend of frankincense (*Boswellia carterii*) and myrrh resin (*Commiphora myrrha*) powdered in a mortar and pestle. (Later in the book you will learn more about blending incense.) Self-igniting charcoal. Fresh air and natural light are also important for a magickal home. Witch's utensils.

Begin with ingredients before you. Pre-light the charcoal.

1. Add incense to the hot charcoal. Hold the censer and turn to cast your circle.

2. Say:

    "I cast a circle, around myself and my home.
    Into the circle I call the magick of the wind gods."

3. Move the smoke around your aura. Say:

    "Magick breathe through this sacred smoke. I purify
    my body, heart, and mind of all unwanted energy."

4. Give this energy a form or colour and imagine it merging with the smoke and transforming into sacred energy.

5. Take the incense into every room of your home and say:

    "Magick breathe through this sacred smoke.
    I purify this home of all unwanted energy."

6. Again, give this energy a form or colour and imagine it merging with the smoke and transforming into sacred energy.

7. Now go to your altar and move the smoke over it. Say:

"I bless this altar with sacred smoke."

8. When you are finished, say aloud:

"I dissolve my circle by the breath of the wind gods."

After the spell: Place an offering to the spirit of your home on the altar. This could be a flower, a candle, a stone, or any significant item.

The Divine Feather: Air

A feather is a natural amulet, holding the vibration of the bird and therefore its domain, the skies. From a bird's perspective, life is seen from above, so their view is inspired by higher thoughts. Birds are messengers between the Earth and the Heavens, a way to communication with the Divine.

The energy of freedom is brought to the witch in the form of a feather, for flying is symbolic of being unrestricted by the mundane, the opposite of being earthbound.

Each bird of the sky has a unique character defined by its nature and skills. Many of the deities were aligned with the powers of the bird. Zeus, Greek god of the skies, called on the golden eagle whose might and strength embodied the command of a ruler.[84] Magickal birds flew above the Welsh goddess Rhiannon as she rode her horse through the dreams of humans. Her birds would wake the dead and render the living to sleep.[85] The owl is the totem of Athena, the Greek goddess of wisdom, and is aligned to knowledge and intelligence. The owl is also of the Underworld, an omen of death and endings.[86]

In some countries, the USA in particular, laws strictly prohibit collecting and buying feathers of native birds and it is important to respect this. Research which feathers you are able to collect. If you find a feather in the wild and you are unsure whether you can collect it, simply give honour to the bird and make a wish. Then leave the feather where it was found.

---

84. Baring and Cashford, *The Myth of the Goddess*, 318.

85. Stone, *Ancient Mirrors of Womanhood*, 71.

86. Baring and Cashford, *The Myth of the Goddess*, 337.

Spell of the Element Air for Freedom

Purpose: To free your mind of negative thinking and to connect your thoughts to the boundless skies and to the flight of birds—a symbol of freedom and limitless possibility. Freedom is always found in the mind. When you live in the present, you become aware of how your mind works. Through awareness you can truly set your mind free by not engaging with worry, fear, and doubt. So, practice transforming negative thoughts into birds.

When to cast: During the waxing moon. Day or night.

Where to cast: Indoors at your altar or outside under the sky.

You will need: A feather, real or imagined.
Begin standing, holding the feather.

1. Hold a feather outright with your arm extended and turn, casting your circle. Imagine birds flying from the tip of the feather as you do so.

2. Move the feather close to your lips and say aloud:

    "I call to eagles, swans, and doves. I speak the words of the old religion. Crows, ravens, and hawks, owls, parrots, and sparrows, set free my thoughts."

3. As you say these words, imagine your thoughts transforming into birds and soaring to the heavens.

4. Imagine the circle ascending in the "breath of the wind."

After the spell: Whenever you begin to worry, imagine your thoughts transforming into birds.

Balancing the Air Element

An idea eventually needs action, otherwise it stays in the invisible world of the mind. Sometimes too much thinking, too much of the air element, stops spontaneity so there is no action. When a creative idea is overthought (air), it may lose its heart (water), or may lose its spark (fire) to manifest. A creative idea can also get "stuck in the mud" by the earthly concerns of financial gain, so never eventuates. Or, an idea of the mind (air) may be propelled by heart's desire (water) and imbue by the energy of strength (earth), then actualize through vitality (fire).

The air element is the intellect and is needed to plan and evaluate, but when relationships fall into the realm of thinking, the true feelings of the water element can be lost. Too much air can create scattered thinking. Words can become "hot air" if ungrounded and then they become meaningless. Air rules freedom and movement, but living always on a whim may result in disconnecting with others or commitment. Air needs water to infuse it with feeling, fire to purify the superficial, and earth to bring stability.

Too much air can result in the illusion of "cleverness." This state of mind is an invitation to trickster energy, embodied in the Norse god, Loki,[87] and the Greek gods, Pan and Hermes. These deities thrive in the slippery slide of relentless ego. Loki is alive in deception, self-gratification, and foolishness, when thinking travels beyond the boundaries of reason. Hermes is the deity of boundaries as well as the breach and defiance of them. He is the ruler of intelligence yet is willing to also be wilful when it suits him as god of thieves. The word "panic" comes from the god Pan.[88] He is a nature spirit and associated with the Earth but also appears out of "air" to create mayhem for those lost in their own thinking.

Tricksters embody the state of shock and surprise experienced when potential trouble is not sensed. They are often associated with air because of their shape-shifting ability and mastery of illusion. You need to know the trickster within because, when left in the shadows, this energy can create a loss of connection with the heart, reason, inner strength, and purpose. The magick of the trickster also teaches the opposite energy, the ability to see life with humour, to be quick-minded and smart. When kept in check, trickster energy brings innovation, freedom from convention, the skill to think differently when resolving problems, the secrets of creating art, and the experience of the wild.

---

87. Lecouteux, *Encyclopedia of Norse and Germanic Folklore, Mythology, and Magic*, 177.
88. Farrar, *The Witches' God*, 75–78.

The element of air in the circle asks you to imagine the vastness of thoughts, to feel the desert wind drying your tears, to conjure a warm breeze of conversation between friends, and to see inspiration as a silent whisper from the spirit world. It is the element of the mind and the intellect. For like air, thoughts are invisible.

Give rise to the power of Saraswati, the Hindi goddess of eloquence, and tell your story through the magick of the element air.

SEVEN

The Element Water

Imagine swimming to the depth of the ocean to meet your true love. Picture holding a mirror of water; look into it and see the past, present, and future. Visualise rain cleansing your soul, a river taking you into the unknown.

Water
Element of Feelings
Heart of the Goddess
Stillness and Intuition
Depth

The oceans move as the moon waxes and wanes and this same element falls from your eyes as tears. Water moves into you and through you. You are mostly water, you sweat; you drink. You entered this world with the breaking of water from your mother's body.

Water is the oceans, the rivers, the lakes, and the streams beneath and on the surface of Earth. Water evaporates from the earth to become the rain, sleet, and snow. It is the river of mystery, the seven seas, the pond of prophecy, as well as morning dew on the grass. The moon and water spin the magick of water together. Both are reflective; they are partners, akin to the realm of the heart and the secrets of the heavens.

Once your ancient kin thought all water, rain, oceans, and rivers came from the Goddess. Water and life became one.

A personification of water is also the Hindu deity, Ganga. She is the Ganges River and holds the power to wash away the sins of past lives and to bestow health, happiness, and good fortune.[89] Ran,[90] the Norse sea goddess, is the "queen of the drowned," but her realm also speaks of the depths of love and the power of fertility.[91] Indigenous Australians gave rise to the powerful Rainbow Serpent, central to their creation myth, an embodiment of sacred water and divine resident of the water hole. This divine entity is also the rainbow, water's divine signature of the sky.[92]

Water is a still pond. It is the rolling, crashing power of waves in a stormy ocean; it is a river moving, a waterfall. Water is built-up emotions ready to burst from a thunder cloud. It is the unfathomable depth of the seas, akin to the unknown—limitless and mysterious. It is the element of feelings, ever-changing, light and dark.

The water element rules relationships—how you feel about others. Relationships are pure heart. They are not of the mind and when someone says, "I *think* I love her," authenticity is questioned. Feelings are often described as deep or shallow, words also used to describe water. An outburst of crying that has been supressed is described as "opening the floodgates." Tears taste salty like the ocean. They express opposites joy and sadness, and mysteriously they soothe and bring release and relief. An example of the unity of moon, water, and humanity is found in the Levanah, the Chaldaean name for Moon Goddess.[93] She is considered both ruler of the tides and oceans as well as the nature of women.

---

89. Monaghan, *The New Book of Goddesses and Heroines*, 132.

90. Monaghan, *The New Book of Goddesses and Heroines*, 264.

91. Cotterell and Storm, *The Ultimate Encyclopedia of Mythology*, 189.

92. Willis, ed. *World Mythology: The Illustrated Guide*, 30.

93. Farrar, *The Witches' Goddess*, 240.

In Greek mythology, the world of the living and the world of the dead are separated, as well as connected, by six rivers. These rivers also symbolise feelings that are often pushed into the subconscious, the Underworld, because to recognise their existence within us is uncomfortable. One of these rivers, Styx, is named after the goddess of hatred.[94] This emotion is so forceful and fearful that it creates mystery and suffering both within the person feeling it and the world around them. No one ever wants to experience this destructive aspect of the shadow, but it is a part of the human psyche and needs to be acknowledged and healed.

The opposite of hate is love, the most powerful magick there is. The water element encapsulates love on all levels. It is the deep connection when two people feel they are the one soul; it is love of family, friends, and creatures. It exists in compassion, forgiveness, and sacrifice, in wishing the best for another, and in respect. Love on a universal level is love for strangers, community, and Nature. The Virgin Mary as goddess is also associated with the moon. She is known as the Mistress of the Waters, at one with fertility and birth, yet she is also a goddess who embodies universal spiritual love.

Aphrodite was originally the Great Mother of the eastern Mediterranean, in the islands around Greece, and a deity associated with prophesy[95] and the ocean. When adopted by the Greeks she not only personified sexual desire but was also considered a goddess of platonic love. In Egypt, one of the goddesses of the Nile was Anuket.[96] Her name means "embracer" so her divine essence as water is able to hold and give affection. From Sumerian writings a poem expresses the depths of romance between the goddess Inanna and her lover, Dumuzi. The simple words tell of a true love story. "Like a moonbeam she came forth to him ... He looked at her, rejoiced in her, Took her in his arms and kissed her."[97]

Water, like the moon, rules the unconscious so it rules the realm of the psychic, the seer, and the oracle. Because it reflects, it shows the truth—the way of the past, present, and future. It is akin to the moon in its power to inspire and

---

94. Monaghan, *The New Book of Goddesses and Heroines*, 286.

95. Monaghan, *The New Book of Goddesses and Heroines*, 50.

96. Monaghan, *The New Book of Goddesses and Heroines*, 50.

97. Baring and Cashford, *The Myth of the Goddess*, 210.

heighten the imagination. The potential to explore the depths of the psyche is held in the essence of the water element, its nature is fluid, allowing intuition to flow. Since ancient times "blind springs" have been considered to emanate immense power for healing as well as for prophesy. These are places from which a number of underground waterways radiate. In Europe and the Near East, wells, monuments, and temples were built over them. Blind springs were once places to give birth and meet the Goddess.[98]

Dreams rise in the waves of the water element. They are a fluid realm where the dimension isn't fixed. They are the story of your subconscious, what lies hidden from the world and yourself. Every feeling is heightened in a dream and emotions are often experienced in extreme rapture as well as fear. Like dreams, water changes from clear to cloudy to dark. Sometimes dreams take you into the shadows of your deepest feelings and instincts to survive. Like travelling into the darkness, ocean dreams bring wonder and liberate our fears by bringing them to the surface and into the conscious mind of awareness.

The magick of water heals and invigorates. It refreshes the body, so it also refreshes the spirit. It washes impurities; therefore, it is spiritually cleansing. In England, the water a blacksmith used to cool metal was valued for its healing powers.[99] Certain springs and wells throughout Europe were known to possess healing magick and were associated with the womb of the goddess Hel, as well as the divinity of the Celtic goddess Brigid.

Water is associated with the ability to adapt and with truthfulness. When someone is natural, words, thoughts, and actions seem to flow from them with ease.

A connection with the magick of water is made when you allow the sea to wash your troubles away, when you "sail" into the realm of sleep to hear messages and meet your guides. When you "bathe" in the moon's bewitching glow, see your emotional life as a vast ocean of feelings and feel peace listening to the rain; you are united with the beauty and magick of the element.

At one also with water is Sobek, the Egyptian crocodile god who resides in the Nile River.[100] Tiamat in Mesopotamia was the primordial creation goddess

---

98. Sjöö and Mor. *The Great Cosmic Mother: Rediscovering the Religion of the Earth*, 125–126.

99. Franklin, *Working With Fairies: Magick, Spells, Potions, and Recipes to Attract and See Them*, 206.

100. Lurker, *An Illustrated Dictionary of the Gods and Symbols of Ancient Egypt*, 117, 118.

of the ocean and Great Mother.[101] A spirit of the Yoruba religion is Yemaya. She is an *orisha*, at one with the living oceans, embodying the power to heal through the mystic energy of water.[102]

The Element Water in the Spell

The magick of water is present at a spell in a sacred vessel or container. A shell, crystals associated with water, and natural items from the sea, rivers, and waterways also bring the vibration of water into the circle.

The colour associated with water is blue and the ruling planet is the moon. Water is feminine in many traditions because of its connection to birth. It calls the magick of the undine elemental and to the mystical forces of the west direction.

The water element is of the heart. It rules the realms of feelings, cleansing, healing, forgiveness, compassion, relationships, the psychic, dreams, and the subconscious.

Water is the element of emotions, balance, and reflection. In acts of magick, water is used for love on all levels, for all relationships, to bring balance and depth. Water cleanses and *washes away* anything tarnished. Its energy calls you to contemplate the unfathomable mystery of the ocean, to go with the flow of the *river of life* and to gaze into the depths of a pond. Water magick is reflective and brings insight through stillness. Just as the moon reflects the sun's light, water's magick is reflection. It mirrors the soul, is the harbour of true love, friendship, compassion, true beauty, and grace.

Water brings the energy of reflection and true feelings into the circle.

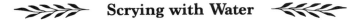 **Scrying with Water**

Purpose: To seek an answer, for divine guidance, and to heighten your psychic abilities.

When to cast: Any phase of the moon but will be particularly powerful on the full moon. Day or night.

Where to cast: Indoors at your altar or outside under the sky.

---

101. Monaghan, *The New Book of Goddesses and Heroines*, 296.
102. Monaghan, *The New Book of Goddesses and Heroines*, 320.

You will need: A bowl of water and a silver coin.

Begin by placing the coin into the bowl of water.

1. In your imagination "see" a "circle of moons" descending from the sky. The circle surrounds you.

2. Gaze into the bowl of water.

3. Breathe and empty your mind of all thinking.

4. Say:

   "I invite the Goddess of the Moon to sit by me. To speak through the coin."

5. In your imagination, allow the coin to become the moon.

6. Listen; the moon will speak to your heart.

7. Observe what comes to you; accept, surrender, and allow the symbols to "talk to you."

8. Take the coin out of the bowl and hold it to your heart. Pour the water onto the Earth or a potted plant.

9. When you are finished, imagine the "circle of moons" ascending to the sky.

After the spell: Keep the coin in a magickal place and use for future scrying or spells.

The magick of water is woven into the myths of Aphrodite, the Greek goddess of love, born from the foamy seas. Water magick speaks of the sacred ponds, mermaids, sirens, and water spirits. It is found in the lotus of Kuan Yin,[103] the Eastern deity of mercy, and in the shape-shifting powers of the German river entities, the bewitching Nix.[104]

---

103. Stone, *Ancient Mirrors of Womanhood*, 28.
104. Lecouteux, *Encyclopedia of Norse and Germanic Folklore, Mythology, and Magic*, 211.

Water in the form of morning dew was associated with Eos, the Greek goddess of the dawn, and was thought to contain the essence of fertility.[105] In ancient Sumerian images, dew along with milk, semen, and honey are symbols of fertility and the moon.[106] Italian witches would also collect dew for blessing and purification magick.[107]

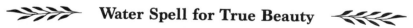

Water Spell for True Beauty

Purpose: True beauty is a state of the heart and shines through you when you are kind and connected to purpose.

When to cast: At dawn, during the waxing moon. Any morning when dew is present on the ground.

Where to cast: Outside where there is grass and plants.

You will need: Dew.

Begin by going outside to find the dew.

1. Say "good morning" to the dawn. To the rise of the sun. To the beginning of day.

2. Look around you and imagine a "circle of faeries" forming around you.

3. Say:

    "By morning dew, beauty true.
    By faery dance, may grace enhance.
    By kindness bright, By morning light."

4. Move your hands over the morning dew.

5. Place your hands onto your face.

6. Then move them again over the morning dew and hold them to your heart.

105. Raven Grimassi, *Encyclopedia of Wicca and Witchcraft* (St. Paul, MN: Llewellyn Publications, 2000), 98.

106. Baring and Cashford, *The Myth of the Goddess*, 211.

107. Grimassi, *Encyclopedia of Wicca and Witchcraft*, 99.

7. When you are finished, dissolve your circle by imagining the "circle of faeries" moving into your heart.

After the spell: See the beauty in others and in Nature.

Water cleanses your heart and transforms sadness into a creative force in your life. Magickal cleansing is like washing. With each wash you come closer to a pure energy and truth. Sometimes cleansing takes time because pain can be very deep and often hidden within you. Always be gentle with yourself and have no expectations. There may be some hurt you will always have but over time you can change it into a powerful part of yourself. You just need to be aware of the pain and want it to evolve. However, with every cleansing spell your story will brighten.

 ## Water Element Spell to Cleanse the Heart

Purpose: To move closer to an awareness of your feelings. To cleanse what depletes you.

When to cast: On the full moon. Day or night.

Where to cast: Indoors at your altar and then outside under the sky. At the end of the spell you will leave your bowl of water under the moon.

You will need: A fallen leaf and a bowl of water.

Begin outdoors with the leaf and the bowl of water before you.

1. Imagine light coming from the moon and forming a glowing circle around you.

2. Still your mind. Hold the leaf to your heart. Allow any pain, disappointment, and fear to rise within your heart.

3. Imagine these feelings entering the leaf.

4. When you are ready, place the leaf in the bowl of water.

5. Say:

"Spirits of water take my pain to Mother Moon."

6. When you are finished say:

"Circle of light enter my heart."

7. "See" the circle around you moving into your heart.

After the spell: Leave the bowl under the moon for three nights and then empty it onto the Earth.

A broken heart is a deep mystical experience. Often only desired experiences are considered so, but when you understand magick at a deep level you realise it is a part of the witch's journey. When something is broken it will never be the same again, but when mended it can hold the power of experience and endurance. To travel into a state of brokenness is to truly feel alive, to become aware of the crashing seas of the heart and its shadow. At some stage feelings do break. Mending a heart doesn't mean forgetting the pain or grief, it means healing, that is, changing it into something magickal.

Spell for a Broken Heart

Purpose: To heal the heart after loss of love, sadness, grief, anger, and deep disappointment.

When to cast: At the new moon and then the following new moon. At night.

Where to cast: Indoors at your altar then outdoors under the new moon.

You will need: Paper (around 3 in. x 3 in. or 7 cm x 7 cm). A pencil. A bowl of water. Five small stones.

Begin standing with the items before you.

1. With arm extended and index finger pointed, turn as you imagine a "circle of blue water" around you.

2. On the paper draw a heart crying tears. Write your name across the heart.

3. Hold the paper to your own heart. Imagine tears from your heart moving onto the paper.

4. Place the paper into the bowl of water.

5. Add the five stones to the bowl. With each stone say:

    "Grandma Moon, hold me in your arms."

6. When you are finished, leave the bowl outside until the next new moon.

7. Dissolve your circle by imagining it disappearing into the bowl.

After the spell: At the next new moon, return to the bowl you've left outside. Imagine Grandma Moon beside you. Together pour the contents of the bowl onto the Earth. Keep the stones near your bed. When you feel the birth of change within your heart, place the stones on the Earth.

The water element incites true flow, the natural movement of the energy of the heart. It opens feelings and takes you to a depth of truth and the potential to love completely. Water spells that attract energy include many intentions. You must open your heart fully to attract divine energy into your life. You must create a story in your heart that will reflect into the great world. Through attraction spells you weave magick threads that bring energy to you. This energy prepares your life for change and wonder.

Attraction spells include love on all levels; true love, romance, family, and friends. It also includes love of life, humanity, nature, and creatures. When you wish to attract love it is important not to think of a particular person. Instead, surrender to the Divine to weave your destiny and have faith in your own worth. Sacred intentions are also peace, forgiveness, hope, faith, healing, compassion, and acceptance. Listen to what your spirit is prepared to invite in.

Water Element Attraction Spell

Purpose: To open the heart to divine intervention. To attract love, luck, or any other purpose or wish.

When to cast: During the waxing or full moon. Day or night.

Where to cast: Indoors at your altar or outside under the sky.

You will need: A bowl of water. Seven flower petals. A small piece of paper (around 3 in. x 3 in. or 7 cm x 7 cm). A pencil.

Begin standing with items before you.

1. Point your index finger of either hand, extending your arm fully and turn in a circle by way of the sun. As you turn, imagine you are casting a "circle of flowers" around you.

2. Imagine taking one of these flowers and placing it into your heart.

3. Write or draw what you wish to attract on the paper. Imagine the silvery glow of the moon coming from the pencil as you write.

4. Breathe onto the paper as the "circle of flowers" begins to spin.

5. Place the paper into the bowl of water.

6. Using your finger, write your name in the water.

7. One by one, place each of the seven petals into the bowl. Each petal is an offering to the Goddess.

8. When you are finished, imagine the "circle of flowers" moving into your heart.

After the spell: The next day, pour the contents of the bowl onto the Earth.

Balancing the Water Element

When the water element is out of balance, you can find yourself drowning in tears. When this happens the fire of willpower is extinguished, earth becomes mud, and thoughts of the air element are "washed away." The Scandinavian myth of the water spirit, called *neckan,* lured humans into their watery realms.[108] Entranced by the beauty and music of the creature, the human drowned under a spell of bewitched attraction. A similar story is associated with the Germanic *nixie*; they cast irresistible love spells through their singing and those who fell under their magick were rarely seen again. These stories may well be speaking of how emotions can completely consume, if left unchecked. When you only live through the water element, when you can't "think straight" (air) or have a connection with reality (earth), it is possible to lose yourself and become entranced by an illusion.

Oversensitivity, and feeling hurt too often, needs the element fire to define boundaries and activate confidence and self-preservation. Too much water element makes it hard to see a situation objectively and needs the element air to elevate vision, reason, and fairness and the element earth to connect with purpose and strength. Prolonged sadness and extended disappointment need the will (fire) to want to change and take action and strength (earth) to endure.

The stillness and reflectiveness of water can mesmerize, rendering ideas and plans constantly adrift in the ocean of wishes and hopes. Fire brings the action, air the planning through using the mind, and earth connects the idea to structure and foundation.

The Greek god of the sea, Poseidon, and his Roman counterpart, Neptune, embody the vastness of the water element's extremities, where emotion holds potential for beauty as well as rage and destruction. Both gods are vulnerable and moody, and easily driven to anger. Poseidon's symbol of power was the trident and he rode through the waters in a horse-drawn chariot. This god is the embodiment of extreme emotion. His disappointment and jealousy created floods, droughts, and raging seas. Emotions out of control can be depicted as dangerous seas and the "shutting down" of feelings is found in the energy of drought.

---

108. D. J. Conway, *Magical Mythical Mystical Beasts: How to Invite Them into Your Life* (St. Paul, MN: Llewellyn Publications, 1996), 73.

The element of water in the circle calls you to the kiss of the Goddess and to explore the realms of your dreams and your power as an oracle. You are at one with its power when you want to heal and transform, when you want to be your true self. You have raised its energy in the circle when you wish for a kind, loving heart.

Emerge from the foamy seas with the goddess Aphrodite and create your own deeply complex story of true beauty and romance with the element water.

EIGHT
The Element Earth

Imagine your home is a burrow in the warm lands of Earth, a dark hole, dry and warm. The colours of the red earth stain your skin. It is night and you curl inside to sleep. With your ear on the dusty earth, you hear the beating heart of Mother.

Earth is the ground beneath your feet, the sand, salt, plants, trees, moss, rocks, clay, caves, hills, mountains, and crystals. It is a place to dwell and take shelter. Earth is your home. It is stable, enveloping, soft, hard, crusty, rocky, slippery, and cracked. The colours of this element hold every hue and every shape is found on the planet. Earth is the name of the planet and everything birthed from the surface and beneath it (that is not water, fire, or air) is of the earth element.

Earth
Element of Matter
Belly of the Goddess
Connection and Purpose
Grounding

Earth rises with mountains and tunnels with caves. She is rainforests, desserts, beaches, swamps, tundras, moors, valleys, quicksand, and woodlands. There are around 60,000 different species of trees on the earth and each extends below the earth, what you see above.[109] There are around 350,000 types of plants.[110] The character of Earth is vast and ever-changing according to the light of the sun, the frequency of rain, and the strength of the wind. It is through Earth you see the marriage of the elements most clearly.

Earth is the roots of a tree anchored into the ground. It is every leaf on that tree, the lichen, the bark, the flowers, and the fruit. You taste earth when eating. Earth is the countless grains of sand on a beach and the creatures of this planet, it is a spider's web, a beehive, and a hut made of grass. This element is soft mud between your toes, sand on your skin, and pollen floating in the air.

You are flesh—you are made of earth. You eat what grows in earth. You will become a part of earth, as well as the Earth. In the Babylonian creation myth, the god Enki and the goddess Ninhursag created humans from clay.[111] The same story is told in the Bible about the creation of Adam. In Egyptian myth the shapes of humans were thrown on a potter's wheel by the gods Khnum and Ptah.

Pregnant and abundant with life, earth is the fertility goddess, the Great Mother, and growth itself. She is the goddess Gaia of the Greek myth who created herself out of chaos before life existed. From her womb all life was birthed. In Egypt, the earth goddess took the form of a pregnant hippopotamus deity, Taweret, or Tauret, carrier of the protection scrolls.[112] Earth itself was also Tellus, the Roman goddess, who was ripe and waiting to be seeded. Her existence was entwined with her sister-goddess, Ceres, personification of Earth's harvest.[113]

---

109. E. Beech et al, "GlobalTreeSearch: The first complete global database of tree species and country distributions," *Journal of Sustainable Forestry* 36:5, (2017): 454–489, doi: 10.1080/10549811.2017.1310049.

110. "350,000 types of plants," B10NUMB3R5, The Database of Useful Biological Numbers, accessed December 28, 2020, https://bionumbers.hms.harvard.edu/bionumber.aspx?id=113395&ver=0&trm=plant&org=.

111. Baring and Cashford, *The Myth of the Goddess*, 425.

112. Monaghan, *The New Book of Goddesses and Heroines*, 293.

113. Baring and Cashford, *The Myth of the Goddess*, 403, 404.

The energy of the element earth is centring, purposeful, and nurturing. It anchors you to home and asks you to find meaning in your journey on Earth. Earth grounds and steadies you, reminding you that you are on the Earth. Because of its own nature this element embodies the energy of fertility. At the core of this energy is fertility of body, but fertility expands to include creating life from your own existence so the ability to create and have a fertile effect on the world. The earth element also lives through the energy of abundance and prosperity. What is abundant and prosperous is also a state of being; however, money, work, and the workings of the world are of this element.

A connection with the magick of earth is made when you centre your spirit, when you know Earth is your mother, and when you nurture yourself. When you think of a mountain as "She" and see a tree reaching into the heavens, you are interfacing with the magick of the earth element. See the sand on the beach and know that every grain holds the story of Earth. Hold a rock and feel your spirit strengthen. Hold a coin and recognise that its value is formed by how you value yourself.

The Element Earth in the Spell

The magick of earth is present at a spell with all that comes from the Earth: salt, all plants, fruit, vegetables, herbs, natural oils, leaves, earth crystals, stones, sand, and soil. Coin and other money also hold the element as does natural materials, such as fabrics, threads, and metals.

This element's colour is green and gender is feminine, as Earth births all life. The elemental of the earth is the gnome.[114] Earth calls the magick from the north in the Northern Hemisphere and from the south direction in the Southern Hemisphere.

The earth element is of the body. It rules the realms of health, growth, strength, purpose, work, and the home. Health, fertility, and steadfastness are of this element.

The energy of the earth resides over your earthly life and practicalities, the vitality of the physical body and your relationship to everyday matters, home, work, and society. As a grounding force, the element earth calls you to connect

---

114. Conway, *Magical Mythical Mystical Beasts: How to Invite Them into Your Life*, 210.

with life and to find belonging. Earth magick dispels illusion and wishful thinking and helps to connect with the reality of a situation or person.

Earth in the form of fruit, grains, and cakes are often used as offerings to deities and the departed in many cultures and mystical traditions. Like all other elements, earth is also used to scry and connect to other worlds. This is done through reading patterns and shapes both in nature and psychic readings.

Scrying with Earth

Purpose: To divine an answer, direction, or message from a shape or pattern. To develop your intuition, imagination, and connect with other realms. You may see a picture or symbol before you or you may "see" something in your mind or feel a sensation in your body while scrying.

When to cast: During any phase of the moon. Keep in mind any psychic work is potent on the new or full moon however frequently a scryer reads. Day or night.

Where to cast: Indoors at your altar or outside under the sky. Scrying may take place in a friend's home or at a gathering.

You will need: Anything from the earth you can create a pattern or shape with like salt, rice, seeds, or grains (called "material" in the spell). You need at least two handfuls of the "material" on a large plate.

Begin sitting down with the items before you.

1. Holding your hands over the pile, say:

    "I cast a 'circle of psychic eyes' around me. I invite into the circle the Goddess of insight."

    Imagine her.

2. Close your eyes.

3. Bring a question to mind, then slowly move the material on the surface. Flatten, shape, move your fingers through it, allowing your intuition to guide you.

4. When you are ready open your eyes and look at the form before you.

5. The first thought in your mind will bring the message.

6. Continue scrying until you are finished.

7. Dissolve the "circle of psychic eyes" into your brow. As you do, imagine your third eye opening. The third eye is positioned in the middle of your forehead and brings you higher vision and psychic insight.

After the spell: Keep any earth material for future scrying.

The Magick of Salt

Salt is used to represent the earth element in a spell. By its nature salt preserves as well as purifies. When you taste salt, the sensation will bring awareness to where you stand on the Earth. It will ground you, bringing you to the present moment. Salt water is used for healing and is a substitute for blood in a ritual. It can be used to create a circle, to cleanse objects, and when scattered it will banish unwanted energy. Salt can also be used as an offering to the deities. It is associated with the goddess Aphrodite, who was born from the ocean.

 ## Spell for Healing

Purpose: To heal sadness, pain, and past wounds.

When to cast: On the full moon. However, this spell can be cast whenever you need. Day or night.

Where to cast: Indoors at your altar or outside under the sky.

You will need: Three handfuls of salt. Warm water in a bowl.
Begin with the ingredients before you.

1. Using half the salt, create a small circle in front of you. Say:
   "With salt of the earth, I cast a circle before and around me."

2. Place the remaining salt in the warm water.

3. Now imagine where any energetic wounds reside in your body. You may "see" them as a colour or a form.

4. Using your hand, stir the salt water four times. Then place your hand on the "wound" or "wounds." Continue to do this until you feel healing energy. The form of the wound may start changing shape in your imagination.

5. When you are ready, place the circle of salt into the water.

6. Place both hands into the bowl and move around your aura to heal your energy field.

7. When you are finished, say:

> "I heal through Mother Earth. My circle is dissolved."

After the spell: Pour the salt water onto the Earth.

The power of earth is aligned with the shape of the square, with foundation, strength, and growth. Earth magick weaves the energy of abundance, of plenty, and the splendour of treasures both actual and symbolic. All worldly concerns call on this element.

The prosperity of earth is embodied in the Hindu goddess, Lakshmi. She is present in all forms of wealth, in all coins, precious jewels, and all objects of earthly value. She is the Shakti, the inspiration of the god Vishnu. Without her, his power to enhance life is non-existent. Lakshmi is a cow deity, as giver of milk she is the bringer of life. As well as earthly riches, Lakshmi is the goddess of spiritual prosperity and abundance, therefore purpose and connection.[115]

---

115. Monaghan, *The New Book of Goddesses and Heroines*, 190.

Spell of Coins for Prosperity

Purpose: To attract the energy of abundance. To create prosperous thinking.

When to cast: During the waxing moon. Day or night.

Where to cast: Indoors at your altar or outside under the sky.

You will need: Four coins. Four flowers or leaves. Four stones. Four twigs. Your purse or wallet.

Begin sitting, with your purse and items before you.

1. Cast you circle by saying:

   "I cast a 'circle of golden light' around me."

2. Then say:

   "Into this circle I call the beauty of flowers, the growth of trees, the foundation of stones, and the prosperity of coins." Imagine all in your circle.

3. Position the four coins in the shape of a square. Then connect each corner of the square using the flowers, twigs, and stones.

4. Place your purse into the square.

5. Hold your hands over your purse and say:

   "By the power of earth, I invite prosperity into my life."

6. When you are finished, dissolve the circle by imagining the golden light dissolving into sunlight.

After the spell: Leave the square you created for four days. Return your purse to it when it's not in use. After four days bury the four coins in the earth around your home or in a potted plant. Alternatively conceal them at the four corners of your home. Return the items from the square to Nature.

Earth is also Cernunnos, the Celtic Nature spirit of the forest, a fertility entity whose long stag-like antlers are symbolic of his reproductive powers.[116] Pan, the Greek god of Nature and the Wild, is akin to Cernunnos. Their same fertile essence resides in the Universal Green Man, a nature entity who is covered in vegetation and embodies the fertility of Earth. The abundance of earth is expressed in the Egyptian god, Geb, brother and lover to the sky goddess Nut. Geb wears a serpent or sometimes a goose as his crown. He is god of the harvest and like the Green Man he is depicted with vegetation growing from him.[117]

These deities and nature spirits are personifications of the Earth, completely connected to Nature and therefore their own nature.

 Spell to Connect to the Present

Purpose: To bring you into the moment and help you to connect to purpose and fulfillment. There is no such thing as being happy all the time because is it important to express sadness and fear at times. However, connecting with purpose and meaning brings back a sense of yourself and will ground you in the present moment. When you feel grounded, balance and clarity are birthed.

When to cast: Any phase of the moon. Day or night.

Where to cast: Indoors at your altar or outside under the sky.

You will need: A handful of salt. Ten fallen leaves. A handful of seeds of any kind.

Begin with the ingredients before you.

1. To cast your circle, imagine a "circle of moving leaves" appearing around you. Then "see" a "circle of mountains" and then a "circle of trees."

2. Create a circle with the ten leaves. Say:

    "The present came from the past."

---

116. Farrar, *The Witches' God*, 96–99.
117. Lurker, *An Illustrated Dictionary of the Gods and Symbols of Ancient Egypt*, 55.

3. Around the circle of leaves, create another circle with the rest of the salt. Say:

> "The present is now. This moment."

4. Around the circle of salt, create another circle with the seeds. Say:

> "The present holds the seeds that create tomorrow."

5. Hold your hands, palms down, over the three circles and say:

> "The present came from the past.
> The present is now. This moment.
> The present holds the seeds that create tomorrow."

6. When you are finished, bring your mind back to the three circles and imagine them fading into each other and disappearing.

After the spell: Leave the three circles of leaves, salt, and seeds for three days. Then merge them together and place them on the Earth.

The Sacred Tree of Earth

The tree is the home for birds, who carry the souls of the dead and whose songs speak of the rise and sleep of the moon and sun. Each tree has a spirit, its own personality. The Greeks called the spirit who inhabits a tree a *dryad*.[118] The dryad takes our breath and returns it as oxygen. In this way the trees hold history, the essence of everyone, the essence of you.

The World Tree is an enormous mystical tree supporting the Heavens, connecting that divine realm to the Earth and then Earth to the Underworld.[119] In Scandinavian mythology gods created humans from two tree trunks[120] and in Europe trees were made into maypoles and their branches placed on houses to

---

118. Thomas Bulfinch, *Bulfinch's Complete Mythology* (London: Hamlyn Publishing Group Limited, 1989), 120.

119. Roy Willis, ed. *World Mythology: The Illustrated Guide* (London: Duncan Baird Publishers, 1996), 20.

120. Carole M. Cusack, *The Sacred Tree: Ancient and Medieval Manifestations* (Newcastle Upon Tyne: Cambridge Scholars Publishing, 2011), 12.

bring the blessing of the tree-spirit.[121] The Kabbalah's central symbol is the Tree of Life. The branches of the Tree of Life depict divine realms as well as the mystical influences of life's journey.[122]

Buddha sat under a Bodhi tree. He became the tree itself and gained enlightenment through the energy of compassion. Through the tree, he experienced complete transformation, relinquishing all his earthly riches for a spiritual destiny.[123] In ancient Egypt one of the earliest stories of the Tree of Life is found in the myth of Osiris. His jealous brother, Set, tricked him into climbing into a chest before throwing it into the Nile River. Eventually the chest came to rest under a tamarisk tree and as the tree grew it encased the chest. The tree was not only the place of Osiris's death, it was also the place of his resurrection.[124] This theme is found again in the death of Christ, another story where the tree is the central motif linking life and death and then rebirth.

Odin, the Norse god, hung on the ash tree, Yggdrasil, to acquire the cosmic knowledge of the runes: powerful divination symbols. Yggdrasil was central to Norse mythology and connected the nine worlds of their cosmos. The branches of Yggdrasil were brimming with activity. Four stags grazed on the branches, snakes slivered at its roots, and a residing squirrel took messages to the eagle watching from the tree's highest point. This sacred tree was fed by three wells. Each of these wells were attended by the three sisters, the *Norns*, who are past, present, and the future and, like the Greek Fates, were weavers of destiny.[125]

Temples across Europe were once sacred groves where trees were worshipped and alive with spirits. To the Greeks, Italians, Slavs, and Norse, the oak tree was revered and believed to hold the magick of their thunder gods Zeus, Jupiter, Perun, and Thor. Because the oak attracts lightning strikes, it was deemed to be at one with magickal forces. In the ancient groves of Aricia, Italy, a priest of the goddess Diana guarded the mystic oak that held the life of their sky god, Jupiter.[126] To the Celtic Druids, this same tree was the foundation of their magick. Their priests ritualistically cut the mistletoe that grew on the sacred oak for use

121. Frazer, *The Golden Bough: A Study in Magic and Religion*, 120.

122. Ronnberg and Martin, eds. *The Book of Symbols: Reflections on Archetypal Images*, 142.

123. Cotterell and Storm, *The Ultimate Encyclopedia of Mythology*, 368.

124. Lurker, *An Illustrated Dictionary of the Gods and Symbols of Ancient Egypt*, 93.

125. Lecouteux, *Encyclopedia of Norse and Germanic Folklore, Mythology, and Magic*, 323.

126. Monaghan, *The New Book of Goddesses and Heroines*, 103.

in ceremony. Their mistletoe was known as thunder-besom and was believed to hold the essence of lightning's power and the force of the gods.[127]

The apple tree is also one of the many trees of life. The fruit holds the essence of love as well as the secrets of the dead and knowledge itself. The acquisition of this knowledge caused the banishment of Eve from Paradise in the Abrahamic myth. The magick of the apple tree also belongs to the Hesperides,[128] the evening stars and guardians of the golden apple. They are the daughters of Nyx, the Greek night goddess. They reside in the west, the direction of the setting sun where red, green, and yellow hues transform the sky.

The west is the direction of the realm of the dead, Avalon, the Land of Apples. In the tradition of Samhain, the apple is used for divination, as ghosts walk the Earth heading towards sunset.[129]

The apple tree holds the opposite essence as well, the magick of life and fertility. It has love-drawing powers and is sacred to Aphrodite, the Greek love goddess. It is a symbol of initiation, of transformation and surrender to the spiritual.

You create earth element magick when you cast a spell under a tree, hide a charm within it, or hang a written wish from a branch. Listen as the tree tells you of its divine essence. It is the connection between the three realms and this connection also exists within you. The Heavens in the tree's highest branches reflect your spirit; your body is held by the Earth in the tree's trunk; and your unconscious, the hidden, your dreams, are found at the roots.

The *Tree* symbolizes the integration of the three realms. It embodies growth, reaching for something greater, and anchoring to purpose yet remaining in contact with the mysterious and unknown. To cast a spell with a tree, by its power and magick and with its essence, is potent, awe-inspiring, and majestic. A tree will always take your wish to the Divine. Have no expectations of the outcome of a wish, for it can take you to places beyond the imagination. However, when a wish is made with a pure, open heart, a beautiful change always begins ...

---

127. De Cleene and Lejeune, *Compendium of Symbolic and Ritual Plants in Europe, Vol 1*, 411–420.

128. Cusack, *The Sacred Tree: Ancient and Medieval Manifestations*, 13.

129. McCoy, *Sabbats: A Witch's Approach to Living the Old Ways*, 40, 41.

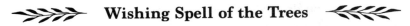 ## Wishing Spell of the Trees

Purpose: To spin the threads of tree magick around an intention. To ground and anchor a wish to the earth element. As the tree reaches to the sky your wish is deemed ethereal, through the journey down the trunk the wish comes to earth and through its roots it becomes bound to the unknown, the mystery of the future.

When to cast: For attraction wishes during the waxing moon. For dispelling wishes during the waning moon. Day or night.

Where to cast: Indoors at your altar then outside under the sky.

You will need: A dried leaf from any tree. Paper (3 in. x 3 in. or 7 cm x 7 cm). Pencil. String (9 in. or 22 cm). A wish. Witch's utensils. Begin sitting with items before you.

1. Say:

   "I cast a circle of trees around me. They are living beings, ancient and all knowing."

2. Light the dried leaf with a match, blow out the flame, and allow it to smoulder.

3. Move the smoke around your body to purify any unwanted energy.

4. Write your wish on the paper and imagine the trees from the circle are watching.

5. Now move the smouldering leaf around the wish. You may need to relight.

6. Roll the paper into a scroll, tie it with string, and fasten with three knots.

7. Go outside and tie your wishing scroll to the branch of a tree.

8. Acknowledge the residing dryad by simply nodding your head.

9. When you are finished, imagine your "circle of trees" disappearing back into the Earth.

After the spell: Place the remaining part of the leaf on the earth. Leave the scroll on the tree.

Balancing the Earth Element

When the earth element is out of balance it can create stagnation. When this happens, you become a stranger to your dreams and in alignment with the mundane. Too much earth can create resistance to trying something new because stability is valued above all else. Material concerns, money, and practicalities are earth element qualities. But when these energies are paramount in all decisions, opportunity and wonder may be lost. When the earth element is out of balance, fire is needed to activate passion, air to bring flexibility, and water to connect with the imagination.

In the Greek myth of King Midas, his wish to turn everything he touched into gold is soon realized to be a curse. He cannot eat the food of Earth and even his beloved daughter is turned to gold by his touch. Through loss Midas comes to understand that he values survival and love more than the power of wealth. Dionysus, the god of wine, who originally granted the king's wish, eventually instructs Midas to wash in a river in order to restore everything as it was. He does so and through his connection with the healing powers of water, the true flow of life, Midas is cleansed of his own imbalance and attachment to the material world of Earth.[130]

The element of earth in the circle calls you to feel the ground beneath you and to connect with its character and essence. It calls you to the incredible nature of Mother Earth, her vast beauty, power, and vulnerability. You are one with this element when you want to grow, when you choose to be strong, and when you search for purpose. It is the element of the earthly matters and how you imbue this with a spiritual force.

Speak to the spirits of the trees and ask them to whisper your story to the wind.

---

130. Cotterell and Storm, *The Ultimate Encyclopedia of Mythology*, 63.

NINE
The Witch's Purpose

Rising smoke assisted the Oracle of Delphi with her visions of the future; a child's spiritual life has been acknowledged by water when baptised; the ancient people of Europe lit fires at seasonal festivals to conjure the energy of life; and rice was thrown at weddings to entice fertility and good fortune.

Entering the mysterious realm of a spell, you will weave your story with the energy of the four elements, either with one element or all combined. Your intention is to unite your mind, body, heart, and spirit with their magick to liberate, to love, to find meaning, and to transform. When you cast a spell, you will join with ancient prayers and enter a place of unexplainable beauty, an energy as old as time.

You can create many types of spells. The act of lighting a candle is a spell, so is making a wish on a falling star.

You can call in energy during a spell and you may also dispel it. Your purpose may be to attract something new or to protect and build boundaries around your heart. When you invoke energy, you are creating an invitation to a divine power to enter your life. When you banish, you create a way for negative energy to leave your life. Magick can be created to release, to relinquish, to liberate, or to anoint, bless, and consecrate. A spell can be created as an initiation, a passage, a beginning. It can be cast to acknowledge the importance of the divinity of a time or place. Spells can be a way of making offerings or petitions to the departed or to sacred beings.

The spell is created through your imagination and the language of symbolism. Weave your story with threads from the visible to the invisible and you will feel closer to your own heart and the Divine. Visualise the following images in your mind. Close your eyes...

From the bowl of water, within the circle, Yemaya of the Ocean arises and moves around your heart. She is the depth of true love, the beauty of attraction, and the magick of surrender.

From a flickering candle flame, Hephaestus, the Greek god of Fire, hands you his mighty hammer, a symbol to attract the energy of action and creation.

A bird soars from the feather you hold in your hand. Its song is carried by the wind and calls to the spirits of freedom to lighten your mind.

From the flowers of the Earth, the Roman goddess Flora arises, passionate and ready to create life. She merges into your body inspiring desire.

When you enact your sacred story in the circle, something changes in you, a profound energy is activated and everything in your life shifts.

Spells to Attract or Call in

Feathers are used in spells to attract the magick of the bird. The feather holds the creature's essence so creates the sympathetic relationship attracting the qualities of the creature to the witch as well as raising these qualities from within her. Gold crystals are used in a spell to attract money and abundant thinking. The colour gold is of the Sun as well as of the valuable metal gold. The magick inherent in the feather or crystal is contagious and rubs off onto you. Incense smoke attracts the energy of change because it is in constant movement. Salt is preserving, so attracts the energy of protection, and fire's ability to consume calls in the energy of purification.

Attraction is magnetic, sympathetic. A wish or desire begins with the will to connect, absorb, and become. In attraction spells you create what you want to attract. You infuse the desired energy into your energy through the creation of your magick threads. You entwine what you want to attract into your story during the enactment of the spell through symbols, actions, and words. So, a setting is created to connect your wish to the sacred and in that setting you act out the wish. Just like an actor does in a play, though you are not acting—you are in fact purely yourself.

A spell will imbue your thinking with sacredness so the energy attracted to you will also be sacred. If it is true love you wish to attract, true friendship, honesty, or insight, you will merge this intention with the divine essence of the elements, and by doing this your intention becomes magickal.

To attract love, you may imagine the candle flame as the light in your heart or weave your vision to the mysterious depth of the oceans. You can move a letter of love through incense smoke so your message is taken to the Goddess. Or you may wear rose oil (*Rosa spp.*) on your heart to awake the energy of Venus within you.

Any of the elements, or all four, can be used in the creation of attraction spells. Intentions to bring love, friendship, prosperity, luck, attainment, peace, confidence, creativity, and happiness are some of the sacred hopes to be fulfilled.

A Love Attracting Spell

Purpose: To rise to true love within. To deem your journey to love sacred.

When to cast: During the waxing moon. Day or night.

Where to cast: Indoors at your altar or outside under the sky.

You will need: Paper. A pencil. Five drops of rose essential oil (Rosa spp.) and five drops of ylang-ylang essential oil (Cananga odorata) in a teaspoon of almond oil (Prunus dulcis). A stone. A bowl of water. Witch's utensils.

Begin with ingredients before you.

1. Cast a circle by imagining stars coming from your heart to create a circle around you.

2. Write a love letter to your true love. Psychically it will come to them.

3. Anoint the letter with the oils.

4. Place the letter under a stone outside.

4. When you are finished, dissolve the "circle of stars" into the letter.

After the spell: After three days, place the letter in a bowl of water under the moon. Then bury the letter in the Earth the next day. Pour the water from the bowl over it.

Dispelling Spells: to Purify, to Banish, to Cleanse.

In your imagination you "see" the elements and their energy, alive and moving during your spell. With them you can banish unwanted energy and clear mundane thinking and outmoded habits. Stagnant feelings and thinking can be purified and banished in a spell. The ability to do this is found in awareness and the will to change.

Fire symbolically drives away self-doubt because of its power to eradicate. Incense transforms the atmosphere with scent, so anything not aligned with its heavenly vibration is banished. The salt of the Earth anchors energy to strengthen and resolve, dispelling anything unstable.

Energy is created through feelings and thoughts, through words and actions as well as stillness. Energy seeps into places, into objects. It "rubs off" and melts. It has a place of residence. Unwanted energy will also "live" somewhere. You can sometimes feel it in places, objects, and also within your body and your aura.

Through your imagination, allow energy, your wish to banish, to come into your mind. It may be an old habit, something that depletes you, something unkind or wounded within. Allow the energy to evolve into a symbolic form, or a smell, a taste, a colour, a sound, or a texture—or any combination of these. A form may be grey smoke for a hurtful feeling, a smell of rotting flesh for the energy of abuse, the taste of mud for stagnation, the feeling or vision of prickles for re-occurring agitation.

Giving energy a form defines it and is similar to the power of knowing a name. This knowledge draws you closer to awareness and understanding. For the deeper something is known, the easier it is to dispel.

During the creation of a banishing spell, you "move" the imagined form out of your body or aura and into one of the elements present in the circle. The act is the opposite of an attraction spell where you bring the energy to you. To dispel or purify you "give" the unwanted energy to the element to eradicate, dissolve, cleanse, or take away.

The flame of the candle brings light into the darkness of fear. Imagine fear as barbed wire around your mind. The energy of the candle flame moves into your mind and melts the wire encasement.

Imagine your heartbreak is an injured bird. You "lift" the bird from out of your heart and place it in rising incense smoke to awaken it in a heavenly breath.

Imagine a bowl of water is a portal to the soul of Kuan Yin, the Buddhist bodhisattva of compassion. Sorrow, in the form of a grey cloud, "moves" from your heart into the bowl, into Kuan Yin's temple of healing. The colour of the smoke changes to turquoise blue as it merges with the water.

"See" the energy of regret as the image of a tear falling from the eye onto salt. The healing power of the salt is the medicine of the Great Mother who always forgives.

Spell to Banish a Hex

Purpose: To banish negative energy from your body, heart, and mind.

When to cast: During the waning moon. Day or night.

Where to cast: Indoors at your altar or outside under the sky.

You will need: A small white candle. A sewing needle to carve the candle. Witch's utensils.

Begin with ingredients before you.

1. In your imagination, cast a "circle of white light" around you.
2. Carve words or symbols that represent the energy of the hex into a white candle.
3. When you ignite the flame, say:

    "I banish all negativity to the Light."

4. When you are finished, dissolve the "circle of white light" by imagining it disappearing into the candle.

After the spell: If any of the candle remains, relight in the future with this same intention in mind.

Spells to Release, to Liberate

Captive birds are released in an Eastern ceremony to liberate the energy of hope and freedom. In the ancient Celtic tradition of Samhain, dressing up as a demon, faery, or witch liberates this same energy from within the psyche. Releasing magick is depicted in the ancient festivals of Europe. During Saturnalia in ancient Rome, the structure of society was symbolically freed through disregarding what was considered normal. At the festival, a person of low status was appointed ruler of the day and known as the "Lord of Misrule." This symbolic act released the energy of wildness and frivolity into the community as structure of society was "turned on its head."[131]

Turn your own life upside down to see it in a new light, to free old patterns and thinking. Releasing energy in magick is liberating. It awakens you, giving life to something within you that has been supressed or hidden away. Releasing spells require surrendering to the new as well as sacrificing what is no longer needed.

 A Spell to Release Old Patterns

Purpose: To become aware of and to let go of depleting patterns of thinking and outworn habits.

When to cast: On the new moon. At night.

Where to cast: Indoors at your altar or outside under the sky.

You will need: A red candle of any size. Paper (3 in. x 3 in. or 7 cm x 7 cm). A pencil or any art materials. Frankincense resin (Boswellia carterii). Self-igniting charcoal and a bowl of water. Witch's utensils.

Begin with the ingredients before you.

1. In your imagination, cast a "circle of swords" around you.

2. Light the candle and the charcoal. Add a pinch of resin to the hot charcoal.

3. On a small piece of paper draw the patterns of your mind.

---

131. Nozedar, *The Illustrated Signs and Symbols Sourcebook: An A to Z Compendium of Over 1000 Designs,* 483.

4. Be creative and allow the pencil to move without controlling it. Draw anything that depicts your current thinking.

5. When you are finished, move the paper through incense smoke.

6. Say:

   "Release now."

7. Burn the paper on the candle flame. Place the end of the burning paper in the bowl of water.

8. When you are finished, dissolve the "circle of swords" by imagining them disappearing into the candle.

9. Snuff out the candle.

After the spell: If any of the candle remains, relight in the future with this same intention in mind. Pour the water onto the Earth.

Spells to Invoke or Evoke

When you invoke during a spell, you call to or summon magickal energy or a divine presence into your circle. This energy is brought into the circle as a witness, an inspiration, a guide, and a participant in the weaving of your story. Invoking is an invitation and when you invite, you open yourself to change, to be inspired by what you invoke, to receive messages from this source, and to become or live by this energy. The pure intention of wanting to unite forces with a pure energy is powerful and manifesting.

You can also evoke an energy or spiritual presence during a spell. Evoking is when the energy remains separate from you, whereas invoking draws the energy into your spiritual being.

Ancient Romans carried small statues of their deities in their clothing as a way to invoke divine power into everyday life. The famous sixteenth century philosopher and diviner Dr. John Dee invoked angels. He scripted their ethereal language, called Enochian, with information he received from his assistant, Edward Kelly, who channelled the angelic realm. John Dee claimed he invoked a daemon, a divine guide, into the circle by way of the elements and commanding words.[132]

Invoking is partnering with a magickal state of being, a spiritual force or a divine entity. The elementals, deities, ancestors, angels, familiars, daemons, and fae are invoked into the circle to be part of the quest or intention. Invoking can be enacted with words, symbols, actions, and with the elements. Imagine what is taking place during these invoking acts.

Invoke a wild dog with you in the circle. She watches protectively as you create your story.

As you create a circle of flowers, invoke the goddess of joy, Hathor, to enter your life through the circle. Imagine her entering your heart.

To invoke Hathor's guidance, light incense and say, "This incense be my message to invoke the goddess Hathor to come close to me and guide me."

Call on the brilliance of the god Apollo when you light a candle flame. Imagine the sun moving into your body, illuminating your being.

Invoke the energy of good fortune into your home by placing coins and flowers in a bowl.

To invoke is the same as forming a bond or having a mystical conversation with divine energy. During the spell, a kinship and commitment is forged with the invoked energy. This sacred essence melds with you, strengthening your will to manifest change.

 ## A Spell to Invoke Cerridwen for Creativity

Purpose: This spell invokes the Celtic goddess Cerridwen. She is the keeper of the cauldron of rebirth and creativity. The spell is to liberate your imagination and innovation.

When to cast: On the full moon. Day or night.

Where to cast: Indoors at your altar or outside under the sky.

You will need: Paper to write a poem on. A pencil. A bowl of water.

---

1. In your imagination, cast a "circle of cauldrons" around you.

2. Say:

   "I invoke the goddess Cerridwen into my circle."

3. Allow your imagination to be free and, without hesitation, write a poem to anyone—human, creature, or mystical—about anything.

4. Place the poem into the bowl of water.

5. When you are finished, dissolve the "circle of cauldrons" into the water.

After the spell: Place the poem and water into the Earth.

Spells to Bless and Anoint

To bless a person, object, place, or creature is to acknowledge hallowed energy. To bless a person is to recognise the sacredness that resides within them. When you bless yourself, you are acknowledging your own sacredness. Blessing also creates protection because a high vibration of energy essence is invoked. The act of blessing is beyond the ordinary world, for when you bless someone, or are blessed, you transcend to a mystical dimension where you see yourself and others as one with the Divine.

To bless a place or an object is to imbue it with magickal essence, to infuse it with a pure power and potential. Once blessed the object or space will hold that energy and will emanate an otherworldly vibration. Blessings can be made with magickal words, symbols, gestures, or the elements. An object or talisman is blessed with the elements, with a kiss, your breath, or by holding the object to your heart or raising it upwards to the heavens.

Anointing imbues spiritual significance and will raise the mystical vibration within a person or an object. Spiritual oils or water can be placed on your brow, heart, or hands to bless. Any part of the body can be anointed. A room can be blessed with the burning of incense or the speaking of holy words.

During a spell, you may anoint parts of your body to awaken desired energy or to create the magick of healing. You may anoint the middle of your brow before psychic work, your heart to activate forgiveness, or your hands to empower creativity. Candles, the written word, and other significant objects are also anointed to imbue them with magickal influence during the weaving of a spell.

A Spell to Bless a Ring

Purpose: Rings are significant, and most rings are symbolic of a relationship, a memory, a belief, or an intention. This spell deems the ring sacred.

When to cast: On the full moon. Both during the day and at night.

Where to cast: Indoors at your altar and outside under the full moon.

You will need: A ring you own. Salt to sprinkle.
Begin, with ingredients before you.

1. In your imagination, cast a "circle of magick rings" around you.
2. Hold your ring and say:
   "Sacred and divine."
   Kiss the ring.
3. During the day, hold it towards the sun (fire).
4. Move it in the wind (air).
5. At night, hold it towards the moon (water).
6. Sprinkle with salt (earth).
7. When you are finished, dissolve the "circle of magick rings" into your ring.

After the spell: Remember, your ring now belongs to the divine realm.

A Spell to Anoint Your Heart

Purpose: To remind you that your life is a sacred journey. To bring lightness and magickal intent to the heart. Anointing also dispels depleted energy.

When to cast: During any phase of the moon. Day or night.

Where to cast: Indoors at your altar or outside under the sky.

You will need: Six drops of rose essential oil (Rosa spp.) in a teaspoon of almond oil (Prunus dulcis) in a small bowl. Witch's utensils.
Begin with ingredients before you.

1. In your imagination, cast a "circle of roses" around you. Touch your heart three times with the oil.

2. Each time say:

   "I anoint my heart. I heal, I love, I create."

3. When you are finished, dissolve the circle by imagining it disappearing into your heart.

After the spell: If there is any oil remaining, anoint your heart every day until it is gone.

Spells of Initiation and Rites of Passage

The Sumerian goddess Inanna was initiated into the energy of courage and willpower through her journey into the Underworld. Odin, the god of the Norse, hung on the sacred ash tree for nine days, initiating himself into enlightenment through sacrifice. In many legends, the bridge-guarding troll initiates the traveller with a challenge before permission is granted to cross to the other side. On meeting the troll, the traveller is often unaware that he is being tested with a riddle. To cross to the other side of the bridge, the traveller must be spiritually ready. The readiness is the entry point of initiation into a new life.

Spells of initiation define a rite of passage, a beginning of something significant. Initiation asks for a sacrifice. Something needs to end in order for something to begin. This sacrifice is the trial that initiation follows. The maze and the labyrinth are both symbolic and actual places of initiation. They are a passage from the old to the new, as well as a place of trial. In the maze, you lose yourself before finding the way out. The state of confusion while in the symbolic maze separates you from what you have known, your conception of reality. So, when in the maze or labyrinth, between endings and beginnings, hold on to the thread of divine thought, of otherworldly assistance, to find the exit. This will be your new beginning.

A rite of passage acknowledges a new way of being in the world. The phases of life are also initiations. The step from one phase to the other often involves pain and always a sacrifice. Childhood innocence is lost with maturity and innocence gained again with old age. There are many phases you go through, but to truly "cross the bridge," a part of the old self needs to end. This happens through a symbolic death within your psyche.

There are other phases that are often not seen as initiations, though they are. These initiations can be intoxicating and exhilarating, like falling in love or bringing new life into the world, or they can be dreaded experiences like heart-break, grief, and sickness. All these experiences are a passage from what was to what is and to what will be. All these initiations are magickal, life changing, and take you closer to who you truly are.

An initiating spell involves the imagination, conjuring images of a passage, a door, a portal, or bridge. The cauldron is another symbol of initiation. It is the womb, so speaks of birth both symbolically as well as actually. It is also the entry to the afterlife. It also speaks of death on all levels.

 ## Initiation into Becoming the Witch

Purpose: A rite of passage to make your life sacred. This initiation makes sacred your journey into witchcraft. To deem your reinvention as Witch, a divine intention.

When to cast: On the new moon. Day or night.

Where to cast: Indoors at your altar or outside under the sky.

You will need: A purple candle of any size. Dried mugwort (Artemisia vulgaris). Self-igniting charcoal. A bowl of water. Container of salt. Witch's utensils.

Begin with ingredients before you.

1. Cast your circle by imagining you are standing at a forked crossroad. Surrounding you is a "circle of flaming torches."

2. Say:

> "I call on Hecate, goddess of witches, to initiate me as Witch."

3. Imagine you are entering a maze. With each element invoked, stop and "see" where you are. Allow images from your imagination to flow.

4. Light the candle. Hold your hands to feel the warmth of the flame.

5. Say:

> "I weave my spirit to the flame."

Look to see what surrounds you in the realm of your circle.

6. Light the charcoal. Add mugwort (*Artemisia vulgaris*) to the hot charcoal.

7. Move your hands through the smoke.

8. Say:

> "I weave my mind to the wind." Look to see what surrounds you in the realm of your circle.

9. Bless your heart, brow, hands, and feet with water.

10. Say:

> "I weave my heart to the moon."

Look to see what surrounds you in the realm of your circle.

11. Touch your heart, brow, hands, and feet with salt.

12. Say:

> "I weave my purpose to Mother Earth."

Look to see what surrounds you in the realm of your circle.

13. Close your eyes and imagine Hecate embracing you. She points to a door at the end of the maze. You open and walk through as the Witch.

14. When you are finished, dissolve the circle by imagining the flame from the torches extinguished.

15. Snuff out the candle.

After the spell: If any of the candle remains, relight in honour of the initiation. Place the water from the bowl and any used salt on the Earth.

Offering Spells

Coins are used as an offering to water deities when thrown into wells, rivers, ponds, and the sea. This is done to bring luck and for the granting of wishes. Norse sailors carried gold coins as an offering to their sea goddess, Ran. Their offering was a fare into her realm of the Afterlife in case of their drowning.[133] In Mexico, small metal folk charms called *milagros* are used as offerings to petition the saints or to give thanks. Offerings also appease magickal forces in the faery-faith of the ancient Celts. Milk and honey were gifted to the wee folk in Cornwall where the resident "piskies" are gifted a "dancing platform." This small structure is built on the roof of the home and is called a "pisky-pow."[134]

"Ghost money" or joss paper is an offering burnt at Asian funerals to ensure a good afterlife.[135] Flowers placed on graves and at the actual place where someone died are an offering. In mystical traditions, incense and candles are burnt for the dead and placed on altars and shrines. Incense takes messages to the departed and the light of a flame symbolises eternal life and the spiritual light that binds both worlds. These offerings are made as an expression of grief, the joining of both worlds, and also to acknowledge the continuation of life after death.

Offerings are made to connect with, acknowledge, and venerate spiritual entities, deities, and loved ones. They are sometimes a petition for assistance and can be part of invoking spells or any other intention. They are a symbolic gift, an appreciation, devotion, and acknowledgement of the sacred.

The offering is a physical representation of your relationship with the divine energy. Like all symbolism, it is a way to communicate without words. An offering usually takes the form of flowers, stones, food, candles, incense, or any meaningful object.

---

133. Monaghan, *The New Book of Goddesses and Heroines*, 264.
134. W. Y. Evans-Wentz, *The Fairy Faith in Celtic Countries. Library of the Mystic Arts Edition* (New York: Citadel Press, 1994), 164.
135. Mankey and Zakroff, *The Witch's Altar: The Craft, Lore and Magick of Sacred Space*, 233.

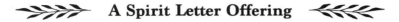 ## A Spirit Letter Offering

Purpose: To communicate with a loved one.

When to cast: During the waning moon. Day or night.

Where to cast: Indoors at your altar or outside under the sky.

You will need: Paper of any size for your letter. A pencil. String (9 in. or 22 cm).

Begin with ingredients before you.

1. In your imagination, cast a "circle of sunsets" around you.

2. Write your letter to a loved one. Know this is an offering of love.

3. When you are finished, roll the paper into a scroll or fold it into a small parcel.

4. Bind it with string, tying nine knots.

5. Go outdoors and find a tree. Tie the letter to a branch.

6. When you are finished, dissolve the "circle of sunsets" by imagining the suns fading into night.

After the spell: In time the spirit letter will be taken by the elements. It will fade with the sun, turn to pulp with the rain, be blown by the wind, and eventually return to the earth.

Spells to Charge, Consecrate, and Enchant

Objects hold energy; so do houses and clothes. Energy seeps from one thing to another. Energy also influences, inspires, and remains forever the same through time. A wedding ring may emanate love even though it is basically a gold band, a book holds the energy of thinking even though it is made of paper, and a shoe always speaks of movement.

An intention or a desire, and even the spoken word, can also change the energy of an object—take it beyond the five senses and make it magickal. This act is also called enchanting, consecrating, or charging. It is to imbue, invigorate, and infuse with otherworldly energy.

As a witch you will charge your talismans, jewellery, and the objects you use to weave your spells. When you do this, you invest these objects with sacred intention. They will then hold this vibration and reflect the energy back to you. This magickal act brings *life* to the object, awaking it, acknowledging its mystical purpose. The charging activates a spiritual vibration within the object, transforming it into a divine muse. The charging melds your intention into the physical object so they collaborate energetically. This magickal act can also align jewellery or an object with a spiritual force, such as a goddess, creature, or pantheon. After the charging, the object is no longer of the world of matter. It becomes otherworldly, a talisman.

Jewellery and significant objects are charged within your circle. There you move the object through, or near, the four elements as you hold your intention strongly in your mind.

A Charging Spell with the Four Elements

Purpose: To infuse an object or jewellery with sacred energy and to invest it with your intention. This intention becomes the purpose of the talisman. The purpose is also to transform an object from material to magickal.

When to cast: On the new or full moon. Day or night.

Where to cast: Indoors at your altar or outside under the sky.

You will need: A candle of any size. Choose the colour of the candle according to your intention. (See colour chart in the Appendix.) An incense blend of five parts frankincense (Boswellia carterii) and five parts white sage (Salvia apiana). Self-igniting charcoal. A bowl of water. A container of salt. Witch's utensils.

Begin standing at your altar with items before you.

1. With index finger pointed, turn in a full circle. Imagine the elements fire, air, water, and earth coming out of your finger to cast the circle.

2. Light the candle and the charcoal. Add a pinch of incense to the hot charcoal.

3. Say:

> "By way of magick I invoke fire, wind, water, and rain into my circle."

4. Hold the object you wish to charge and breathe onto it to connect your lifeforce with it.

5. Pass the object through (or near) the candle flame for purification (fire).

6. Through incense smoke for transformation (air).

7. Touch with water for the Moon Goddess (water).

8. And then sprinkle it with salt for the Earth Goddess (earth).

9. Hold the object to your heart and imagine a "bridge of light' connecting your heart to it.

10. The object is now a charged talisman.

11. When you are finished, imagine the "circle of elements" disappearing into your talisman.

12. Snuff out the candle.

After the spell: Always acknowledge the magick of the talisman. If any of the candle remains, relight in honour of the talisman. Pour the water from the bowl on the earth or a potted plant. Place any used salt on the Earth.

Once charged, your talisman has an ethereal personality. Its purpose is to tell your magickal story. Remind you who you truly are. Speak of your dreams and potential. And so, a fantastic communication comes into play. Your talisman has been deemed hallowed, so wearing it or connecting with it through the senses will have a profound influence on you. When you wear or make a connection with this object, you will make contact with magick.

Natural items, such as crystals, shells, wood, or feathers, will always hold their own magickal energy. Anything from the Earth, stones, plants, and parts of animals will emanate a unique vibration that melds its own story with yours. There is no need to activate it. Instead, the charging of a natural item creates a bond or alliance with the force that is already present in the object.

Objects and jewellery that once belonged to someone else or are inherited will hold the energy of the former owner. Sometimes it is important to retain this energy if a significant bond exists between the former owner and the new. Instead of charging inherited jewellery with an intention, you may want to weave a spell to acknowledge the person it belonged to or to bless it. You may use this object to make spiritual contact with the former owner, to feel close to them, or to be inspired by the qualities of that person or creature.

An alliance between you and your talismans will prevail. A deep magickal relationship has been forged in the circle. Talismans and blessed objects become messengers of power, protection, and love. They are your contract with a divine being, a beautiful thought, a pact with magick, and part of your sacred witch's weave.

Throughout time certain objects have been deemed inherently auspicious due to their symbolic nature. Because of this they have been used in the creation of magick. They are still used this way. These are the *witch's tools*.

TEN

The Witch's Tools

The creation of a spell can include symbolic tools and objects. A symbol transcends words and the mind. Symbolic tools not only represent intention, they hold that energy within their physical form and resonate a magickal vibration.

Each of the four elements: fire, air, water, and earth have a corresponding tool that is used to invoke, dispel, bless, attract, and heal. Some of these tools hold or contain the actual element as well. They are used to communicate with the divine. Like all magickal tools, they also speak of your story, purpose, and spiritual lifeforce. They hold within their symbolism sacred concepts that will align the mind to divine meaning and purpose.

You will charge or consecrate your tools and objects with the element it represents, sometimes all the elements. When a tool is "charged" it is deemed sacred, and a profound alliance between the tool, you, and magick is created. During the charging you merge your intention with the tool's physical form, just as a ring is transformed into a symbol of the union during a wedding ceremony. A strong relationship then forms between you and the tool and it is no longer "seen" as belonging to the ordinary world. It is then understood to be at one with divine power, knowledge, beauty, and something extraordinary. The creation of every spell needs your complete focus. Through every action and word, you imbue sacredness. Everything you do and say aligns with a magickal energy and entwine with the threads that connect your story to the world around you. In your imagination a divine tapestry is been created.

Magickal tools must be "fed" energy and interacted with. The more you interact with it, the deeper you consider the sacred quality and character of the tool, the stronger the magickal vibration will be between you.

Traditionally each tool is also aligned with a gender, male or female, according to its shape and energetic properties. Gender in this sense is a way to define opposites and does not belong to limitation, identity, or concepts of biology. The concept of gender, when pertaining to the elements and the witch's tools, refers to two independent forces; when united, these forces create transformation.

You will collect and acquire your witch's tools over time. You can purchase tools new or second hand, make them, or have them made for you. The cost of the tool has no value within the circle of your spells, for every charged object holds limitless magickal value. Sometimes you might receive a gift or inherit an object and decide it would be a beautiful tool to consecrate. There are no limitations because witchcraft liberates the imagination. When choosing a tool, the object must "speak to you." You need to feel a connection with its physicality and energy. Each object is symbolic so there are guidelines to keep in mind when collecting; however, the symbology doesn't limit the shape, colour, and size of your witch's tools. Keep in mind the wand and athame are directional and the chalice and cauldron are receptive. Apart from this, there are no limitations.

An athame or witch's knife is always blunt and traditionally the blade is double-sided. However, you may find a fascinating knife at a market that doesn't necessary fit the traditional description. You may decide to use a bowl instead of a traditional chalice or your grandmother's compact mirror instead of a "black mirror." A pentacle is easily made because it is basically a geometric symbol. This tool can be etched in clay or wax, drawn on paper, carved in wood, or purchased at many occult stores.

Every witch's tools are an expression of your story, so bring joy and freedom with each choice you make, and over time deepen your mystical relationship with each object.

The tools are kept on your witch's altar, a mystical place that changes according to the moon phases, the seasons, celebrations, and significant events. This is where you create your spells and is the heart of magick in your home.

The Wand: The Witch's Power
Element Fire

The word wand is an old Indo-European word meaning "to turn, wind or weave."[136] Wands are phallic, so are masculine in character, action-orientated, and outward.

In ceremonial ritual magick, and in the Tarot, the wand represents the element fire, though there are some mystical schools that align it with the air element. The Magician in the Rider-Waite Tarot holds a wand to the heavens, activating a flow of energy from the divine realm through his being. With his other hand he points to the Earth, manifesting his will in the realm of matter.

Wands of astounding splendour are found in the myths. The magick wand of the Celtic faery race, the Tuatha Dé Danann, is an apple branch of silver. The Irish Druids created wands from the yew tree (*Taxus baccata*) to gain power over the faeries and spirits.[137] Wands are symbols of power, mystical knowledge, and divine authority. They hold the potential for transformation as well as destruction. Asclepius, the Greek god of medicine, has a wand on which a snake is entwined.[138] Hermes, Messenger of the gods and guide to the Underworld, holds a staff of olive wood, or in some stories, laurel wood. Hermes' wand, called the caduceus, has wings and two snakes entwined, representing opposites, will and destiny, beginnings and endings. Zeus has a wand of oak and Dionysus, the Greek god of wine, holds a fennel wand, wound with ivy and tipped with a pinecone.

The power of the wand to transform is also found in the Bible when Aaron, Moses's brother, transformed his *rod* into a serpent. The wand's ability to transform aligns it with the serpent's power to shed its skin and become anew. Circe, the

---

136. "Wand," Online Etymology Dictionary, accessed August 21, 2020, https://www
.etymonline.com/word/wand#etymonline_v_4817.

137. Evans-Wentz, *The Fairy Faith in Celtic Countries. Library of the Mystic Arts Edition*, 343–344.

138. Becker, ed. *The Element Encyclopedia of Symbols*, trans. Lance W. Garmer, 24.

witch goddess of magick, turned men into animals with her wand and in ancient Egypt the falcon god, Horus, held a wand as a symbol of divine command.

Like the tree, the wand is a symbol of the World Axis, a link between the Heavens, Earth, and the Underworld. Like all tools of power, it brings you the ability to create magickal thinking, mystical energy, and spells.

The Ace of Wands in the Tarot calls you to action, to purify the mundane, to manifest, to take the burning torch and search through the darkness for truth.

A wand is a directional tool, a muse to influence your energy, to activate the imagination and ignite passion and desire. Wands can be made from wood, metal, stone, crystal, or any material. The wood of the tree or the metal or crystals used in the wand's creation will create the character of this magickal tool. A wand can be a simple stick, or it can be crafted, bejewelled, plain, or embellished.

A name is usually given to a wand. If it is made of wood, oils can be rubbed onto it to nourish its spirit. The wand, like all magickal tools, will harbour a spirit, a vibration that can never be reversed or banished. It will forever hold your energy and intention.

Every wand has a unique character and, if this isn't understood, you and your wand will remain strangers and will not be able to create magick together. A mystical relationship must exist between you and explored in the imagination. Your wand will remind you that you are a magickal being. It will speak to you of possibilities, other realms, and will imbue your thinking with a mystical quality.

Under the force of the wand the imagination wakes, worry is dispelled, and the ability to take action becomes possible.

When you point a wand you direct energy. You cast circles, "draw" invisible symbols in the air, and with the point of the wand, imprint mystical symbols in sand, salt, and earth. The wand focuses energy, directs your mind to magick, and tells you: You are powerful. You are a creator. You are the witch.

All tools of magick are charged to connect your spirit to the object. For objects belonging to a particular element, that element is often used alone in the spell.

A Spell to Charge a Wand with the Fire Element

Purpose: To bring a magickal purpose to the wand, to acknowledge its divine use, and to invest it with your intention. Then the wand will remind you of your power to act and manifest.

When to cast: At the full moon. The sun by day and the countless stars you see at night are of the fire element, so cast this spell either day or night.

Where to cast: Indoors at your altar or outside under the sky.

You will need: Your wand. A red candle of any size. Witch's utensils. Begin with ingredients before you.

1. Holding the wand outright, turn to cast a "circle of fire" around you.

2. Light the candle. Say:

    "Light my heart and mind."

3. Point your wand to the heavens and imagine it ablaze in flames.

4. From the truth in your heart call:

    "Spirit awake within the wand. Be a bridge to the
    magick world aligned with the sun and stars. Be
    a key to open the portals between the realms. My
    power to dispel, banish, will, and manifest."

5. Move your wand through the candle flame three times.

6. Hold the wand to your heart and imagine fiery threads of magick binding heart and wand.

7. When you are finished, imagine the "circle of fire" disappearing into the sun.

8. Snuff out the candle.

After the spell: Keep your wand in a magickal place or on your altar. You may want to wrap it in fabric or keep it in view. If any of the candle remains, relight when you use your wand.

Connecting with your wand on a deep and imaginative level will heighten the force of your will and ensure your spells are strong. Take up your wand and come to "know it." "See" its power to harness energy and "see" its energetic form in your imagination. Allow your spirit to weave threads around your wand; allow them to become one.

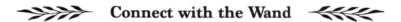

Connect with the Wand

1. Hold your wand towards countless stars in the night sky.
2. Turn to create a circle and "see" this circle in your mind. Imagine the circle is made from stars or flames or red sparkling light.
3. Point to the south (to the north in the Southern Hemisphere) and imagine opening a door to the sun.
4. Allow the wand to "draw" a symbol or a word in the air. What is it telling you?

When you hold your wand, you will connect with the power of your will. Listen as the wand speaks to you of bringing ideas into reality, of action, confidence, and dispelling what is no longer needed in your life.

The wand invokes the magick of fire. It is a tool of action, realisation, and willpower. Its gender is masculine, it belongs to the God. The wand is phallic, thrusting forward, creating, inventing, and actualising ideas birthed in the mind. The tool of the mind is known as the athame, sword, or knife.

The Athame, Sword, or Knife: The Witch's Mind
Element Air

The *athame* is a dagger used for magickal purposes. The name comes from the Latin word *artavus*, meaning a knife that sharpened the quills of scribes.[139] The athame is usually double-bladed to symbolize duality and the blades are blunt for the "cutting" is of a spiritual nature only. An air element tool can also be a sword or a knife. These bladed implements are usually referred to as athames when used in witchcraft.

The athame belongs to air and therefore to the realm of the mind. Its gender is masculine. It masters the world of illusion as it "cuts" through restriction, the pain of the past, and untruths. The double blade reminds us of light and shadow, of choice, of beginnings and endings. The athame or sword is also a protective tool and works with you to dispel unwanted thoughts.

The power of the sword was born from the skill and clarity of intent of the sword-smith. The process of refining the blade is symbolic of intellect, cleverness, and precision. Ancient Japanese smiths would purify and meditate before making a sword to ensure an evil spirit wouldn't inhabit the weapon during the making.[140]

The Vikings gave their swords a name as an acknowledgement of the residing spirit.[141] Durga, the Indian goddess of creation and destruction, wields a sword as one of her seven spiritual weapons. Her sword symbolises freedom from doubt and the determination of will.[142] A mystical knife is found in the medieval book of magick, the *Key of Solomon*,[143] and Fudo Myo-o, the Japanese deity wields a sword of wisdom as a warrior of enlightened thought.[144]

The Tarot's Ace of Swords speaks of choice, devoid of ego and of mastery of the intellect and the self.

---

139. "Athame," Liquisearch.com, accessed August 21, 2020, http://www.liquisearch.com /athame/etymology.

140. Ronnberg and Martin, eds. *The Book of Symbols: Reflections on Archetypal Images*, 492.

141. Ronnberg and Martin, eds. *The Book of Symbols: Reflections on Archetypal Images*, 492.

142. Willis, ed. *World Mythology: The Illustrated Guide*, 82.

143. S. Liddell MacGregor Mathers, tr. and ed. *The Key of Solomon the King* (Maine: Samuel Weiser, Inc., 1989), 96.

144. Farrar, *The Witches' God*, 177.

Like the wand, the sword is directional and can be used to cast a circle by holding it outright and turning. This tool of the element air is used to focus the mind, to draw words and symbols during a spell, and to enact other magickal actions. Because the sword or athame is a weapon by nature, it wields energy. It defeats and eliminates what is not aligned with the divine. The athame as a spiritual weapon is embodied in the sword of the Archangel Michael who yields it to slay demons.

The sword symbolises the magick of victory, justice, clarity, and decisiveness. It bestows honour for bravery, knights rise to its touch, and only the rightful king could dislodge the sword from the stone in the Arthurian myth.

The athame can be charged and bound to the owner by moving it through its element. Breathing onto the sword connects your soul to its soul and awakens your mystical relationship. When you hold your athame, all doubt and limited thinking are eradicated.

To own a spiritual "weapon" brings responsibility. Honour is aligned with awareness of self. When you meditate holding your athame, it will show you how your mind perceives the world. It will heighten your thoughts and allow you to either bless them or transform them.

 ## A Spell to Charge the Athame with the Air Element

Purpose: To bring a magickal purpose to the athame, to acknowledge its divine use, and to invest it with your intention. Then the athame will remind you of your power to think magickally, use the power of your intellect, and create change.

When to cast: At the full moon. Day or night.

Where to cast: Indoors at your altar or outside under the sky.

You will need: Your athame. Any incense stick. (To ignite, place the end of the stick on a flame. Blow out the flame. The incense will smoulder, releasing its scent.) Witch's utensils.

Begin with ingredients before you.

1. Hold your athame and turn in a circle. Imagine you are casting a "circle of flying birds" around you.

2. Point the athame to the east and speak with the full force of your mind.

> "I call to the power of the wind, to the breath of the gods, to the birds of the skies, bring your magick to my witch's knife."

3. In your mind's eye, "see" the blade moving through the wind and birds flying into it.

4. Breathe onto the blade and then move it three times through the incense smoke.

5. Hold the blade to your brow. Then raise it to the heavens.

6. When you are finished, "see" the "circle of birds" flying to the east and disappearing.

7. Allow the incense to completely burn.

After the spell: Always acknowledge the magick of the athame. Place this magickal tool on your altar in the east direction. You may wish to wrap it in fabric or keep in view.

Connecting with your athame on a deep and imaginative level will heighten the force of your mind and your awareness of the mundane. Take up your athame and come to "know it." Bestow a name on it and imagine it "cutting" through energy. Allow your mind to weave threads around it, allow them to become one.

Connect with the Athame

1. Hold the athame and extend your arm.

2. Turn to create a circle and "see" this circle in your mind. Imagine the circle is made of flying feathers, blowing leaves, or rays of golden light. Turn in the opposite direction and "see" the circle fading or dissolving.

3. Point the athame to the east, the direction of the rising sun, and imagine opening a door to the force of the wind.

4. Write your name in the air with the athame. Imagine how the letters vibrate, how they move and speak. What would your name feel like if you could touch it and what would it taste like?

When you hold your athame you will connect with the power of your mind. Listen as the athame speaks to you of purifying worry, transforming, change, cleverness, and freedom.

The athame invokes the magick of air. It is a tool of the intellect and ideas. Its gender is masculine. Like the wand, it is phallic, associated with the God, "cutting" through perceptions of reality as well as untruths, it changes, reinvents, calculates, and inspires. It belongs to the world of thoughts and balances the realm of feelings, symbolised by the chalice.

The Chalice: The Witch's Heart
Element Water

A muse for all the qualities of Water magick, the chalice is shaped like the crescent moon and encapsulates the moon's reflection. It symbolizes wishes to be fulfilled and the fluidity of the dream world. It is the cup of transformation, holding magickal elixirs to change, awaken, heal, and revive. The chalice represents the psychic world and the kiss of insight. A water-filled chalice can be used for scrying and divination, offerings, and to hold flowers. It is a symbol of the witch's imagination, a bowl of countless tears as well as a container of joy.

The cup, vessel, and chalice have been used in sacred ceremony in mystical traditions throughout time as reflective symbols, as a blessing, representations of the womb, and a muse of divine communication. The chalice is a symbol of the Goddess herself and holds your emotional life to the heart of all things. It encapsulates the womb, the gift of life, through the sustenance of water. The stem of the chalice is the link between Earth and the divine. It is receptive, open, and holds the water of life.

The vessel or container has been associated with the goddess since Neolithic times because of her association with water, the element of life itself. The Egyptian goddess, Nut, holds a water vessel aligning her to the life-given rain and rivers.[145] Ancient vessels and vases symbolised the womb that nurtured life and were decorated with water's movement of waves and spirals. Because of its shape, the cup became associated with the crescent moon and the milk of the breast, hence mother and goddess.[146] So too in Islamic writings, the cup is aligned to the heart and in India it is a symbol of the womb.[147]

The magick of the chalice is found in the myth of the Holy Grail. The legend tells that the grail was used to collect the blood, so hence the heart of Christ, when he was on the cross. The grail therefore became the container for divine essence and only Galahad, the knight with the purest heart, who underwent trials of spiritual courage, could find it. From out of this legend, a mystical cult of the Virgin Mary, called the Marian faith, rose throughout Europe. Mary, central to this mystical tradition, was seen as the *Theotokos*, a Greek word meaning "the bearer of God."[148] Her womb was the grail itself and divine vessel. The Virgin Mary is akin to many of the pagan goddesses in her association with the moon and hence the element water. In early Christian myth the chalice also became a symbol of the Goddess, bringer of life, and the sacred feminine.

The Tarot's Queen of Cups holds her feelings, her heart, and her creative dreams in her chalice and the hermetic vessel is the container of opposites merging to create transformation.[149]

The chalice enlivens the heart's energy and can be raised skywards in a spell, as an acknowledgement of divine energy as well as an offering to the Goddess. Water from the chalice can be used to anoint the body, to bless, and to charge other magickal objects.

145. Baring and Cashford, *The Myth of the Goddess*, 58.

146. Baring and Cashford, *The Myth of the Goddess*, 58–60.

147. Becker, ed. *The Element Encyclopedia of Symbols*, trans. Lance W. Garmer, 77.

148. Jean Markale, *The Great Goddess: Reverence of the Divine Feminine from the Paleolithic to the Present*, trans. Jody Gladding (Rochester Vermont: Inner Traditions International, 1999), 15.

149. Cooper, *An Illustrated Encyclopedia of Traditional Symbols*, 186.

A Spell to Charge the Chalice
with the Water Element

Purpose: To consecrate the chalice with the divine force of the Goddess and the energy of the moon. To merge your heart and intention with this tool of magick. The chalice will remind you of the depth of feeling, ways to heal, to love, and to see the invisible.

When to cast: At the full moon. At night.

Where to cast: Indoors at your altar or outside under the sky.

You will need: Your empty chalice. A small jug of water.
   Begin with ingredients before you.

1. In your imagination, cast a "circle of fish" around you.

2. Imagine the full moon above pouring light into your circle.

3. Slowly pour water from the jug into the chalice.

4. Hold the chalice to the west and speak from the truth in your heart.

    "May the Goddess bewitch my cup, vessel of the
    moon, portal to other worlds."

5. Imagine mystical water pouring from your heart into the chalice. The water flows over the sides of the chalice, over your hands, and onto the ground around you.

6. Hold the chalice to your heart and speak any words of love over it.

7. When you are finished, imagine the "circle of fish" returning to the ocean.

After the spell: The following night, take the chalice outside and pour the water over your hands. Always honour the energy in your chalice. Keep this witch's tool in a special place or on your altar. You may want to cover it with fabric or keep it in view.

Every full moon, bless the chalice by placing fresh flowers or herbs into it. Or place a moonstone, aquamarine, or labradorite crystal into your chalice of water. Leave it under the night sky during the full moon. Place a mystical kiss on your chalice on the full moon to connect your heart with the Goddess.

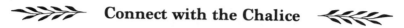

Connect with the Chalice

1. Fill your chalice with water. As you do, imagine tears of joy as well as sorrow pouring into the cup.

2. Hold the chalice with two hands and raise it skyward.

3. Holding the chalice, turn to cast a circle. Imagine the circle is made of water, blue light, or shells.

4. Point the chalice to the west, the direction of the setting sun, and imagine opening a door to the rising moon.

5. Connect your heart to the moon with imagined blue light, then pour this light into the chalice. Look into the water. What do you "see" in your heart?

When you hold your chalice, you will connect with the power of your heart. Listen as the chalice speaks to you of true feelings, healing, purifying, and the psychic power within you.

The chalice invokes the magick of water. It is a tool of the heart, emotions, and intuition. Its gender is feminine, it is receptive and belongs to the Goddess. It speaks of romance, joy, and play as well as heartbreak and the hidden. It is of the moon and the ocean, of ebbs, flow, and depth, and like the cauldron it symbolises *rebirth*.

The Cauldron: Womb of the Goddess
Element Water

The cauldron is a symbol of the Great Goddess herself, the brewing and potency of magick. It is the *vessel of plenty*, a container of the alchemical process, potion-brewer, and omnipotent witch's tool. The cauldron is a symbol of the creative force of life, death, rebirth, and the womb itself.

It is of the water element, an expression of life, initiation, and abundance. It offers transformation. It is the melting pot of the Great Mother. Hecate's cauldron bubbled at the forked crossroads. Into her blend of magick herbs she added wine or milk or blood and sacred stones from the East.[150]

In myth, the cauldron was associated with the cave, the entry to the Underworld. Hecate, in one of her forms, was a guide for the dead, and called their souls into the caves around Lake Averna, a volcanic crater lake in Southern Italy.[151] Hecate's cauldron of rebirth is the symbol of Samhain, the ancient Celtic festival of the dead when the spirits of the departed were appeased with offerings. The cauldron was also one of the treasures brought to Ireland by the Tuatha Dé Danann, an ethereal faery-like race of the goddess, Danu. It belonged to Dagda, the Irish fertility god. It was never empty and satisfied all who took from it. This cauldron is akin to the horn of plenty, the cornucopia, encapsulating endless knowledge and gifts.[152]

The Welsh goddess, Cerridwen, is the keeper of the *cauldron of inspiration*. Kept in the Underworld, it contained a poisonous concoction of herbs and seawater. The poison aligns her cauldron with death, and the seawater with rebirth, so it is a container of magickal opposites. The cauldron of Cerridwen encapsulates the creativity that actualizes only when a death of the psyche takes place. It speaks of transformation as a state where endings and beginnings emerge.

In her cauldron, Cerridwen creates a potion to transform her "ugly" son, Afagdu, into a brilliant visionary. She orders her servant boy, Gwion, to look after the brewing. Gwion, however, tastes the potion when the bubbling mix splashes onto his finger. Immediately he receives the powers of insight and creativity. The magick of the cauldron enables him to shape-shift into fleeing animals when the enraged goddess finds out what he has done. She pursues him as a predatory creature and he the prey. She turns into a greyhound, he a hare; her an otter, he a fish; she a hawk, and he a bird. Gwion finally transforms into a grain of wheat and Cerridwen, in the form of a hen, eats him. Later he is birthed from her to become a great bard.[153]

---

150. Stone, *Ancient Mirrors of Womanhood*, 208.

151. Stone, *Ancient Mirrors of Womanhood*, 206.

152. Farrar, *The Witches' God*, 109.

153. Farrar, *The Witches' Goddess*, 209.

Another shape-shifter called Thetis, a sea-nymph goddess, owned a cauldron and with it created a spell to ensure her infant son, Achilles, was immortal. According to the magick formula, she was to dip him into the cauldron's water seven times. However, because she held on to his heel during the spell, this part of him remained vulnerable and he died in battle when an arrow struck his heel. This myth may speak of our potential downfall when a weakness remains unchecked and unprotected.[154]

Cauldrons are associated with the bewitchment of the moon, the magick of water, and the passages of darkness into other worlds. It is a symbolic opening to the Underworld, the shadow realm of transformation and self-discovery. It is the instrument of blending significant ingredients and the art of transforming the mundane into the sacred. It is the brewing vessel of energies and choices.

The cauldron lures us to taste its contents, yet renders us in awe and fear of its hidden powers. For we never know what change will bring. However, the mystery remains exhilarating.

A Spell to Bewitch Your Cauldron

Purpose: To birth the magick energy of your cauldron. To invest into it your intention to walk the path of the Goddess. Once charged, the cauldron will remind you that a beginning always follows an ending, that rebirth follows death.

When to cast: At the new moon, at night.

Where to cast: Indoors at your altar or outside under the sky.

You will need: Your cauldron. Chalice filled with water. A white candle and a black candle of any size. Witch's utensils.

Begin with ingredients before you.

1. Say:

"I cast a 'circle of water' around me."

"See" the water moving. "Hear" its sound. "Smell" the ocean. "Feel" the water. "Taste" it.

---

154. Farrar, *The Witches' Goddess*, 279.

2. Light the two candle wicks.

3. Hold your hands over the chalice of water.

4. Call to the Old Goddess of the cauldron to enter the circle
   with these words:

   > "Priestess Moon, Sacred flame,
   > Hear my voice and know my name.
   > By power of the stars and seas,
   > By wings of birds upon the breeze.
   > Cauldron charge, below, above,
   > To know, to dare, to will, to love."

5. Pour the water from the chalice into your cauldron.

6. Anoint your heart with the water.

7. When you are finished, "see" the "circle of water" move into
   your heart.

8. Snuff out the candles.

After the spell: Leave the cauldron outside overnight under the new
moon. The following day pour the water over your hands, allowing
it to flow onto the Earth. If any of the candles remain, relight in the
future in honour of the cauldron.

Fill your witch's cauldron with water for your spells. Flowers of the earth element can also be added. Sometimes the cauldron is heated, uniting the element
water with the fire element. Essential oils, herbs, and plants can be simmered
in the water of an iron cauldron on an open flame or stovetop. The aroma from
the cauldron infuses the atmosphere with magick.

With the Goddess, stir the contents in your cauldron and, as you do, stir
life itself, brewing and bubbling tomorrow's promises.

Connect with Your Cauldron

1. Fill your cauldron with water as you cast a "circle of blue light" around you.

2. Place your hands around the cauldron. Close your eyes.

3. Breathe deeply.

4. When you are ready, allow your imagination to take you to a place of beautiful darkness and silence. Breathe.

5. Then, on the "horizon" a sun begins to rise.

6. Imagine this is the first light you saw at your own birth.

7. With your finger, write the word "birth" in the water of the cauldron.

8. When you are finished, dissolve the "circle of blue light" by imagining it moving into your heart.

Through time this tool has been associated with the myth of the witch. Originally a pot to cook food and brew remedies, it became known for its healing potential and ability to transform and bring life. Associated with the transformative spells of the goddesses, the nurture of woman, of mothers and grandmothers, the realm of the cauldron was the crossroads of Hecate as well as the kitchen and the herbal apothecary. Like the womb, it had the ability to hold water, to transform and reinvent, and therefore become a symbol of *life* and *rebirth*.

The cauldron holds potential, mystery, and flow. It is a passage and vessel of elixirs and, like the pentacle of the element earth, it symbolises the magick of fertility.

The Pentacle: The Witch's Coin
Element Earth

When the pentagram, the five-pointed star, is drawn within a circle, a *pentacle* is created. Like the pentagram, the pentacle is a symbol of mysticism. In ritual magick, occultism, and witchcraft it is a symbol of the element earth. The pentacle as a tool of the earth element can be made of wood, metal, or clay, or can be drawn on paper or any natural material. It is a protective grounding emblem, solid, centring, and defined. It is also a token to other worlds.

The symbol of the pentacle also introduces the fifth element, Spirit. Spirit is the divine, the sacred, the witch's purpose and truth. The upper point of the star is the symbol of spirit. It is positioned at the highest point denoting that the spiritual realm always presides over the physical.

All talismans in the ancient grimoire, the *Key of Solomon*, were called pentacles and were invested with the energy of a spirit in accordance to astrology, timing, and metallurgical influences.[155] The sixteenth century occultist, Dr. John Dee, used an elaborate pentacle in his evocations of angels. It was made from wax and was used to protect his magickal workings.[156] In the Tarot, the Queen of Pentacles holds her pentacle as a symbol of her connection to Nature and awareness of her physical well-being as well as her purpose on Earth. Her counterpart, the King of Pentacles, loves what he does on Earth and is the master of his work because he is spiritually aligned with it.

The pentacle is a portal for spirit communication and connection. It calls divine magick to the Earth, to your spell, and, like the talismanic pentacles of old, it invokes and evokes energy.

Just like a coin, the pentacle is a unit of exchange between the realms of Earth, the Heavens, and the Underworld. It is an entry token to the worlds of the divine and encapsulates the ability to move between them and to unite them. It is a key to open ethereal doors while simultaneously anchoring you to the physical world.

Coins also represent the earth element in a spell. Like the pentacle, the coin grounds the witch during her otherworldly experience in the circle and reminds her of purpose.

As tokens, coins are *obols* and placed on the eyes and in the mouth of the departed. Obols were the fare for Charon, the ferryman of Hades in Greek

---

155. Mathers, tr. and ed. *The Key of Solomon the King*, 66–79.
156. Guiley, *The Encyclopedia of Witches and Witchcraft*, 84.

myth. Charon transported the dead to the Afterlife across the rivers Styx and Acheron.[157]

A Spell to Charge the Pentacle with the Earth Element

Purpose: To transform the pentacle into a mystical tool. To birth with it the energy of grounding, strength, and growth. To consecrate it as a token into other realms.

When to cast: At the full moon. Day or night.

Where to cast: Indoors at your altar or outside under the sky.

You will need: Your pentacle and a handful of salt.
Begin with ingredients before you.

1. Hold your pentacle outright and turn, casting a "circle of green light" around you.

2. Speak through the power of strength:

    "I invoke Gaia, Earth Goddess, the trees, the mountains, and creatures of Earth to charge this tool with the magick of earth."

3. Sprinkle the pentacle with salt. Imagine plants of the Earth growing from the pentacle.

4. When you are finished, dissolve the "circle of green light" into your heart.

After the spell: Always acknowledge the power of your pentacle.

As a drawn symbol the pentacle can be cleansed or activated by covering it with salt, sand, soil, herbs, or flowers. Your circle can become a pentacle by imagining the pentagram inside it. The pentacle on paper can be placed in a wallet to connect with the energy of prosperity, and created with clay to actually feel the Earth while creating the symbol.

---

157. Willis, ed. *World Mythology: The Illustrated Guide*, 33.

Connect with the Pentacle

1. Hold your pentacle to your belly. Imagine mystical green threads binding you to this magick tool and then to the Earth.

2. Holding the pentacle, turn to cast a circle. Imagine the circle is made of plants, stones, or sand.

3. Hold the pentacle to the north in the Northern Hemisphere (the south in the Southern Hemisphere) and imagine opening a door to a forest.

4. What do you "see" in the forest? What do you "hear, smell, taste, and feel" there?

When you hold your pentacle, you will connect with your purpose. Listen as the pentacle speaks to you of your home, work, nature, your money, and your body.

The pentacle invokes the magick of earth. It is a tool of connection, growth, and anchors you to conviction. Its gender is feminine, it is fertility and belongs to the Goddess. It speaks of health, stability, the way you live your life, and your relationship with prosperity and food. It is of the Earth, abundant and expansive. It enlivens the five senses in limitless ways and, unlike the *besom*, anchors you to your home, the Earth.

The Besom: The Witch's Ride
Element Air, Fire, and Earth

Brooms sweep away the old and are a magnificent symbol of witchcraft, the spell, and the freedom to be wild, untamed, and to fly with the wind.

The besom is associated with feminine power and represents great magick disguised as a practical earthly tool. Brooms were of the woman's domain in an oppressive past, a tool of the kitchen and housework. The witch now breaks the shackles of history's chains by transforming this domestic tool into a vehicle of magick, of higher thoughts and ideals.

All tools that venture skyward transport the mind from the ordinary to a higher way of thinking. From above, life is viewed from a higher perspective, free of restraints and expectations. When the witch "rides" her broom, she is closer to the Heavens, bathed in the madness of the moon's dreamy influence.

The power of the broom is also born from ancient tree worship and honours the dryad. Hence the broom's element is earth as well as air. The broom, due to its directional shape, can also be a wand or a staff, also aligning it with fire. You can use your besom to energetically clear your circle. In your imagination it can transport you to other realms.

Brooms have been used through history to magickally cleanse a space. In ancient Rome, midwives would dispel unwanted energies from a house after a birth with a broom.[158] In Japan, a broom made out of grass was used to purify the home in spring festivals.[159] The broom is aligned to the concept of wisdom and purity in Zen Buddhism.[160] In some world traditions, the marrying couple jump over the broom to conjure good fortune.[161] Hence the besom is seen to be enchanted with the energy of luck.

 **Bless Your Besom**

Purpose: To bless what the broom symbolises: the divine feminine. To enchant the broom with magick and give rise to a residing spirit within. This witch's tool will remind you of the need for freedom, wildness, and embracing what is unique within you.

When to cast: On the night of a full moon or at one of the witch's sabbats, either Imbolc or the spring equinox (see The Witch's Wheel). At the full moon the energy of magick comes to fruition and peaks. The sabbats are a gateway where beginnings and endings merge. At night.

Where to cast: Indoors, standing by your altar or in your kitchen.

---

158. Barbara G. Walker, *The Woman's Dictionary of Symbols and Sacred Objects* (London: Harper-Collins, 1995), 123.

159. Cooper, *An Illustrated Encyclopedia of Traditional Symbols*, 26.

160. Ronnberg and Martin, eds. *The Book of Symbols: Reflections on Archetypal Images*, 596.

161. Walker, *The Woman's Dictionary of Symbols and Sacred Objects*, 123.

You will need: Your besom. Water in chalice. A green candle of any size. Salt to sprinkle. An incense blend of five parts copal resin (Bursera odorata, B. fugaroides), three parts mugwort (Artemisia vulgaris), and two parts patchouli (Pogostemon cablin or P. patchouli). Self-igniting charcoal. Witch's utensils.

Begin with the besom and ingredients before you.

1. Hold the broom and imagine a "circle of silver moons" around you.

2. Say aloud:

>"By power of the plants and trees.
>By sprouting seeds and falling leaves,
>I invoke the charms of blooms and bees,
>To charge this broom, as Gaia weaves.
>So mote it be, so magick rise,
>By moonlit night, by sunlit skies."

3. Ignite the candle. Imagine the light merging into the besom.

4. Light the charcoal on the flame and add a pinch or two of incense blend.

5. Pass the broom through the candle flame three times.

6. Pass it through the incense smoke three times.

7. Sprinkle it with water three times.

8. Sprinkle it with salt three times.

9. To infuse your spirit into the besom, breathe onto it and then hold it to your heart.

10. When you are finished, imagine your "circle of silver moons" moving into the besom.

11. Snuff out the candle.

After the spell: Your besom is now a tool of your magick and within it a spirit resides to guide you. Interact with the spirit and place it in any special place in your home, by your altar, at the front door, or in the kitchen. It is up to you. If any of the candle remains, relight it in honour of the besom. Pour the water and any used salt on the Earth.

Throughout time this magick vehicle has transported witches to ceremony and the circle, to the woods, and to faery lands. Brooms may sweep floors, but also tell us that beyond what we consider to be ordinary lies the extraordinary.

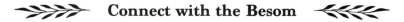

Connect with the Besom

1. Hold your besom. Say:

   "I invoke a guiding spirit to inhabit my witch's broom."

2. Feel the energy change.

3. Close your eyes and allow the broom's name to come to you. When it does, the relationship between you, the witch, and the besom begins!

4. Allow any messages from the broom to come into your mind.

5. Add bells, ribbons, or any other significant embellishments to your besom.

The besom "carries" you skyward, to higher thinking, to other realms, and beyond the ordinary life. Its power lies within your imagination and its magick symbolism. The broom is ethereal, and its flight is invisible. It belongs to the trees of earth, the fire of the wand, and, like the written word, the realm of the element air.

Book of Shadows: The Witch's Word
Element Air

Before spells and mystical lore were written in books, they were inscribed on objects and on buildings. Before this they were drawn and etched in Nature. Magickal acts, depictions of the divine, and the power of animals were once painted in the caves and on rocks when humans were completely at one with the natural world. A drawing of a shaman in a mask known as "the sorcerer" was found in Ariege in France. The drawing depicts a figure, a fusion of man and animal, and dates to 13,000 BC.[162] On the surfaces of prehistoric caves in Chauvet, France, the fantastic energy of animals running calls us to revere the power of herd.[163]

The desire to connect, understand, and communicate with the divine is primordial and with this comes the need to hold knowledge in a tangible form and to pass it on to others. The actual recording and depicting of magick in writing or images is also a way to acquire its power, as well as a way to honour it and also share it with others.

"Grimoire" is a word of French origin meaning "grammar."[164] It is the name for a book where magickal information is written and drawn. Spells, invocations, spiritual experiences, dreams, symbols, and thoughts are entered into a grimoire, also called a *Book of Shadows.*

Creating a Book of Shadows is a spell in itself, a record of your divine story. The act of writing the words or drawn symbols adds to the potency of manifesting your intention. Like all your witch's tools, the type of grimoire you choose it up to you. It can be a simple notice book, an art folio, or an elaborate book encrusted with crystals and mysteriously locked. Flowers can be pressed into a grimoire. It can be painted, can include wax seals, photos and drawings, or a cat's whisker. Once created, the grimoire holds a magickal vibration and becomes a sacred object.

Spells and incantations were once written in cuneiform on clay tablets in Mesopotamia in the fourth and fifth century BC. Fragments of the first book containing astrology and angelic lore were found with the *Dead Sea Scrolls,* also called the *Book of Enoch.* In the manuscript, mysticism and magick are intertwined with ancient religious writings.

In antiquity, the Egyptians were revered as the most adept magicians of the time. They inscribed their esoteric knowledge on objects and tablets in hieroglyphics and their spells were mostly created for protection and health. Their

---

162. Guiley, *The Encyclopedia of Witches and Witchcraft*, 321.
163. Ronnberg and Martin, eds. *The Book of Symbols: Reflections on Archetypal Images*, 313.
164. Aaron Leitch, *Secrets of the Magickal Grimoires: The Classical Texts of Magick Deciphered* (St. Paul, MN: Llewellyn Publications, 2016), Title page.

belief in the power of the written word is embodied in Thoth, their god of writing, wisdom, and magick.

Later, in the first to fifth century BC, the Egyptians created a writing system with the Greeks and used papyri to record their mystical beliefs. These written spells often invoked magick to advance the success and prosperity of the spell-caster.

The merging of the Greeks and Egyptians gave rise to a mythological entity that united Thoth with the Greek god of communication, Hermes. This entity, called Hermes Trismegistus, was said to be the divine author of one of the greatest grimoires, the *Emerald Tablet*. Thought to have originated in the Hellenistic period, between 323 BC and 31 BC, the *Emerald Tablet* may well contain the most profound of all magickal writing: "That which is above is the same as that which is below."[165] How you think is what your world will be. The mind and the world around you are reflections.

The mythical Hermes was said to have written countless books and they appeared everywhere, dating from ancient biblical times to the medieval era. The knowledge contained in these grimoires included alchemy, astrology, and ritual practice. Although ancient occult scholars, physicians, and alchemists from Egypt, Chaldea, Near East, and Greece speculated Hermes was the author, the author or authors of the books remain shrouded in mystery.

The *Key of Solomon* is a Renaissance grimoire of great renown and includes descriptions of how to create talismans and the evocations of spirits. This manuscript is said to combine the alchemy of the Middle East and the mysticism of the Kabbalah. Versions have been found written in Latin, Greek, Italian, and Hebrew.

Many old grimoires were studies in the summoning of demons and dark angels. The purpose of this fascination was not to align with these entities, or to join forces with them, but to learn of their nature and motivations. By doing this the magician hoped to gain an understanding of how to control these forces in the psyche as well as around him.

In the eighth century, Arabic magick flourished in the libraries of the Moors and conveyed studies of medicine, mysticism, alchemy, and, in particular, astral magick. The Hebrew *Kabbalah*, a collection of mystical knowledge, was birthed

---

165. Trismegistus, *The Emerald Tablet of Hermes*, 19.

between the twelfth and thirteenth century in Spain and France. Its magick explores the connection between humanity and the Universe and its central symbol is the Tree of Life.

Other grimoires of the past include the *Leechbooks* of medieval England that combined herbal remedies with charms and elven cures.[166] Cornelius Agrippa, a German occultist, wrote the *Three Books of Occult Philosophy* in the fifteenth century. His grimoire included the power of nature, colours, numbers, and the elements.

Within the pages of these grimoires, science, healing, and the health of the body are found alongside spells, the invocation of spirits, natural magick, and astrology. The ancient grimoires brought together the astrologers, alchemists, and magicians of Islam, the pagan world, Christianity, and Judaism. The knowledge within them has inspired and influenced ritual methods, spellcraft, folklore, and nature worship.

In the Icelandic world, a grimoire called the *Galdrabók*, written around 1600, combines Christian and Norse gods as well as sigil and runic magick.

A washing verse (20) "I wash myself in thy dew and dales … I set thy blessed form between my eyes. I wash away all my foes and their spells … the world shall be kind to me …"[167]

Another grimoire, *Pow-Wows: Or, Long Lost Friend* by Dutch healer, John George Hoffman, holds knowledge of folklore, herbal cures, hex signs, and invocations.[168] It was published in America in the early nineteenth century and includes a mysterious word square, a Latin palindrome called the Sator Square. This palindrome is depicted in the *Key of Solomon*, found in the ruins of Pompeii and in locations and documents all over Europe.

---

166. Owen Davies, *Grimoires: A History of Magic Books* (New York: Oxford University Press, 2009), 22.

167. Stephen E. Flowers, *The Galdrabók: An Icelandic Book of Magic.* Second, Revised Edition (Smithville Texas: Rûna-Raven Press, 2005), 45.

168. John George Hoffman, *Pow-Wows: Or, Long Lost Friend* (Middletown, DE: Forgotten Books, 2007).

Figure 1: Sator Square

Charles Leland's *Gospel of the Witches* was published in 1899. The book can be considered a grimoire because it writes about the mysteries, the "old ways," and goddess worship in Italy. The American folklorist transcribed the practices and beliefs of witchcraft, the *Old Religion,* told to him by an Italian witch called Maddalena. Within the pages are invocations, spells, and chants of the *stregas,* the witches. A new type of witch emerges in the book as Aradia, daughter of the Moon Goddess Diana. This witch was Goddess made flesh, a messiah sent to Earth to teach spells and fortune-telling. This book can be seen as one of the links between today and a forgotten world where magick spoke through the "voice of the wind." These words are from the *Gospel of Aradia.* They are a recording of the magickal ingredients of a spell, ingredients no different from what you may use in a spell today.

"I bear water, wine and salt and my talisman... and a small red bag which I ever hold in my hand... with salt in it, in it. With water and wine I bless myself."[169]

---

169. Charles G. Leland, *Aradia: Gospel of the Witches* (Washington: Pheonix Publishing Inc. 1996), 15.

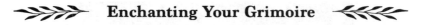 **Enchanting Your Grimoire**

Purpose: To bring a magick vibration to your grimoire. To deem it to be a book of witch's knowledge.

When to cast: On the full moon, at night.

Where to cast: Indoors at your altar or outside under the full moon.

You will need: Your grimoire. Your athame. A found feather (if permitted) or an imagined feather. An incense blend of five parts sandalwood (Santalum album), three parts lavender (Lavandula officinalis or L. vera), and two parts dragon's blood (Daemonorops draco, D. poppinquos). Self-igniting charcoal. Writing or drawing materials. Witch's utensils.

Begin with ingredients before you.

1. Imagine a "circle of feather quills" around you.

2. Light the charcoal and add a pinch of incense mix.

3. Say: "I invoke the power of breath and air,

    By witch's voice, by mystic prayer.
    To charge this book, by owl and crow.
    By Hermes flight, *Above, Below.*"

4. Move the grimoire through the incense smoke three times.

5. Write your witch's sigil on a page. Around your sigil, write words and draw images and symbols as they come to you. Decorate the page according to your imagination.

6. Touch your heart, throat, and brow with the feather and place on the page.

7. Hold your athame to the east and then point it to the page.

8. Say:

    "Ancient quills, and sky birds rise as I write. Words of witches and wind from the east to turn each page. I weave my mind, my word, my breath to the spirit of this grimoire."

9. Breathe onto the page.

10. When you are finished, imagine the "circle of feather quills" ascending to the skies.

After the spell: Always bless the energy of the grimoire before opening it. Keep on your altar or in a secret place. When the charcoal is no longer burning, take some of the white ash and mark the page where your sigil is written. Empty the rest of the ash onto the earth.

Opening the pages transports you into a divine state of mind. Your Book of Shadows is highly personal, a deeply magickal depiction of the microcosm—your inner spiritual world. Like all witch's tools, it will reflect to the macrocosm—the world around you.

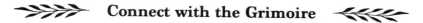 ## Connect with the Grimoire

1. Hold your hands, palms down, above your grimoire. Say:

   "Your name appears before my eyes. On wings of
   birds from realm of skies."

2. Close your eyes and allow the grimoire's name to come to you. When it does, the relationship between you, the witch, and your grimoire deepens.

3. Flick through the pages of the grimoire, breathing onto them.

4. Your spirit and the book become closer.

Your grimoire is a highly personalised document of your magickal experiences, your dreams, and your thoughts. Each word, symbol, or drawing in the book is a silent spell. Over each page, your breath, a feather's touch, or the sound of a bell will bless.

The Bell: The Witch Rises
Element Air

The Hindus say that the echo of a bell is akin to the primordial vibration of the Universe.[170] Their gatekeeper and divine bull, Nandi, wears a bell around his neck as a symbol of dignity. The Russian orthodox thought of the bell as "God's own voice" and believed that living entities resided in the sound. Bells were rung at Beltane, one of the ancient Celtic seasonal festivals, to repel troublesome wee folk and then, at other times, bells were rung to invoke the faeries.

Tibetan ritual bells include a small object called a "dorje," representing male energy and compassion. This combines with the bell's feminine sound that resonates with the wisdom of emptiness. Together they symbolise the state of enlightenment. A traditional-shaped bell combines sacred opposites, uniting male in the phallic handle and female in the dome-shaped opening.

Although the bell is the tool of the air element, the sound calls in all the elements. It will be one of your enchanting tools and is used in most magickal and spiritual traditions. It is of the air element because sound is invisible to the eyes and travels on the wind. Bells also announce a magickal act is taking place. The sound honours a place that is deemed sacred and calls the heart to celebrate. A bell is rung to summon the divine, the spirits, or a familiar. When words are spoken during a spell, bells are sometimes rung to unite sacred energy with the words, to heighten the magick.

The sound of a bell raises the vibration of the heart and connects feelings to the divine realm, so it is akin also to the water element. Rung over the heart, the bell awakes wonder and virtue; around the aura, dispels low vibrations; and over charms, tools, and talismans the ring blesses, charges, and welcomes all that is sacred. A bell is sounded at the beginning and end of a spell, or to herald profound actions or words. Bells clear unwanted energy from a house and the mind. The sound is of the heavens as well as of the faery world. Bells call you to silence, to reverence, and to play.

---

170. Ronnberg and Martin, eds. *The Book of Symbols: Reflections on Archetypal Images*, 872.

 **Bless Your Bell**

Purpose: To consecrate your bell as a witch's tool. To open your psychic abilities to hear its voice and feel its power to purify and dispel unwanted energy.

When to cast: At any phase of the moon. Day or night.

Where to cast: Indoors at your altar or outside under the sky.

You will need: Your bell. Incense stick of any kind. Witch's utensils. Begin with ingredients before you.

1. To cast a circle, turn around as you ring the bell. Imagine the sound as light emanating from the bell and filling the circle.

2. Light the incense stick.

3. Move the bell through the smoke three times.

4. Ring the bell over your heart.

5. Close your eyes. Remember your first breath on this Earth, your mother's arms around you, your first tear, your first kiss. Ring the bell.

6. Through the sound of the bell, be at one with the Goddess, at one with your dreams, part of life's mystery. Ring the bell.

7. When you are finished, dissolve the circle by turning in the opposite direction as you ring the bell.

After the spell: Always know your bell has a sacred voice. Allow the incense to burn out.

The bell is a tool to summon the divine and banish the unwanted. The sound of a bell heralds a sacred occurrence, a magickal event, profound words spoken. A bell marks the beginning and the end of a spell, so it is a tool of opening and closing and also of messages, for petitions to the deities are transported through the beauty of the ringing.

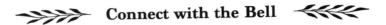
Connect with the Bell

1. Create a magickal conversation between you and the bell.

2. Ring the bell very gently, then just gently, louder and louder again. Slowly then fast.

3. Listen to its "voice." What is it telling you?

4. Think of a wish and ask the bell to take the wish to the Goddess.

5. Hold the bell and allow it to sound out your wish.

Bells ask you to be still and silent, to hear the voices from other realms. They tell you to look within and, like the witch's mirror, they ask you to reflect.

The Witch's Mirror: The Witch's Window
Element Water

As mirror is symbolically seen as "fixed water," so holds the magick of this element, speaking to your imagination, heart, and insight. It is ruled by the moon for it reflects the past, present, and future. Mirrors reveal the truth and transform the reflected image to another dimension, so you see it removed from the greater world. By doing this it brings focus to what it reflects. As if in a painting, the face or object reflected is revealed to you in a different way and with greater meaning. The energy of the subject is explored in the mirror, its power and secrets too. You will always see something different when you look at a person or object in a mirror's reflection. They seem to hold enchantment, the ability to reveal another side or aspect of a person or thing. They have a bewitching nature because they seem to have a "voice" that speaks of what they reflect. Nothing in a mirror ever appears mundane because the mirror tells its magickal story. This is what you will learn to read.

See the mirror as a portal, a window, or a door to other realms. So travel into it and as you "listen" to the "voice," you will experience the mystical and the wonder of a true psychic. Never try to "see" into your witch's mirror; instead "fall" into it and allow it to show you a changing face, symbols in your mind, and feelings in your body. Allow your imagination to merge with the mirror and know that you may not "see" things as they normally appear. The mirror is a type of dreamscape and speaks in the language of symbols and visions. Every witch will "see" and "hear" her mirror in different ways. Sometimes while scrying, an image may appear in your mind or a thought, word, or symbol may present itself. Everything that comes to you will be significant and will require your interpretation. Other times a certain knowing or an answer may come to you as you gaze into the reflective surface. A profound relationship will begin when you relinquish the thinking mind and embrace the stories told by your mirror. So, look into your mirror and say, "Once upon a time" and then tell the rest of the story.

Mirrors capture a sacred view of the world. Every mirror has a personality and no two mirrors ever seem to reflect in the same way, hence why they are thought to have a soul or spirit. There are superstitions of bad luck connected to breaking a mirror and vampires having no reflection in them because they have no souls. The belief that a mirror should be covered if there is a death in the house is another practice associated with the ability of mirrors to capture a soul. Like all new friendships, yours with the mirror will deepen and the way your mirror communicates will become clearer. The name of this witch's tool will be revealed, and through the reflection, you will begin to also know yourself deeply.

Your witch's mirror is also a tool to call the Goddess into the circle because, like the chalice, it is aligned with the moon, the heart, and your ability to see life beyond the surface. As a witch you will reflect on your life, feelings, and thinking so the mirror is both a symbolic and practical tool.

The herb mugwort (*Artemisia vulgaris*) is used to charge, enchant, and cleanse a witch's mirror. Mugwort conjures psychic ability, the understanding of dreams, and the heightening of the imagination. Always have this herb if you have a mirror. Using fresh or dried mugwort, you can create a brew, just like making tea. Submerge and rinse a clean cloth in the infusion and wipe the surface of your mirror. Mugwort can also be burnt in dried form, and the mirror passed through the smoke to invigorate the vibration.

"… if a smooth shining piece of steel be smeared over with the juice of mugwort, and made to fume, it will make invocated spirits to be seen in it."—Cornelius Agrippa[171]

---

171. Agrippa, *Three Books of Occult Philosophy,* 134.

An enchanted mirror will assist you in many ways as a witch. With practice, your psychic powers will heighten, your imagination will broaden, and your knowing of magick will strengthen. The mirror will guide you, reflect the truth, and always show you possibilities.

 ## A Spell to Enchant Your Witch's Mirror

Purpose: To consecrate your mirror. To invoke a spirit into it and know its name. To see the truth in its magick reflection and to bewitch the mirror with the energy of the moon.

When to cast: On the full moon at the height of the moon's enchanting powers. At night.

Where to cast: Indoors at your altar then outside under the full moon.

You will need: Your mirror, chalice with water, and bell. A white or silver candle of any size. Mugwort (*Artemisia vulgaris*) to burn as incense and to make an infusion with. Self-igniting charcoal. Clean, soft cleaning cloth. Witch's utensils.

You need to prepare an infusion: Place fresh or dried mugwort in a bowl and add hot water (though allow to cool a little after boiling). Allow the brew to infuse for ten minutes.

Begin with ingredients before you.

1. Pour the mugwort infusion into the chalice. Holding it, turn to cast your circle.

2. Imagine you are casting a "circle of moons" around you.

3. Light the candle flame and ignite the charcoal.

4. Add a pinch or two of dried mugwort to the hot charcoal.

5. Move the mirror through the rising smoke. Imagine spirits dancing through it.

6. Wet the cloth with the mugwort infusion. Wipe the surface of the mirror. As you do this, imagine the mirror surface becoming water.

7. Say aloud three times:

> "By ocean, shell, and silver moon.
>
> Awake spirit of the mirror and tell me your name."

(You may receive a name "written" as a word in your mind or see an image that will inspire a name for you to choose. You may also feel an emotion that brings you closer to the spirit of the mirror and therefore a name to bestow on it.)

8. Breathe into the mirror three times, connecting your lifeforce with its spirit.

9. Ring the bell over the mirror as a blessing.

10. Snuff out the candle.

11. Go outside and leave the mirror under the full moon.

12. When you are finished, dissolve the "circle of moons" by imagining it disappearing into the mirror.

After the spell: Bring your mirror inside early the next day. If any of the candle remains, relight in honour of the spirit in the mirror. Place any infusion from the chalice on the earth. Always acknowledge it is a divine object. It is traditional to cover a witch's mirror when it isn't being used so only the images you choose are captured in the reflection. Only use your mirror for magickal purposes.

Early Egyptian mirrors were made from polished copper and were used as ritual items as well as household decorations. Hathor, the Egyptian goddess of love, music, and dancing, had a shield through which she could see all things in true light. From this shield she created an all-seeing magick mirror. One side was endowed with Ra's Eye of the Sun. Through it she could see everything, no matter the distance or how far into the future. The other side of the mirror was able to reveal the true nature of the glazer and only the bravest person could look into it without flinching. Some depictions of Hathor show the goddess holding a mirror above her head.

Obsidian makes a traditional black mirror. An obsidian sphere was used to channel the Enochian or angelic language by the sixteenth century occultist Dr.

John Dee. However, you can use any mirror for divine reflection and scrying. Some witches create their own black mirror using a glass frame and black fabric or paint. Simply place the fabric behind the glass and attach the frame or alternatively paint the back of the frame behind the glass.

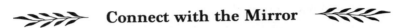

Connect with the Mirror

It is important not to try too hard when connecting with the psychic realm. In fact, it is important not to try at all. The mirror will often "speak" in symbols; interpretation is up to you. It is important to always ask about your own life unless someone has requested a reading from you.

Surrender and dream and be at one with your imagination.

1. Hold your mirror and look beyond your face. It is important not to look at the physical. Try to soften your focus.

2. Ask the mirror to reveal something you need to know about yourself. Does your face change? What rises in your imagination? How does your body feel?

3. Ask the mirror to show you something from the past, the present, and the future.

4. Ask the mirror for direction. What do you "see," "hear," or "feel"?

5. Ask the mirror for a message from a loved one.

You visit a mirror, and for that moment, it captures you, showing you a time in your life. You visit your witch's mirror to ask for truth, to see the invisible, to dream while awake, and to connect with deep knowing and guidance.

Mortar and Pestle: The Witch's Alchemy
Element Earth

The Chinese Moon Goddess, Ch'ang O, has a rabbit as her familiar. He resides on the moon and pounds his mortar and pestle. Look up to the full moon and you will see his shadow.

A mortar and pestle are used to blend herbs, plants, and oils for charms and sprinkles. The blending itself needs to be imbued with your intention. Because the blend will be used for a magickal purpose, the implements used to blend need to be invested with a magickal essence. Therefore, the mortar and pestle become an instrument of alchemy or transmutation, a part of the act of changing a combination of plants and oils into a mystical concoction.

Like all magickal tools, a gender is attributed to each part. The mortar being receptive is female and the phallic pestle is male. Symbolically when the two tools combine, *creation* takes place through the meeting of opposites.

 ## Connecting with and Enchanting
Your Mortar and Pestle

Purpose: To transform a kitchen utensil into an instrument of magick.

When to cast: Any phase of the moon. Day or night.

Where to cast: Indoors at your altar or in your kitchen.

You will need: Four small candles: black (base energy), white (knowledge), yellow (refinement), and red (awakening). These colours symbolise the four phases of alchemy, the art of transmutation. Salt to sprinkle. Witch's utensils.

Begin with the ingredients before you.

1. In your imagination, cast a "circle of light" around you. See it change from black, to white, to yellow, then to red.

2. One by one, light each candle in that same order.

3. Move the mortar and pestle over each flame. Say:

    "To know, to blend, to create, to transform."

4. Sprinkle the mortar and pestle with salt.

5. When you are finished, imagine the colours of your "circle of light" dissolving into the mortar and pestle.

6. Snuff out the candles.

After the spell: Always see your mortar and pestle as an instrument of transformation. If any of the candles remain, relight them in honour of your own transformation. Place the used salt on the Earth.

The witch's tools are used practically and symbolically during the spell to create your story as an act of magick. These tools are the pillars of your altar. They will remind you that you are a spiritual being. Your tools will always hold your magickal intention and emanate a sacred vibration. When life's hardship weighs you down, when you disconnect from hope, love, and courage, hold one of your witch's tools, look into your mirror, or sound your bell and you will be transported to a place out of the ordinary, a better part of yourself, connected to everything with magickal threads.

Often the tools are placed in their own direction in the circle and on your altar. Sometimes only one tool is used in a spell; other times you will combine them. The witch's mirror should be covered or wrapped in fabric between your scrying. All your tools should only be used for magickal purposes. They are not of the physical world. They have their own lifeforce now aligned with your story and the story of witchcraft.

The actual presence of the four elements—the flame, incense smoke, water, and salt—bring the vibration of the actual element into the circle. The symbolic tools become your intention as you enact your magick. They are an expression of your voice, keys that open mystical doors within you and around you; they communicate with the divine and with you. Every time you use your witch's tools, you will discover more about yourself and deepen your relationship with the sacred.

As well as the witch's circle and tools, there are other symbols that mysteriously open portals to magickal thinking and mystical worlds. They are geometrical designs and act as keys to unlock new vision, for they too speak of concepts beyond actions and words.

ELEVEN
Magick Shapes

Within the circle, geometric symbols weave your story and work like keys to unlock mystical knowledge and divine relationships. Symbols are the language of the divine and transcend the limitations of words and the mind. This mystical language expresses the heart and also invokes the energy it represents. Symbols can be worn, drawn with your witch's tools in the air or on paper, or they can be created using salt, flowers, or rice.

Candles and other tools can be positioned in the shape of these symbols to heighten the power of the spell. The meaning of symbols is universal, deeply embedded in the psyche and you can speak to the divine through them.

Like the circle, geometrical shapes are expressions of magickal concepts, petitions to hallowed worlds, and keys to doorways of power and beauty. They call you to speak in perfect truth, in a perfect moment.

Look into the symbol,
A world to find.
A bridge to a feeling,
Beyond words and time.

+	△	□	☆	✡	✳	✴
Cross	Triangle	Square	Pentagram	Hexagram	Heptagram	Octagram

Figure 2: Geometrical Shapes

The Cross: The Meeting Place: Power of 2

The cross is one of the oldest symbols used to depict a mystical concept. It was used in ancient Sumerian and Assyrian times where it depicted the Sun.[172] It has been found on objects all over ancient Europe. Its symbolism is thought to include Heaven itself as well as the powers of protection and good luck. The Egyptian ankh is a form of a cross and is thought to represent the key to the Afterlife.[173]

Long before the European invasion of America, the cross was a magickal sign representing the four winds for the land's First Nations. It is depicted on medicine wheels to symbolise this divine concept where it is drawn within the circle of life.[174] The cross, in Christian symbolism, is the ultimate sacrifice. It also represents the hallowed tree of the cosmos: the Universal Tree of Life. It symbolises the four directions, north, south, east, and west, as well as the four elements and the seasons. The horizontal line is the material plane and the vertical is the spiritual plane. The point where the two lines meet is where the Heavens and Earth connect, where all is centred and balanced. In numerology, the power of 2 vibrates with this symbol. It resonates duality, the combining of opposites to create transcendence.

Magickally, the cross is used to protect, banish, and ward off all opposed to truth and goodness. It is a divine guardianship, a sacred signpost that stops anything harmful from advancing.

Like the five-pointed star, the cross is symbolic of a human figure and at its centre, the heart. It calls you to acknowledge the divine. The symbol is still and forceful. It denotes a meeting point and is a gateway to spiritual potential.

---

172. Cooper, *An Illustrated Encyclopedia of Traditional Symbols*, 45, 46.

173. Becker, ed. *The Element Encyclopedia of Symbols*, trans. Lance W. Garmer, 19.

174. Chevalier and Gheerbrant, *The Penguin Dictionary of Symbols*, trans. Buchanan-Brown, 257.

The cross represents the "crossroads," a mythological place of ritual, sacrifice, and profound magickal intervention. The cauldron of the goddess Hecate bubbles away at the crossroads, brewing the secrets of transformation.[175] Although Hecate's crossroads are a fork-road, she is still present where all roads cross, especially in isolated places and in Nature's secret realms. You find yourself at the crossroads during times of waiting, when the motion of life has stopped, and you are unsure of the future. At the crossroads you contemplate. It is a time to surrender to the unknown and embrace mystery. In the Tarot this concept is found in the card of the Hanged Man. His waiting involves viewing life from a completely new perspective symbolized by hanging upside down. Only when he stops, he can transform.

The crossroads are a turning point, a contemplation of opposing feelings and thoughts that need to be brought together to bring growth and change. The cross is the symbol of the beginning and the end, representing the magick of stillness, ritual, choice, then transformation.

Spell of the Crossroads: Surrender to Wisdom by the Magick of 2

Purpose: To receive clear direction and inspiration when at a "crossroad" or during a time of waiting when life feels at a standstill.

When to cast: The new moon to invoke the crone aspect of Hecate, the goddess who resides at the crossroads. At night.

Where to cast: Indoors at your altar or outside under the new moon.

You will need: Your wand. If you haven't a wand, use your pointed index finger or find a stick. A black candle of any size. Paper (3 in. x 3 in. or 7 cm x 7 cm). A pencil. Container of salt. Witch's utensils. Begin with ingredients before you.

1. Hold your wand outright. Turn to cast your circle. As you do, imagine crossroads appearing as two paths in a faraway place.

---

175. T. C. Lethbridge. *Witches: Investigating an Ancient Religion.* 6th Edition (New York: Routledge), 21.

2. Light the candle to honour the fall of night.

3. In this hallowed place, call to the ancient goddess Hecate:

> "Hecate, I ask you to meet me at the place of wait-
> ing in my heart. Bring to me knowledge."

4. In your imagination, "see" the goddess transforming from
   crone into her familiar forms: horse, dog, and bear. Now
   merge these creatures in your mind.

5. Take Hecate's hand and draw the symbol of the cross on
   paper. Now write your own name where the two lines meet.

6. Place salt over the cross and name to ground your magick.

7. When you are finished, dissolve the circle into Hecate's cauldron at the crossroads.

8. Snuff out the candle.

After the spell: Leave the written spell, covered in the salt, under the
waning moon for two days before burying salt and paper in the earth.
If any of the candle remains, relight in the future in honour of the
goddess Hecate.

The Triangle: Vessel of Magick: Power of 3

Triangles are mountains and hills as well as funnels and wells. Triangles point
and seem silent. They call us to pray and be still; they also call us to purpose
and direction.

Pointing towards the skies, the triangle represents the spiritual realm. Three
is the first number of dimension and symbolizes manifestation. So, the three-
sided triangle holds the power of creativity and actualization. Three is the number that is associated with spells, for wishes always come in threes, as do faeries.
Three is the hallowed number of the Triple Goddess, the mystical trinities, and
the Fates. There are three Worlds: the Underworld, Earth, and the Heavens;
three passages on this Earth: birth, life, and death or childhood, maturity, and
old age. There are the three concepts of time: past, present, and future and three
phases of the moon: waxing, full, and waning.

The shape of the triangle conjures the imagination of alchemy: imagine
using its shape as a vessel to pour elixirs. The upward pointing triangle is solar,

as fire always reaches to the sky and the downward triangle is lunar, as water always descends. Air rises so its symbol is the upward triangle with a line across the top and earth is beneath us, so its triangle points down, also with a line drawn through it.

The triangle is used to direct energy as well as contain it. It can be drawn with a pen or created with salt or other materials. Candles and other magickal tools can be positioned in its shape. The triangle can be imagined inside the circle and also meditated on.

 ## Divine Mirror of the Triangle to Call in Love by the Magick of 3

Purpose: To invoke true love.

When to cast: During the waxing moon. Day or night.

Where to cast: Indoors at your altar or outside under the sky.

You will need: A red candle of any size. Pencil and paper (3 in. x 3 in. or 7 cm x 7 cm). String (9 in. or 22 cm). Something to draw on your skin like non-toxic paint, an eye-pencil, or lipstick. Witch's utensils.

Begin with ingredients before you.

1. Imagine a "circle of red moons" surrounding you.
2. Light the candle.
3. Draw the symbol of fire on one of your palms and on the other the symbol of air.
4. Draw the symbol of water on the top of one foot and on the other the symbol of earth.
5. On the paper draw a circle and then within it a triangle.
6. In the triangle write: To love's own quest I bind my heart.
7. Imagine this symbol entering your heart.
8. When you are finished, dissolve the circle by imagining the red moons fading.
9. Snuff out the candle.

After the spell: Place your written spell under your pillow for three nights, then tie it to a tree branch using the string. If any candle remains, relight in the future and say: "To love's own quest I bind my heart."

The Square: Foundation and Order: Power of 4

The square is a symbol of the Earth realm and foundation. It is a firm base for a physical structure and this same structure is reflected in its symbolism. Squares symbolise order and logic, a realm of step-by-step analyses, where the mind resides over the heart. The square is aligned with the number four and is associated with Jupiter, the planet of prosperity and expansion. Your money is of the world of matter and is a unit of exchange. It most often requires plans and the intellect, an ordering of the mind, how much to spend, and how much to save. Even the counting of money requires a logical progression of the mind.

Like the cross it represents the four directions. Pythagoras, the ancient Greek mathematician, saw the square as the four elements united.[176] It has been used as the shape of altars and for ancient word and number configurations called palindromes. Palindromes vibrate defined magickal energy, according to the letters and numbers used with their squared design.

The square is also symbolic of the mundane, fixed ideas, and walls that limit the mind. The square doesn't have the movement of the circle. It seems to be still and rigid, hence the encouragement to "think outside the square" when innovation is needed.

Enclosing the symbol of the square inside a circle unites your earthly quest with a spiritual force. The square is steadfast and strong. It is the symbol of building an idea, structure, the working world, and the physical plane.

 ## A Witch's Square for Prosperity by the Magick of 4

Purpose: To attract the energy of abundance. To create prosperous thinking.

When to cast: During the waxing moon. Day or night.

---

176. Cooper, *An Illustrated Encyclopedia of Traditional Symbols*, 157, 158.

Where to cast: Indoors at your altar or outside under the sky.

You will need: Your pentacle (if you don't have a pentacle, a coin can substitute). Four small green candles. Container of salt. Four coins. Your purse or wallet. A piece of green cloth (8 in. x 8 in. or 20 cm x 20 cm) and string (16 in. or 40 cm). Witch's utensils.

Begin with ingredients before you.

1. Holding your pentacle, turn and cast a "circle of coins" around you.

2. Position the four candles in the shape of a square. Inside the square place a small heap of salt.

3. Place your purse on the salt and then place the four coins onto the purse.

4. As you light each candle say:

   "I unite this purse with the power of four. With the force of Jupiter. With a seed that forms a tree."

5. Wrap the coins and some of the salt in a small bundle of green cloth. Tie the bundle with string and fasten with four knots.

6. Dissolve the "circle of coins" by imagining them dissolving into sunlight.

7. Snuff out the candles.

After the spell: If some of the candles remain, relight in the future and say: "With a seed that forms a tree." Place any salt on the Earth. Keep the four coins on your altar or in a sacred place.

The Pentagram: The Alliance: Power of 5

The pentagram is a gateway to the sacred realm, to a place of perfection. This symbol is Universal and emanates a forceful vibration. It represents many mystical concepts. It is the symbol of the five elements as well as the five senses.

The pentagram is a perfect binding seal, representing a magickal alliance between you and witchcraft. Of all symbols it may be the one most associated with the modern witch.

The mysticism of the pentagram represents spirit presiding over the physical realm, as the point of spirit rises above the extremities of matter: fire, air, water, and earth.

The pentagram also depicts the human figure with the head, hands, and feet at each point. It is a symbol of balance, protection, and power. It holds the force of the number five. Combining the feminine two with the masculine three, it represents a union. The pentagram embodies the microcosm, the world within you, and can be drawn with one motion. Within the circle, the five-pointed star becomes the pentacle, a witch's earth element tool.

The pentagram has been found on pottery in Mesopotamia and to the ancient Hebrews it represented the concept of truth and perfection.[177] It is considered divine in Eastern, Egyptian, and Indian mysticism. In the middle ages, knights wore the pentagram on their armour to represent the five wounds of Christ as well as the five virtues of knighthood: friendship, generosity, chastity, courtesy, and piety. The pentagram is also viewed as an endless knot and was placed for protection on windows in medieval times.

The Pythagoreans called the pentagram "health." It was an emblem for perfection, and they aligned it with Hygenia, the Greek goddess of health. Cornelius Agrippa attributed the five elements to the pentagram. It is also found in the Kabbalah, and in the magick of the alchemists. The magickal significance of this symbol was revered in ancient Arabia and it also appeared on the abraxas talismans, the divine charms of the Gnostics, a pre-Christian mystic cult that spoke of god as female as well as male.

The power of this symbol has been invoked as a "closed gate" to harmful energy throughout time.

Talismans in the ancient text the *Key of Solomon* include the pentagram in designs. And the symbol was used in the complex ceremonies in magickal societies, such as the Golden Dawn. The rebirth of paganism and witchcraft in the mid-twentieth century reclaimed the pentagram from the shadows of time, and it has come to be known as the ultimate symbol of witchcraft.

---

177. Chevalier and Gheerbrant, *The Penguin Dictionary of Symbols*, trans. Buchanan-Brown, 747.

The symbol of the pentagram belongs to no one and also to everyone. It is used to raise the energy of magickal power within you: truth, bravery, kindness, and the search for meaning.

 ## A Spell for Magickal Knowledge by the Magick of 5

Purpose: To know yourself and understand the workings of magick. To make your spells stronger.

When to cast: On the new moon to learn of the mysteries or on the full moon to brighten illumination to your magick workings. Day or night.

Where to cast: Indoors at your altar or outside under the sky.

You will need: Chalice of water. Pentagram (either drawn or a talisman). A white candle of any size. White sage (Salvia apiana). Ten drops of frankincense oil (Boswellia carterii) in a teaspoon of almond oil (Prunus dulcis). Salt to sprinkle. Witch's utensils.

Begin with ingredients before you.

1. Stand with arms and legs extended. Imagine you are a living pentagram. Now imagine a circle appearing around you.

2. With your pointed index finger, "draw" the pentagram above your head and also beneath you.

3. Light the candle.

4. Burn the sage leaf and call to your ancestors with these words:
   "Take my message to the divine.
   I wish to walk a magickal path."

5. Using the oil, anoint your heart and top of your feet by drawing the pentagram onto them.

6. Now move your pentagram five times through the flame and sage smoke. Then sprinkle the symbol with the water and salt.

7. When you are finished, imagine your circle is taken away by the wind.

8. Snuff out the candle.

After the spell: If any candle remains, relight in the future and say: "I wish to walk a magickal path." Place water and used salt on the Earth. If your pentagram was drawn on paper, keep it in your grimoire or any other significant place.

The Hexagram: The Beautiful: Power of 6

Combining the two triangles, fire and water, creates the Hexagram. This potent symbol is the elements as one, ascending and descending, it is male and female united, consciousness and the unknown, the union of Heaven and Earth.

The hexagram represents "as above so below" and is thought to represent the macrocosm—all that is.[178]

The symbol's origins are found in Hebrew, Islamic, and Christian lore. It is found in the ancient books of mysticism and etched on talismans and seals. In the *Key of Solomon,* instructions are written on the creation of an auspicious ring called the *Seal of Solomon.* The central symbol on the ring is an interlaced hexagram and was thought to hold the power to bind demons and bestow commanding magick.[179]

This six-pointed star became a symbol of faith as the Star of David in Judaism.[180] In Hinduism it is known as Shatkona and represents the constant embrace of Shiva and Kali, the union of male and female, creation and destruction, beginnings and endings, birth and death.[181]

The hexagram in alchemy was used to symbolise the seven ancient planets and their corresponding metals. The sun and gold were placed in the middle of the star. From the top point and moving clockwise: Saturn's metal was lead,

---

178. Cooper, *An Illustrated Encyclopedia of Traditional Symbols*, 83.

179. Mathers, tr. and ed. *The Key of Solomon the King*, 44–47.

180. Chevalier and Gheerbrant, *The Penguin Dictionary of Symbols*, trans. Buchanan-Brown, 504.

181. Alexander Roob, *Alchemy and Mysticism*, trans. Shaun Whiteside (Koln: Taschen GmbH, 2005), 469.

Jupiter was associated with tin, Venus with copper, the moon with silver, Mercury with quicksilver, and then Mars with iron.[182]

The hexagram has a solid personality. It holds the elements in a firm embrace. It is a magick shield, a divine instrument that calls in opposites and reminds us of the power created by combining opposing energies and connecting to the forces of the elements.

 ## Spell of the Hexagram to Clear the Mind by the Magick of 6

Purpose: To invoke clarity and to dispel worry. To think magickally and powerfully.

When to cast: Over six nights of the waning moon, at night.

Where to cast: Indoors at your altar or outside under the waning moon.

You will need: Chalice with water. Six yellow candles of any size. The candles will be snuffed and relit six times. Leave enough of the candle for six burning times. A plate large enough to stand your six candles. An incense blend of three parts lavender (*Lavandula officinalis* or *L. vera*), two parts rose (*Rosa spp.*), three parts copal (*Bursera odorata, B. fugaroides*), and two parts sandalwood (*Santalum album*). Six pieces of self-igniting charcoal. Container of salt. Paper (6 in. x 6 in. or 15 cm x 15 cm). A pencil. Witch's utensils. This spell is created over six nights.

Suggestion: Position the six candles on a large plate. Always be careful with burning the paper. As the burning paper nears its end, place the paper into a bowl of water.

Begin with ingredients before you.

1. Cast your circle by imagining a "circle of hexagrams" around you. "See" each symbol as a portal to another world.

---

182. Migene González-Wippler, *The Complete Book of Amulets and Talismans* (St. Paul, MN: Llewellyn Publications, 1991), 197.

2. Light the charcoal and add a pinch or two of the incense blend.

3. Position the six candles in the design of the hexagram on the plate.

4. As you light each flame in turn, imagine this same flame igniting in your mind, illuminating thinking, and banishing worry.

5. Begin to write any worries or fears on the paper as the candles burn.

6. When you are finished, snuff out each flame.

7. Dissolve the circle by imagining the hexagrams moving onto the paper.

Continue the spell the following night:

1. Over six nights cast your circle and relight the candles. While the candles burn, again write down your doubts and fears.

2. On the sixth night, tear the paper into six pieces and draw a hexagram onto each piece.

3. One by one, burn each piece of paper on a candle flame.

4. The circle is dissolved every night and re-cast.

5. Snuff out the candles each night.

After the spell: If any candles remain, relight in the future as you imagine a hexagram in your mind. Place any used water and salt on the Earth.

The Septagram: The Elven Door: Power of 7

The septagram, or heptagram, was used in early alchemy to represent the seven ancient planets. It holds the vibration of seven, a highly mystical number combining the spiritual three with the earthly four.

This star mirrors the magick of movement and light. It is said in recent times to be associated with the fae, the faery realm, and is known in witches' circles as the Elven Star. In the Tarot the Chariot is numbered seven. This card heralds a breakthrough after a time of hardship and asks you to strengthen your will and align your thinking to sacred intent.

 ## A Spell to Open a Gateway to Start Again by the Magick of 7

Purpose: To refresh and invoke a new start. To let go of regret. To reconnect, reinvent, or redefine the past.

When to cast: On the new moon. At night.

Where to cast: Indoors at your altar or outside under the new moon.

You will need: Purple candle of any size. Paper (3 in. x 3 in. or 7 cm x 7 cm). A pencil. An herbal blend of five parts rose (*Rosa spp.*), three parts mugwort (*Artemisia vulgaris*), and two parts thyme (*Thymus vulgaris*). String (9 in. or 22 cm). Witch's utensils.

Begin with ingredients before you.

1. Say:

   "By the power of magick, I cast a circle of seven
   mystical doors around me." Imagine these doors.

2. Draw the number seven on paper, then draw a door around the number. Write your name on the door.

3. Place the herbal blend onto the paper and then fold the paper into a parcel.

4. With string, fasten the parcel with seven knots.

5. Breathe onto the parcel, then hold it to your heart.

6. Close your eyes.

7. In your imagination, look around your circle at your seven doors. Now choose one of the doors and imagine walking through it.

8. As you do, all other doors dissolve around you.

9. Snuff out the candle.

After the spell: Place the parcel under your pillow for seven nights. After the seven nights, bury the parcel in the earth. If any of the candle remains, relight in the future and, as you do, bring the number seven into your mind.

The Octogram: Star of Ishtar: Power of 8

The eight-pointed star was called the Star of Ishtar in the ancient Near East.[183] The goddess Ishtar was the embodiment of all feminine characteristics and attributes. She was the initiate as well as the gatekeeper to the Underworld. She is the nurturing mother, the lustful pursuer of lovers, and at the same time the constant virgin. She therefore embodies all possibilities and powers.

The octogram is also thought to be the Star of the Magi, so it is a guiding light, the heralding of something auspicious. This message of hope is felt in its depiction in the Star card in the Rider-Waite Tarot, where it is aligned with freedom, faith, and renewal.

It is a protective symbol that speaks of regeneration and balance. It holds within its magick the divine number eight, aligned with the heavens, a divine realm beyond the seven spheres of the known planets. In Babylonia the number eight was the number of the gods, representing a hallowed state of being.[184] It has also been considered lucky and auspicious universally. The eight lotus petals in Indian tradition symbolize good fortune and in China the doubling of the number four represents strong material foundation and results in the bestowing of luck in life.

Spell for Courage by the Divine 8

Purpose: To invoke courage and dispel fear. To centre energy, to give rise to self-worth and belief, and to connect with guidance. To liberate divine strength and conviction.

When to cast: During the waxing moon. At night.

---

183. Annemarie Schimmel, *The Mystery of Numbers* (New York: Oxford University Press, 1993), 157.
184. Schimmel, *The Mystery of Numbers*, 156.

Where to cast: Indoors at your altar or outside under the waxing moon.

You will need: Your wand and chalice of water. A red candle of any size. Container of salt. Sandalwood incense stick. Paper (3 in. x 3 in. or 7 cm x 7 cm). A pencil. Five drops of pine essential oil (*Pinus spp.*) in a teaspoon of almond oil (*Prunus dulcis*). Witch's utensils.

Begin with ingredients before you.

1. Stand holding the burning sandalwood stick outwards. Turn around to cast your circle.

2. Say aloud:

   "I am the witch who in the dark of night walks in the light of the moon."

3. Light the candle and feel the warmth of the flame.

4. Take some salt and rub between your hands.

5. Bless your heart with water.

6. Anoint your feet, hands, and the back of your neck with the pine oil (*Pinus spp.*).

7. Draw the number eight on paper and anoint with the oil.

8. Sprinkle the paper with salt and move it over the heat of the candle flame.

9. Imagine the number merging into your body as a shield of protection.

10. Raise your wand skyward and call to the Goddess:

    "I stand with Ishtar. Complete, centred, and power-ful." Repeat this eight times.

11. When you are finished, imagine the circle rising and dissolving into eight distant stars.

12. Snuff out the candle.

After the spell: If any of the candle remains, relight in the future and say: "I stand with Ishtar." Place any used salt and water on the Earth.

There are countless magical designs and symbols. You use them to communicate with the divine, to banish and to invoke, to weave your story.

Along with geometric designs and sometimes included within them, there are symbolic charms, talismans, and amulets that capture sacred concepts in a physical object or an image. They may be worn as a ring, a necklace, carried, hidden, or drawn. They whisper possibilities, align your mind with magickal thinking, and your heart to meaning and intent.

TWELVE
Keys to Unlock

Magick has been activated using symbolic objects since ancient times. These objects are used to invoke spirits, summon familiars, increase power, attract luck, heal, acquire knowledge, and call on mystical assistance. They have also been used for protection, psychic enhancement, and to banish and dispel. They represent a sacred force, a magickal agreement. They encapsulate your intention and are an expression of your inner world made visible in the outer world.

Ancient symbols of the Great Goddess included the horn, the crescent moon, the cosmic tree, the labyrinth, and the egg. Neolithic altars were horn-shaped, a depiction of the moon. Crescent horns became divine symbols and were worn as crowns to connect with the power of the Goddess. Horses left a crescent symbol in the dirt with their hooves and so they also became aligned with the Goddess, with her moon and with dreams, hence the word "nightmare" and the lucky horseshoe. The Cosmic Tree was etched onto Sumerian seals[185] and was depicted with the moon and the serpent long before the story of Eden in the Bible. The symbol of the labyrinth and the spiral is a form of the serpent. These symbols denote initiation, a place between the worlds and the passage of oneness with the Goddess.

Symbols, images, and sacred objects draw the mind to higher thinking, beyond the mundane, imbuing thought with the quality of beauty and mystical vision. They liberate innovation, magnetise what they represent, ward off lower energy, and remind you of magick. Worn as jewellery, carried, and placed somewhere significant or concealed, they represent an intention or invocation. They encapsulate your sacred story, a story often unexplainable in words or needing more words than is possible. A vast number of charms are universal, reflecting the story of humankind and our relationship to the divine.

Like a key they open your mind and heart to wonder. They can also repel, protect, and guide by strengthening the courage, awareness, and resolve within you. Some appear to be under a "rapture of glamour," the illusion of the faery realm. Some are symbols that belong to ancient pantheons and speak of the deities, mystical systems, and beliefs. Other symbolic objects contain an inherent natural vibration expressing the might of the animal world or the forces of Nature.

There are many names given to these symbols and objects, including *charms.* When an object is charmed it resonates a purposeful energy that is compelling and contagious, because it changes you. A charm holds a mystical intent and speaks to you of your wishes, potential, opportunity, passion, and truth. Many objects in the ordinary world seem to have a charm because of what they symbolise beyond their practical purpose. A button is considered a charm because of its ability to bind and fasten. It brings what "fits" together, so in the realm of magick it attracts the right energy and is carried to attract luck. A key is also a charm because it opens. It conjures the idea of a door and the wonder of what lies behind it. It is a charm of initiation and the promise of beginnings and opportunity. To the witch, so-called ordinary objects become extraordinary in the realm of spells. Always keep an old key and pick up a button if you see one.

---

185. González-Wippler, *The Complete Book of Amulets and Talismans,* 15.

Charms are often defined as amulets and talismans. An amulet is most often thought to possess inherent power due to its design, such as the pentagram, or because of its natural composition. An animal's tooth, a wand made from oak, and a crystal of any type is an amulet because in contains a mystical essence that doesn't need "activating" nor can it be removed. An amulet often has a general purpose like to attract luck or create protection. A talisman is a charm that is charged or concentrated by the witch for a specific purpose, say to heal a broken heart. A charm is also something created by you, an item crafted in your hands that encapsulates your intention.

The realm of charms, amulets, and talismans is immense; I have only mentioned some in this book. Every mystical tradition has charms and symbols to connect humanity with a higher purpose, with good fortune, love, and protection. As a witch you will discover the charms that express your story and most often, they will discover you.

The Witch's Amulet

Abracadabra Amulet

The ABRACADABRA symbol was an ancient charm used by the Romans to cure illness. This charm depicts a diminishing sequence of the word *abracadabra* to form a downward triangular shape. On each line of the design a letter from the end of the word is omitted until the only letter left at the bottom of the triangle is A. Although mysterious in origin, this charm is thought to have derived from an older formula, the Chaldean words ABBADA KE DABRA, meaning "perish by the word," or is the origin of the word Abraxas, the name of the Gnostic god that was used on charms to protect against the evil eye.[186]

The diminishing word, written or read, has a direct influence over unwanted energy, causing its power to fade as the word does. You can use this ancient charm to diminish unwanted thoughts or habits. When writing each diminishment of the word, imagine unwanted thoughts disappearing into the void. The ABRACADABRA charm speaks clearly of how the act of magick works, a physical enactment or symbolic depiction of the desired change.

---

186. Mathers, tr. and ed. *The Key of Solomon the King*, 476, 481, 482.

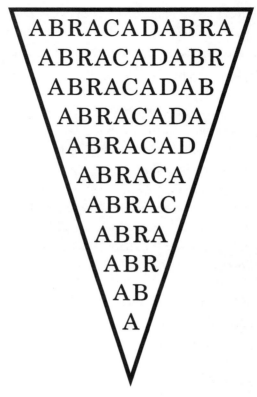

Figure 3: Abracadabra Amulet

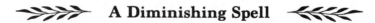 **A Diminishing Spell**

Purpose: To dispel unwanted thinking.

When to cast: During the waning moon. Day or night.

Where to cast: Indoors at your altar or outside under the sky.

You will need: Chalice filled with water. A pencil. Paper (3 in. x 3 in. or 7 cm x 7 cm). A black candle of any size. Nine drops of hyssop oil (*Hyssopus officinalis*) in a teaspoon of almond oil (*Prunus dulcis*). An incense blend of four parts myrrh resin, two parts juniper berries (*Juniperus communis*), and four parts copal (*Bursera odorata*, *B. fugaroides*). Self-igniting charcoal. Salt to sprinkle. Bowl of water.

Begin with ingredients before you. Pre-light the charcoal in the censer.

1. Point your wand skyward. Then as you bring it downward, image a "circle of mystical fire" descending from the sky to surround you.

2. Light the candle. Say:

   "The Light."

3. Hold in your mind what you wish to eliminate from your life. Then allow a word to come into your mind that encapsulates this energy (e.g., "DISAPPOINTMENT," "UNWORTHY," "BITTER").

4. Write the word. Then, according to the ancient enchantment of ABRACADABRA, continue to write the word omitting the last letter. Create the shape of an inverted triangle as you write.

5. Move the paper five times through the candle flame. Say:

   "By fire diminish."

6. Move the paper five times through the incense smoke. Say:

   "By air diminish."

7. Sprinkle the paper with water five times. Say:

   "By water diminish."

8. Sprinkle the paper with salt five times. Say:

   "By earth diminish."

9. Breathe onto the enchantment, then burn on the flame.

10. Place the remains of the burning paper in the bowl of water.

11. When you are finished, stand and hold your wand. Point it to the ground. Imagine your "circle of mystical fire" entering the wand as you move it skyward.

After the spell: If any of the candle remains, relight in the future and say: "Diminish." Place the water on the Earth.

While a talisman is infused with specific intentions, an amulet is mostly used to banish energy and is for protective purposes. In ancient Babylon, clay cylinder seals were carved to ward off evil[187] and when the Dutch immigrated to America, they brought with them protective hex signs and painted them on their houses.[188]

The Cimaruta

In Italy the *cimaruta* is a witch's amulet worn as a necklace. Cast or etched in metal, it includes a combination of magickal images. Its central form takes the form of a sprig of rue (*Ruta graveolens*), a highly protective herb. Attached to the rue other images are depicted, including the moon, a key, animals, flowers, a heart, and a helmet. Every symbol brings to the amulet a connection to the protective force it represents. The *cimaruta* also aligns you with the *strega,* an ancient witch's cult dedicated to the Moon Goddess, Diana.[189]

The Eye

The symbol of the Eye is a universal amulet for protection, a mirror reflection of the power associated with the eye to hex or control another. There is a belief that to look at someone with jealousy is to give the person the "evil eye." The energy from the jealous eye projects a destructive force affecting the person who it is cast upon. In Rome, Greece, and the Middle East, the symbol of the *eye* has been worn as an energetic shield.[190] Like the coin and the mirror, the eye also contains a mystical reflection of opposites. The ability of the eye to see the physical world renders it divine, so it must be able to also "see" the invisible. This all-seeing eye is located in the middle of the brow and in Hindu mysti-

187. González-Wippler, *The Complete Book of Amulets and Talismans,* 15.

188. González-Wippler, *The Complete Book of Amulets and Talismans,* 156.

189. Raven Grimassi, *The Witch's Craft: The Roots of Witchcraft and Magical Transformation* (St. Paul, MN: Llewellyn Publications, 2005), 188.

190. Francis Huxley, *The Eye: The Seer and the Seen* (London: Thames and Hudson, 1990), 74.

cism. This is the sixth chakra vibrating the colour violet.[191] Kali, the Hindu goddess of death, was born from the brow of her younger counterpart, Parvati. Kali is the *Shakti*, the power of the god Shiva. Both deities have a third eye on their brow symbolizing their supreme knowledge.

The Norse All-Father, Odin, sacrificed one of his eyes to acquire the power of insight.[192] In ancient Egypt, the Eye of Horus, or Udjat, was used for protection. Horus's right eye was of the sun and amulets sometimes combine his right eye with his left eye, the moon, again partners of source and reflection.[193]

Figure 4: Eye of Horus

A Mexican amulet called the *"eye of god"* is crafted from two sticks forming a cross and yarn tied around it in the shape of a diamond. It is hung in the home to energetically guard those living there.[194]

The image of the hand is also a universal protective symbol. The hand stops harmful energy while it welcomes good with a beckoning gesture. The hand blesses, anoints, and points the way.

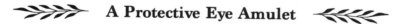

A Protective Eye Amulet

Purpose: To create a protective amulet for your home. Energetic protection raises the vibration of magick in your home, deeming it to be a place that aspires to sacredness under any circumstance.

When to cast: On the new moon. Day or night.

191. Nozedar, *The Illustrated Signs and Symbols Sourcebook: An A to Z Compendium of Over 1000 Designs,* 398.

192. Lecouteux, *Encyclopedia of Norse and Germanic Folklore, Mythology, and Magic,* 213–217.

193. Becker, ed. *The Element Encyclopedia of Symbols,* trans. Lance W. Garmer, 106.

194. González-Wippler, *The Complete Book of Amulets and Talismans,* 169, 170.

Where to cast: Indoors at your altar or outside under the sky.

You will need: Your athame. A white candle of any size. Paper (3 in. x 3 in. or 7 cm x 7 cm or larger if you choose). Pencil or any art material. A button of any shape or size. Needle and black thread. Witch's utensils.

Begin standing with items before you.

1. Holding your athame outward, cast a "circle of eyes" around you.

2. Light the candle. Say:

   "To see and reflect."

3. Draw the image of an eye on the paper. Decorate it in any way you wish.

4. When you have finished your drawing, hold the button near the warmth of the flame. Say:

   "To banish."

5. Now sew the button on the pupil of the eye.

6. Move the paper through the flame and breathe onto it.

7. Place it above your front door or somewhere significant in your home.

8. When you are finished, imagine your "circle of eyes" disappearing into the image you have created.

After the spell: If some of the candle remains, relight and say: "To see, to reflect, to banish."

Amulets are often natural items like stones, crystals, herbs, branches, fruit, vegetables, and minerals. Parts of animals and humans have been used as magick amulets through time, though these amulets must be ethically sourced and used sacredly. In Victorian England, jewellery was created from the hair of the departed and worn to invoke memories and express devotion. Parents often keep a lock of their child's hair or first teeth to treasure the memory of this time.

In many mystical traditions, animal parts are worn or used in ceremony to conjure the power of the creature. They hold a magickal vibration from Nature and their essence can never be altered or changed because it exists within an amulet as an innate energy. This energy is sometimes called *mana,* a spiritual power that exists in something physical.[195]

Natural amulets call to the energy of their source—the creature, the person, the plant, the stone—as well as liberating the characteristic of the element or the creature within you. Amulets will also deflect energy opposed to their nature, so they are used for energetic protection. A snake's skin attracts change and opposes stagnation, a cat's whisker calls to curiosity while defying submission, and honey speaks of life's riches and never of lack.

The Goddess Necklace

The goddess Artemis, in her incarnation in ancient Ephesus, wore a necklace from acorns, symbols of fertility. The Hindu goddess, Kali, wears a necklace of skulls, natural organic objects that symbolize her role as the destroyer of ego as well as divine Mother of Time. The actual wearing of the skulls as an adornment speaks of her divine understanding of the spiritual life beyond the flesh as well as of her power over life and death.

The Witch's Necklace

A traditional witch's necklace is created from the witch's stones, jet and amber. Jet is ancient petrified wood, once alive as a tree, and amber, the sap from ancient trees, said to be the tree's tears. Both these stones, born from the sacred tree, raise powerful energy when combined. Together they create a sacred marriage, bringing sunlight and night, life and death, together as one.

The Hag Stone

A hag stone is a powerful and sought-after witch's amulet. It is a stone with a naturally formed hole through it. Hag stones found on the beach are of the water element, as well as the earth element, as they also hold the energy of the

---

195. González-Wippler, *The Complete Book of Amulets and Talismans*, 3.

ocean that has formed them. This stone inspires psychic abilities and allows you to "see" faery through the opening.[196]

The "hag" or "seer stone" gives you a magickal perspective. These stones vibrate a powerful "glamour," gifting the ability to see beyond this world and to transform through the spell of illusion. Like all magickal charms, hag stones have the power of insight, so their powers must also be acknowledged and respected. The magick of a hag stone was also known to the strega. Here is a quote from the witch Maddalena when she refers to a hag stone as hallowed.

"I have found
A holy stone upon the ground.
O Fate! I thank thee for the happy find."
From Maddalena's story to Charles Leland[197]

Magnetic Amulets

Lodestones are naturally magnetic stones and are also a witch's amulet or charm. They are used to attract energy. They are sometimes purchased as a pair, called male and female, with iron shavings, their symbolic food. Like lodestones, black sand is naturally magnetic and is used magickally to attract and magnetise energy. The sand can be carried in a pouch or used as the earth element in a spell.

 **Amulet to Attract Peace**

Purpose: Place in the home to remind you to choose to be peaceful and to attract the energy of nature to your home.

When to cast: Begin seven days before the full moon, at night.

Where to cast: Indoors at your altar or outside under the sky.

You will need: Loadstones and iron fillings. A selenite crystal (for the moon), a carnelian crystal (for the sun), a small stone (for earth), a feather (for air). Natural cord like bamboo or hemp (18 in. x 18 in. or 44 cm x 44 cm). A small cloth pouch.

---

196. David Pickering, *Dictionary of Witchcraft* (London: Cassell, 1996), 122.
197. Leland, *Aradia: Gospel of the Witches*, 23.

Begin with ingredients before you.

1. Create a circle using the cord. Imagine this circle extending out so it surrounds you.

2. Place the loadstones into the middle of the circle. Say:

   "Attract peace into this home."

3. Place the carnelian and the selenite into the circle. Say:

   "By the light of the sun,
   By the glow of the moon."

4. Place the stone and the feather into the circle. Say:

   "By Mother Earth,
   By flight of bird."

5. Hold your hands over the circle and say:

   "By the power of fire, air, water, and earth,
   I call to the spirit of peace to reside here."

6. Sprinkle a pinch of the iron shavings over the loadstone to symbolically strengthen its power.

7. When you are finished, dissolve the circle by imagining it disappearing into the loadstone.

After the spell: For six more nights, sprinkle iron shavings onto the loadstone. When completed, place the two crystals and the stone into the pouch. Place the end of the feather into the pouch. Using the cord from the circle, hang in your home.

All sacred objects symbolize as well as hold a pure, focused energy. They are a magickal language, an encapsulation of otherworldly concepts, and a way to create mystical communication. They are keys to the divine and remind you that you are magickal. They embody your sacred wishes, speak of the invisible worlds, and remind you of the quest to live authentically. They are part of your magick weave.

The Witch's Talisman

From the Greek "teleo," talisman translates "to consecrate."[198] It is a symbolic item, worn as jewellery, carried, or placed somewhere significant to attract energy. It has a defined intention or purpose; it can be an object found or acquired. A talisman needs to be charged by the power of a spell to activate its lifeforce. This enables your intention to merge with it.

Talismans can take the form of an image, a depiction of a goddess, animal, or tree. Sometimes a talisman is worn as a necklace, a ring, or a tattoo. Talismans can represent the elements, heavenly realms, or the Underworld. They can be household objects, spell tools, or a piece of clothing that vibrates a mysterious energy. Objects become talismans when they have been imbued with magick energy in a spell or have absorbed the energy of an incident, place, or person. Enchantments can hold light as well as dark energy, as can any charm, amulet, or talisman.

The creation of talismans is an ancient art. Intention and will are the most powerful components in the making, yet other energies may also be used to deepen the manifestation. In the Renaissance grimoire, the *Greater Key of Solomon*, the crafting of talismans and seals includes invocations of the planets, the vibration of numbers, and the power of the angels. These ancient talismans were created according to significance of day with planetary metals and were aligned to the phases of the moon. They were very specific and involved a great amount of time and precision.

The wearing of the talisman as jewellery or in a charm pouch affects your energetic force. The energy from the object will merge with you. The relationship between you and your talisman flows in two directions; your energy also seeps into it. This merging of energies is told in the myth of Freya, the Norse goddess. To acquire her own talisman, a necklace called *Brisingamen*, she agreed to spend a night with each of the dwarfs who created it. Her unreserved sexuality was the energy that manifested her talisman. As goddess of love, she offered sexual favours to gain ownership over what would become an emblem of her erotic power.[199]

---

198. González-Wippler, *The Complete Book of Amulets and Talismans*, 203.

199. Lecouteux, *Encyclopedia of Norse and Germanic Folklore, Mythology, and Magic*, 100.

Many talismans have universal significance, their origins rooted in ancient mysticism. They speak of the cycle of beginnings and endings and the power manifested through the union of opposites.

The Ankh

The *ankh* was carried by the gods and goddesses of ancient Egypt and was thought to be the key to knowledge. Its shape is thought by some to depict the joining of male and female. It is a fertility talisman as well as the key to the Afterlife. The ankh reflects the perpetual cycle of birth and death, beginnings and endings, and aligns the wearer to the ancient magick of Egypt.[200]

Figure 5: The Ankh

The Caduceus

The *caduceus,* or wand, of the Greek god, Hermes, depicts the four elements, the connection between the realms and of opposites unified. The two serpents entwined on the wand have the power to poison as well as to heal through their venom. The wand itself is the axis mundi and, like the sacred tree, it connects the three realms of the Heavens, the Earth, and the Underworld. The serpent's movement between these worlds speaks of the need to connect and explore these realms within yourself, to find meaning and purpose.

The symbol of the caduceus is far older than Hermes' wand. The depiction of two entwining serpents has been found in ancient Sumerian magick.

---

200. Chevalier and Gheerbrant, *The Penguin Dictionary of Symbols*, trans. Buchanan-Brown, 27.

Their goddess Inanna carried a staff with two entwined serpents.[201] The serpent embodies the activation of life in Eastern tantric mysticism. This is depicted in the serpent, called the *kundalini*. It coils at the base of the human spine and is the source of energetic activation for the body, mind, and spirit.[202]

Figure 6: Caduceus

The Ouroboros

The serpent appears again in the alchemical talisman, the *ouroboros*. Here the snake forms a circle devouring its own tail. This talisman depicts the relationship of endings and beginning and the unbreakable bond between life and death. The *ouroboros* is a symbol of regeneration and the cycles of life.[203] When it appears in contrasting black and white, it is thought to correspond to the Chinese symbol *yin-yang*, the bringing together of opposite forces, light and dark, male and female. The wearing of these talismans reminds you of the cycle of change and the marriage of opposites.

---

201. Baring and Cashford, *The Myth of the Goddess*, 175.

202. Chevalier and Gheerbrant, *The Penguin Dictionary of Symbols*, trans. Buchanan-Brown 142–145.

203. Cooper, *An Illustrated Encyclopedia of Traditional Symbols*, 123, 124.

Figure 7: The Ouroboros

The Coin

A coin speaks of this relationship too, for it has a head as well as a tail. Most coins have a head on one side, but don't depict a tail on the other. However, intuitively we know the two sides are opposite. Hence the choice "Heads or tails?" is offered when leaving a decision up to chance. Like the coin, every characteristic within you also harbours its opposite energy. All your strengths exist alongside their opposing traits. So, willpower will exist with stubbornness, innocence with naivety, bravery with fear.

 ## Coin Talisman for
 Patience and Endurance

Purpose: To connect with the ability to wait and to see things through to completion.

When to cast: At the new moon. Day or night.

Where to cast: Indoors at your altar or outside under the sky.

You will need: A coin: new, old, from any country. Container of salt. Begin with ingredients before you.

1. Holding the coin, turn to cast a "circle of gold and silver metal."

2. Holding the coin say:

   "Day and night,
   The moon, the sun,
   To end, to start.
   My spell is spun."

3. Breathe onto the coin.

4. Leave on your altar and place salt over it.

5. When you are finished, dissolve your "circle of gold and silver metal" by imagining it disappearing into the coin.

After the spell: Leave the coin covered in salt for eight nights. Gather the salt and throw to the wind. Hold the coin whenever you need to connect with the energy of patience.

Charms, amulets, and talismans aren't completely definable but all hold power. There are other names for these symbolic objects and designs. A "fascination" is an object that has power to conjure and allure. The word comes from the Latin *fascinus*, a divine phallus charm used for protection.[204] An *enchantment* is another term for a magickal object because it engages and has a magickal effect. A *bewitchment* is another name used because the object is created by the witch to make magick. Mystical traditions and belief systems through time have used charms, amulets, and talismans. In some parts of Africa *fetishes and gri-gri* are objects that harbour a spirit,[205] in Italy a red pepper is a natural amulet that repels "the devil,"[206] and in ancient Persia, a necklace of carnelians was worn to repel negativity.[207]

Charms can also describe a magickal object that has been created by you, an item that is highly personalised, unique, and powerful.

204. "Fascinate," Online Etymology Dictionary, accessed August 21, 2020, https://www.etymonline.com/word/fascinate.

205. González-Wippler, *The Complete Book of Amulets and Talismans*, 6.

206. Carole Potter, *A - Z of Superstitions* (London: Chancellor Press, 1993), 7.

207. González-Wippler, *The Complete Book of Amulets and Talismans*, 176.

THIRTEEN
The Witch's Craft

You create something powerful when you craft a charm. A magickal object is created in your hands through imagination. There are countless ways to do this and most often crafted charms will include amulets and talismans. The written word on paper, bound with string, sealed with wax, and then hung on a tree is a created charm. A charm can be a love letter scented with oils or a drawn symbol sprinkled with herbs, folded three times and kept in a secret place. So is a pouch of herbs with an added crystal and a lucky button. The crafting of charms includes poppets, image-magick objects, charm pouches, philtres, potions, spirit jars and bottles, talismans, and other symbolic creations.

All these charms can be blessed, anointed, charged, and given any magickal purpose. They can be an offering or be used to attract something beautiful or dispel something draining. They can be hidden, worn, carried, or placed somewhere significant. All charms are fashioned by your magickal vision.

In the making of a charm you will gather symbolic ingredients and combine them to create an object that tells your story, your sacred purpose. The charm is created to activate the change it represents. The process involves the energy of your heart, mind, and spirit and there will never be another charm like it.

During the making of the charm, thoughts move to inspiration and the heart lightens. The crafting itself is a calming and enchanting process where you will find yourself in the arms of the divine and at one with an auspicious enterprise. You will become lost in the weave of charm-making. The five senses will activate as you see, feel, smell, and symbolically hear and taste your charm as it forms. During the creation you will become closer to the magick that exists within you. The charm represents the microcosm, the world within you. Through its creation, the macrocosm, or the greater world, is energetically affected because something new has manifested in its physical realm. A sacred concept has actualized in physical form and hence everything shifts and changes.

Some charms are united with the elements as you will read in the next chapter, so they no longer exist, however, other charms remain with you to keep. Storing your magick charms reflects your story as you grow. They will always speak of a time in your life and will always resonate the same magickal energy. Charms also create a vision of intrigue and will continue to speak to you. You may wish to keep a charm on your altar for a while until the energy changes. You may have a special shelf or room, or you may wish to conceal it in an attic, behind a book, or under a floorboard.

Charms can be made from all materials and will most often include one or more of the elements. Many items can be used in the making of a charm: plants, earth, stones, salt, clay, paper, wax, fabric, wood, cotton, string, straw, metals, natural oils, bottles, pins and jars, and any natural amulets, such as crystals.

Symbols, colours, numbers (refer to the Appendix), names, and words can be used in the making of a charm. They can be drawn onto the charm, painted, sewn, or inserted into it. All the materials chosen by you need to be meaningful and hold symbolic significance.

Like any art, the charm takes on its own evolution during its creation. Within the circle, you free your mind and allow your hands to manifest something sacred and mysterious.

Clay to Make Dimension: Earth Element

Clay is used to create poppets, seals, symbols, and magickal representations. Using clay, you feel the actual earth element in your hands as the charm is birthed. With it you can create an image of yourself, an animal, or other symbolic image. Clay can be manipulated, and numbers, designs, names, and words can be pressed or etched into it. Herbs and other natural items can be placed into clay and it can also be painted with significant colours.

 **A Clay Poppet**

Purpose: You can create a poppet for any purpose. A poppet is a physical manifestation of your intention. It can represent yourself, an ethereal being, or a creature that reflects the purpose. The making of the poppet is the beginning of change in the greater world.

When to cast: Choose the phase of the moon according to your intention. Day or night.

Where to cast: Indoors at your altar or outside under the sky.

You will need: Witch's tools. Water in your chalice. Candle of any size. Choose the colour of the candle according to your intention (see Appendix). Incense blend of six parts frankincense (*Boswellia carterii*) and four parts copal resin (*Bursera odorata, B. fugaroides*). Salt to sprinkle. Self-hardening clay. A piece of copal. Self-igniting charcoal. Witch's utensils, including carving tools.

Begin with ingredients before you. Prepare to create witchcraft…

1. Raise your pentacle skyward and imagine a "circle of standing stones" around you.

2. Light the candle and say:

    "Manifest."

3. Ignite the charcoal and add a pinch or two of the incense blend. Say:

    "Movement."

4. Take the clay and mould a figure with it. Allow yourself to fall into your imagination and your hands to create your craft.

5. When you have finished the figure, you can carve any details you wish, like a face or hair.

6. When completed, take a piece of copal and push it into the clay in the position of the heart. Imagine the little heart beating as you smooth over the clay.

7. Now move the poppet through the candle flame three times and then through the incense smoke three times.

8. Sprinkle with water and then with salt.

9. To connect your lifeforce with the poppet, breathe onto it and then hold it to your heart. Say:

   "To will."

10. When you are finished, dissolve the "circle of standing stones" by imagining them disappearing into the Earth below you.

11. Snuff out the candle.

After the spell: Place the poppet on your altar for nine days and nights. Some witches bury clay poppets to merge with the earth element and others keep them as talismans. This is up to you. Relight any remaining candle with your intention in mind until it is gone.

Candle and Sealing Wax: Fire Element

Candle wax and sealing wax are powerful witch's materials because of their shape-shifting ability to harden, soften, burn, and melt. Holding all four elements, wax is solid (earth), burns (fire), liquefies (water), and transforms into hot gases (air). Creating charms from wax brings the opportunity for alchemical processes to be part of the magick weave.

Sealing wax fastens and is used to bind magickal agreements, written spells, witch's bottles, and spirit jars. Always have a bowl of water nearby when using sealing wax. If the wax touches your fingers, dip them into the water straight away. Take all care when using the wax.

Bind with Sealing Wax

Purpose: This spell can be created to weave magick around any wish. A wish is a hope or desire, something you would love to happen. Wishes sometimes manifest in unexpected ways, so have no expectations and allow this spell to be a part of your divine story.

When to cast: Cast at night on the full moon.

Where to cast: Indoors at your altar or outside under the sky.

You will need: Witch's tool with water in your chalice. A white candle of any size. Incense blend of three parts rose petals (*Rosa spp.*), two parts lavender (*Lavandula officinalis* or *L. vera*), and five parts rosemary (*Rosmarinus officinalis*). Self-igniting charcoal. Container of salt. String (6 in. or 15 cm long). Paper and pencil to write your wish.

Begin with ingredients before you. Prepare to create witchcraft...

1. Using salt, create a small circle before you. Say:

   "Mother Moon enchant my circle."

   Now imagine a "circle of white light" around you.

2. Light the candle and the charcoal. Add a pinch of the incense blend to the hot charcoal.

3. Close your eyes and bring your wish to mind. Allow any other thoughts, images, and feelings to come to you.

4. Write or draw your wish on the paper.

5. Breathe onto the words or drawing.

6. Fold the paper three times for 3 is the number of manifestation.

7. Tie string around the folded paper and fasten three knots.

8. Hold the lit sealing wax over the knots and allow the wax to drip onto the string and paper to form a seal. The seal can be any size you wish.

9. When the wax has dried, sprinkle the paper with salt to leave overnight in the salt circle.

10. When you are finished, dissolve the "circle of white light" by imagining it merging into the wishing paper.

11. Snuff out the candle.

After the spell: The following day, conceal your written wish in a secret place in your home, outdoors, or in a significant place. If any candle remains, relight it in the future as you bring your wish to mind.

Straw to Add in Luck: Earth Element

Straw provides a home for the faeries and holds the energy of luck. It is traditional to fill cloth poppets with straw or to make a poppet figure from straw alone. A circle, cross, or any geometric design can be created with straw and string and placed on the door of a house, in a room, or on an altar. Straw can be also added to pouches, spirit bottles, and jars.

 ## A Straw Pouch for Psychic Inspiration

Purpose: To enhance psychic ability and intuition. Have the pouch present while using the Tarot, when scrying, or channelling. The pouch can also be placed in the bedroom to conjure prophetic dreams.

When to cast: Cast on the full moon. Day or night.

Where to cast: At your altar or on a craft table.

You will need: Witch's tools. Water in chalice. A piece of fabric (8 in. x 8 in. or 20 cm x 20 cm). Colour of the fabric should ideally be in blue or purple hues but is up to you. A purple candle of any size. Add a blend of three drops of lemon essential oil (*Citrus Limon*), three drops of peppermint (*Mentha piperita*), and three drops of rose (*Rosa spp.*) to a teaspoon of almond oil (*Prunus dulcis*). A handful of straw. String or cord (9 in. or 22 cm). Witch's utensils, including scissors. A bowl for mixing.

Begin with ingredients before you. Prepare to create witchcraft...

1. Hold your chalice to your heart as you imagine a "circle of blue water" surrounding you.

2. Light the candle. Say:

   "To see the unknown."

3. Cut the straw into small pieces and place into the bowl.

4. Pour the oil blend onto the straw and mix.

5. When finished, move your hands through your aura to raise your psychic insight.

6. Place the straw onto the middle of the fabric, then tie in a bundle with the string, making nine knots to fasten.

7. When you are finished, dissolve the "circle of blue water" into your third eye at the centre of your brow.

8. Snuff out the candle.

After the spell: Place the pouch with your psychic tools and have close by during psychic work. If any candle remains, relight during readings or meditation.

Cloth and Stitching to Create a Form: Earth Element

Cloth can be used to create poppets, pouches, and other charms. Ideally, the cloth is a natural material like cotton, jute, hemp, or bamboo. Cloth brings in the energy of colour magick. Significant material, such as used cloth or clothing, can add to the potency of charms, as the material holds the owner's energy. Hand-stitching is an enactment of the Goddess weaving the fabric of life. It also brings you into the moment, at one with the creation, and will manifest a potent charm. However, if you wish you can create the dream pillow from a pouch or something already made. Choose a fabric that speaks to you of dreams.

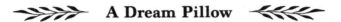 **A Dream Pillow**

Purpose: Dreams are held in the highest regard by a witch. Your dreams bring knowledge from your subconscious and from the realm of magick. Dreams speak in the language of symbols just like a spell does. They tell you about yourself, your strengths, as well as your shadow. They are the portal to other worlds, a way for familiars and guides to speak to you, a realm to meet spirits of the departed and loved ones. Dreams can speak of the future and shed light on the past. You most likely experience the dream world as much as you experience the physical world. The plants and oils in this dream pillow will enhance your understanding and connection with your dreams.

When to cast: Create your dream pillow during any phase of the moon.

Where to cast: At your altar or on a craft table.

You will need: Witch's tools. Water in chalice. Mortar and pestle. Blue candle of any size. Fabric to make a pouch or pillow. The size of the pillow is up to you. Most dream pillows are approximately 5 in. x 4 in. or 10 cm x 12 cm. If you don't wish to sew your own pillow, use a pre-made pouch that can be closed with a drawstring.

Place into a bowl an herbal blend of two parts lavender (*Lavandula officinalis* or *L. vera*), five parts mugwort (*Artemisia vulgaris*), two parts mullein (*Verbascum thapsus*), and one part wormwood (*Artemisia absinthium*). Add ten drops of rose (*Rosa spp.*) and ten drops of lavender essential oils (*Lavandula officinalis* or *L. vera*). Small piece of paper (2 in. x 2 in. or 5 cm x 5 cm). Pencil. Sewing needle and thread. Witch's utensils.

Begin with ingredients before you. Prepare to create witchcraft...

1. Anoint your heart with water from the chalice. Then holding the chalice outright, turn to cast a "circle of divine weavers" around you.

2. Light the candle.

3. Begin to sew your pillow. Allow each stitch to take you into deeper peace and be truly present in time. Leave one end of the pillow open for the ingredients.

4. When you are finished, place the contents of the bowl into the mortar and grind. Allow the blending process to transport you to peace.

5. When you think the plants are blended, place all into the pillow.

6. Write your witch's sigil on the paper and place inside the pillow.

7. Stitch the end of the pillow to close.

8. When you are finished, thank the "circle of divine weavers" and imagine them ascending to the heavens.

9. Snuff out the candle.

After the spell: Keep the dream pillow under the pillow you sleep on or close to your bed. If any candle remains, relight in honour of the divine weavers.

Paper for the Written Word: The Four Elements

Paper is for written spells, words, and magickal designs. A simple poppet can be cut out of paper, coloured, and decorated with drawn symbols. Paper can be scrolled, folded, and hidden. It is easily torn and also burns. Paper also becomes pulp in water, so it is a good material for transformational symbolism.

Banishing the Word

Purpose: To dispel unwanted energy from your heart and mind. This symbolic enactment imbues this intention with a sacred quality and will strengthen your will and courage. When unwanted feelings are given a physical form, an awareness and understanding of them begins. Awareness is power. When you understand the shadow, you can change.

When to cast: Cast during the new moon. At night.

Where to cast: At your altar or outside under the night sky.

You will need: Witch's tools. Water in chalice. Small piece of paper (3 in. x 3 in. or 7 cm x 7 cm). A pencil. Purple candle of any size. Witch's utensils. Always have a bowl of water close by during burning spells.

Begin with ingredients before you. Prepare to create witchcraft…

1. Cast your circle by calling to Hecate, goddess of witches. Say:

   "With all my heart I call to Hecate to cast my
   circle with me. Stand with me, show me the way of
   magick."

   In your imagination, "see" what circle you have cast together.

2. On the paper, write the word "fear" and any other words that described unwanted energy within you.

3. Light the candle and burn the paper on the flame. Place the last of the ash in the bowl of water.

4. When you are finished, dissolve your circle by imagining it disappearing into the bowl of water.

5. Snuff out the candle.

After the spell: Leave the bowl of water under the new moon overnight. The next day, pour the water from the bowl on the earth. If any candle remains, relight it in honour of the goddess Hecate.

Pins and Needles for Binding

Pins and needles can be included in your witch's cabinet. Pins are inserted into candles, the written word, poppets, and other charms. The use of pins in magick is often seen negatively and people often associate the practice with harm or manipulation. This is true, as all magickal practices have been used negatively, which is sad. However, intention is paramount, and the path of the true witch is to create spells that enhance life.

Pins symbolically bind the witch's intention with the physical charm. Pins activate in attraction spells and release and liberate in banishing spells. They are a tool to focus energy and direct intention. When using pins, it is important to acknowledge you are creating a symbolic contract and commitment to a purpose or way of being in the world. If you are using pins in poppet magick, always imagine that part of your own body is open to new energy or is dispelling unwanted energy because the poppet is a symbol of you. Pins are a very powerful witch's accessory and because of this the practice can be either confronting or thrilling.

Needles can be used for this purpose too, as well as for carving words and symbols into candle wax, wood, and other material. Specialised carving tools are also available that will serve this purpose.

Binding to Self-Worth

Purpose: To bring a physical representation of self-worth into the sacred realm of the circle. To bring awareness and strength to your relationship with yourself and to imbue it with magick.

When to cast: Cast on the new moon at night.

Where to cast: At your altar or outside under the night sky.

You will need: Witch's tools. Water in chalice. Self-hardening clay. Yellow candle of any size. Incense blend of five parts frankincense (*Boswellia carterii*), three parts hyssop (*Hyssopus officinalis*), and two parts mugwort (*Artemisia vulgaris*). Self-igniting charcoal. Six pins. Witch's utensils, including a needle to carve or carving tools.

Begin with ingredients before you. Prepare to create witchcraft...

1. Holding your wand outright, turn to cast a "circle of suns."

2. Light the candle and the charcoal. Place a pinch of the incense blend on the hot charcoal.

3. With the soft clay, mould your poppet as a symbol of yourself.

4. When you are finished, etch your witch's sigil on the front of the poppet and the symbol of a pentagram on the back.

5. To release unwanted energy, fear, and doubt, insert three pins into the pentagram. Imagine this energy leaving your body in the form of grey smoke.

6. To activate the energy of self-worth, insert three pins into the "heart" of the poppet. As you do, imagine pink light filling your heart.

7. When you are finished, dissolve the "circle of suns" into your body, just above your navel.

8. Snuff out the candle.

After the spell: Place the poppet on your altar for nine nights and then keep somewhere sacred. If any candle remains, relight in honour of your life and your unique story.

String, Cotton, Cord, and Wool for Binding and Knot Magick

String, cotton, cord, and wool are used for tying the charm. They fasten, so energetically they symbolise binding the intention to the charm or object of power. These materials are also used for knot-magick. Knots strengthen the power of the spell or charm and are combined with numbers and incantations. The number of knots made in the fastening aligns the charm with the numerology, the planets, and other energetic forces. The ritual of handfasting at a pagan wedding uses the power of knots.[208] The couple's hands are tied together to symbolise their union and to acknowledge they now walk the same path.

A Lover's Binding Spell

Purpose: This is a symbolic ritual for two people in a committed relationship. The act of binding the symbolic candles is the celebration of union and the sacredness of love for each other. This spell invigorates your union with romance, honour, and deep magick.

When to cast: Cast the spell during the waxing moon or on the full moon at night.

Where to cast: Anywhere romantic and magickal.

---

208. Guiley, *The Encyclopedia of Witches and Witchcraft*, 151.

You will need: Two free-standing candles: one red for passion and one purple for spiritual love. (The candles should be at least 2 in. or 5 cm wide so they can stand.) Red thread. Ten drops of patchouli oil (*Pogostemon cablin* or *P. patchouli*) in a teaspoon of almond oil (*Prunus dulcis*). Four pins. Witch's utensils.

Begin with ingredients before you. Prepare to create magick together...

1. Together say:

   "In the arms of the Goddess of Love, we cast a 'circle of light' around us."

2. Place some oil blend on each other's hearts.

3. Using the thread, begin to bind the two candles. Start the thread in the middle of the candles, then wind to the top and then to the bottom. Take turns in the threading. The amount of threading is up to you.

4. Now, in turn, anoint both candles with the oil six times by simply touching each candle with oil.

5. When the anointing is complete, take two pins each and insert one of them into each candle (two pins total for each of the candles).

6. Now imagine a bridge of light connecting your hearts.

7. Light the candle flames.

8. When you are finished, dissolve the "circle of light" by imagining it merging with the candles.

9. Snuff out the candles.

After the spell: Relight the candles anytime you are together. As you light the candles, imagine the bridge of light connecting your hearts. Keep relighting anytime until the candles have burnt away. When the pins fall from the candles, reinsert them into the wax. When the candles have burnt way, keep the four pins in a sacred place. You may wish to make a witch's bottle for them or a special pin cushion.

Human and Animal Parts to Influence the Vibration

Historically, animal parts such as feathers and bones, as well as human hair, have been used in charms. These items bring strong energetic influence from the person or creature they were once a part of and will always belong to and invoke the source. These items have a powerful influence and will bind a forceful energetic vibration to the charm. You may wish to use some of your own hair or a captured tear to deeply bind your life to an intention.

Any animal parts used need to be ethically sourced and you need to take all care with your health if you find animal bones or body parts. Never buy animal parts and ensure you are aware of legalities in relation to collecting or gathering items in Nature. However, there may be ways that are ethical. Ten years after our family dog, James, passed away, I felt it was a good thing to keep one of his teeth as a protective amulet because I knew one day the family home, where he was buried, would be sold. I wanted to keep his energy close. With frankincense burning and prayers, I dug into the earth and found the tooth. It is now part of the creation of my jet and amber witch's necklace. It also includes one of our son's first teeth. Another familiar, my cat Levi, used to drop her whiskers. I have three of her whiskers in a special bottle.

 **Bless an Animal**

Purpose: This spell acknowledges the sacred bond between you and an animal. The animal may have died or may still be alive; it may be your pet or ethereal familiar. If it's your pet, this spell is created with the animal present. If the animal is deceased or a familiar, the spell becomes a prayer of your imagination.

When to cast: On the full moon or new moon.

Where to cast: At your altar or anywhere the living animal feels comfortable.

You will need: Just you and the creature. During the spell, speak to the animal as you wish.

Prepare for divine interaction ...

1. To cast your circle, imagine Gaia, Mother Earth, breathing a "circle of stars" around you both.

2. Now imagine the moon on your right palm and the sun on your left palm. Place your hands on or near the animal's head. Say:

   "Divine spirit, I see you and bless you."

3. Breathe onto the animal as you imagine the circle filling with stars.

4. When you are finished, imagine the "circle of stars" merging into the blessed animal.

After the spell: Allow the creature to inspire wonder and gratitude within you.

Plants and Oils to Enchant

Plants, fruit, herbs, and oils can also be added to charms, bringing the magickal vibration and scent of the plant to the charm. Fruit and vegetables can also be used as the "body" of a poppet. Cornhusks are used to make poppets called "corn dollies" in many cultures. In First Nations American tradition, the corn represents the Great Mother.[209] In Northern European tradition the corn poppet symbolizes the Goddess, old and young, the bride of spring as well as the crone of the last harvest.[210]

Wood, fruit, and vegetables can be used to create charms. A lemon decorated with coloured pins is a traditional Italian charm given to someone for good luck[211] and to give someone an apple is an offering of love.[212]

 **A Love Charm**

Purpose: To create sacred energy around the intention to meet your true love. The creation of the love letter will conjure the beauty of

209. Willis, ed. *World Mythology: The Illustrated Guide*, 222–225.

210. Nevill Drury, *The Watkins Dictionary of Magic* (London: Watkins Publishing, 2005), 62.

211. Leland, *Aradia: Gospel of the Witches*, 29.

212. Cooper, *An Illustrated Encyclopedia of Traditional Symbols*, 14.

romance and mystery within you. Psychically it will reach the person it is meant for and the forces of magick will bring you together. It is important not to have a person in mind when you create the spell. Instead trust in the weave of magick; write your letter to the unknown person holding in your heart their spiritual beauty and lifeforce.

When to cast: During the waxing moon. Day or night.

Where to cast: At your altar or anywhere significant.

You will need: Witch's tools. Water in chalice. A pink candle of any size. Oil blend of ten drops clary sage oil (*Salvia sclarea*) in a teaspoon of almond oil (*Prunus dulcis*). Paper and pen for a love letter. A red apple. A ball of string. A flower. Witch's utensils.

Begin with ingredients before you. Prepare to create witchcraft...

1. Hold your chalice skyward. Imagine water coming from it to form a "circle of water" around you.
2. Light the candle and imagine the circle filling with light.
3. Anoint your heart and hands with the oil blend.
4. Begin to write your letter, allowing the words to flow from your heart.
5. When you are finished, anoint each corner of the page with the oil.
6. Wrap the letter around the apple and bind with the string in any configuration. Fasten the string with six knots.
7. Hold the apple to your heart and say:
   "Our hearts to connect."
8. When you are finished, dissolve the "circle of water" by imagining it flowing into the apple.
9. Place the flower into your chalice.
10. Snuff out the candle.

After the spell: Keep the apple on your altar for three days. Then eat the apple. If any candle remains, relight it at any time and say, "Our hearts to connect."

Through the making of a charm, you manifest your intention into the physical. It is a powerful experience to connect with the charm through the five senses: to feel, smell, see, taste, and hear the charm. Not all charms can be heard unless they make a sound through an attached bell or rattle. A charm can only be tasted if made from food. However, you can imagine the experience of sound and taste energetically. When you enliven your relationship with the charm through the five senses and consecrate it with the five elements, a magnificent object is created.

FOURTEEN
Deepening the Magick

There are magickal methods and practices involved in charm making. They involve an act that is not only symbolic, it is also actual. These methods or processes are *Burning, Binding, Blending, Burying, and Brewing.* Each of these processes symbolise an ending as well as a beginning. They encapsulate the mystical intentions of banishment, alliance, completion, and oneness with the power of the elements. Each process creates a story, a physical depiction of transmutation, unification, infusion, mending, or elimination. The way of the process is chosen according to the intention of the spell and the purpose of the charm crafted by you.

Burning: Fire Element
Tool: Candle, the Flame.
Magickal Process: Elimination, Ending.

Burning a charm unites the witch's purpose, represented in the charm, with the element of fire.

Burning eliminates and actualizes an ending, therefore it is also symbolic of the beginning that follows. The process of burning foreshadows a rebirth as well as an initiation. To bring in something new, something else must die. The burning process symbolically ends and eradicates. It also unifies the charm with the magickal state of illumination through brightness and the purification powers of a flame.

When the written word or a drawn symbol on paper is burnt, it no longer exists in the world of matter. It is gone, a part of the ether, symbolically as well as literally. By burning a charm, you are eliminating or bringing illumination to what the words or symbols represent.

If a charm is created to represent unwanted feelings, or to depict heartache of the past, the burning releases this energy. Charms and poppets are burnt to signify the passing of what they symbolize.

Burning creates protection in its ability to keep unwanted energy at bay and to ward off low energies. It is used to create strong resolve and awareness as well as an ethereal barrier between you and harmful energy. Burning also creates banishment and elimination so is used when your intention is to put an end to destructive thinking.

If the charm represents your wish or quest, it is burnt to unify it with the Light, with the warmth of new life, and illumination of mind.

The magick of fire includes the power of manifestation. Burning a charm symbolically energises the object, and therefore your intention, with the passion of will.

The burning of spells and charms is also a part of the magick of secrecy. When a written spell is burnt, the magick remains with you and the divinity of the fire. Secrecy brings reverence to the intention. It renders the energy of the spell contained and sacred. It prevents it from becoming scattered and therefore depleted.

 ## Spell to Banish Unwanted Energy Within

Purpose: To become aware of and transform unwanted energy within. To know the shadow and intend to grow and gain wisdom through unwanted energy, such as resentment, jealousy, bitterness, and spite. These energies reside in the shadow within everyone.

When to cast: During the new moon. Day or night.

Where to cast: Indoors at your altar or outside under the sky.

You will need: Your wand. Three red candles of any size. An incense blend of five parts frankincense (*Boswellia carterii*), three parts rosemary (*Rosmarinus officinalis*), and two parts dragon's blood resin (*Daemonorops draco, D. poppinquos*). Self-igniting charcoal. A pencil. Paper (3 in. x 3 in. or 7 cm x 7 cm). A bowl of water for the burning paper. Witch's utensils.

Begin with ingredients before you. Become the witch and create magick.

1. Holding your wand, turn and cast a "circle of flames" around you.

2. Light three red candles and the charcoal.

3. Draw a symbol or image of the unwanted energy on the paper. Allow your imagination to guide you.

4. Add a pinch or two of the incense blend to the hot charcoal.

5. Move your hands through the smoke and then place them onto your heart. Repeat this three times.

6. Now ignite the paper on the candle flame. Place the last of the paper in the bowl of water.

7. When you are finished, "see" your "circle of flames" dissolving into the sun.

8. Snuff out the candle.

After the spell: If any of the candles remains, relight in the future as you "see" a sun rising in your heart. Pour the water onto the Earth.

Binding: Earth Element

Tools: Pins, cotton, string, ribbon, sewing needles, writing, knots, jars, bottles, boxes, wax, and seals.

Magickal Process: Unification, contractual,
and unbreakable agreements.

Binding is the symbolic act of bringing energies together. It is a magickal contract, a divine unification manifesting the power of oneness and the pledge of your will. During a binding spell you unite your intention with the charm. You do this by actually fastening objects in the physical world.

When you create binding magick, you "fasten" your intention with the charm. You may use any tool that serves this purpose: string ties objects together, wax seals a contract, knots close and strengthen, and the written word binds the intention to divine energy.

Pins are powerful binding tools and are used to unify as well as to release energy. When you insert a pin into a candle charm, you imagine unifying your purpose with the candle and its element, fire. You can also imagine releasing unwanted energy from deep within each time a pin is inserted. When you do this, conjure an image in your mind that depicts the energy you wish to unify or release. Your magick will always be stronger when you give energy an imagined form or name. When you insert the pin, "see" the image moving from your body and entering the candle. For releasing spells, imagine the energy leaving both your body and the candle as the pin is inserted.

If you wish to activate the energy of luck, you may imagine a golden light going into the candle as the pin is pushed into it. If your intent is to dispel energy, such as worry, you may imagine grey smoke coming out of the candle as well as your mind. In binding candle spells, the candle represents you, your story. Through your imagination it is important to thread your body, heart, mind, and spirit to the candle itself.

The process of binding in magick takes many forms and can involve any of the elements.

Binding a Candle Charm

Purpose: A candle holds the power of the sun and shows the way—banishing, purifying, illuminating, and igniting action. You can bind any intention into a candle charm in the most creative ways.

This is a basic candle-binding spell that you can use for any purpose. Another specific candle-binding spell will follow.

When to cast: Choose the moon phase according to your intention. Day or night.

Where to cast: Indoors at your altar or outside under the sky.

You will need: During the candle-binding spell, each imagined step takes the magick to a deeper level. The cotton you wind around the candle, the colours chosen, the oil, and the number and position of pins is your own symbolic creation and has no bounds.

Choose a significant colour for the candle of any size that represents your intention. A sewing needle for carving. Essential oil according to intention or olive oil (*Olea europaea L.*) Pins: the number of pins is selected according to the magick of numbers. Thread of a significant colour. A powder of dried herbs and flowers according to intention. For choices of colour, numbers, oils, and herbs, refer to the Appendix. Witch's utensils.

Begin with ingredients before you. Become the witch and create magick.

1. Hold your intention strongly in your mind as you imagine a "circle of towering candles" appearing around you.

2. The Contract: Take the needle and begin to carve words, numbers, and symbols into the candle. Allow these to come from your imagination.

3. Anointing to make sacred: With olive oil or your choice of essential oil, draw a circle around the middle of the candle.

4. To send your message to the Divine: From the middle of the candle, cover the top half of the candle with the oil using your index finger.

5. To ground your intention: From the middle of the candle, cover the lower half of the candle with oil using your index finger. As you do, imagine your intention manifesting.

6. To bind: Insert pins into the candle wax. Each time you do, the binding becomes more powerful.

7. To weave: Wind thread around the candle in any configuration.

8. To dress: The herbal powder is sprinkled onto the candle.

9. To unite your lifeforce with the charm: Breathe onto the candle.

10. Light the candle.

11. When you are finished, dissolve the "circle of towering candles" by "seeing" them igniting and disappearing.

12. Snuff out the candle.

After the spell: If any candle remains, relight it in the future with your intention in your mind. Keep the pins to use in other charms. The vibration in them will enhance further spells.

 ## Candle Charm for Illumination

Purpose: To invoke spiritual light into any situation that is confusing, difficult, or worrying. To surrender to faith and guidance. To imbue your mind, heart, and spirit with purity and grace.

When to cast: On the full moon, at night.

Where to cast: Indoors at your altar or outside under the sky.

You will need: Your wand. A white candle of any size. Sewing needle for carving. Salt to sprinkle. Six drops of rose essential oil (*Rosa spp.*) in a teaspoon of almond oil (*Prunus dulcis*). Powdered dried rose petals (*Rosa spp.*). Gold or yellow thread. Nine pins. Witch's utensils.

Begin with ingredients before you. Become the witch and create magick.

Imagine: The birds in this spell are "spirits of light" and the "golden threads" are from the Goddess's own spindle. Dedicate the candle to spiritual illumination.

1. Point your wand outwards and turn to cast your circle. As you turn, imagine birds coming from the point of your wand. They fly around you during the spell.

2. Sprinkle the needle with salt to purify.

3. Carve three circles into the candle. Now imagine the birds flying through the circles into the candle.

4. Anoint your heart and then the candle with rose oil. First around the middle, and then cover the top half of the candle to send your message and then the bottom half to ground your intention.

5. Sprinkle a powder of dried rose petals over the candle. Imagine this is food for the "birds of light."

6. Bind the candle with gold thread. As you do, imagine pulling mystical threads from your heart and winding them around the candle.

7. To activate illumination, insert three pins into each of the circles. As you do, imagine a blue bird born in your heart and your mind.

8. Breathe onto the candle.

9. Light the candle and imagine light filling your spirit.

10. When you are finished, "see" the "circle of birds" flying to the heavens.

11. Snuff out the candle.

After the spell: If any of the candle remains, relight in the future and "see" light filling your heart and mind. Keep the pins for future spells to invigorate any other intention with the energy of illumination.

Binding with Poppets and Spirit Dolls

Charms that depict a person, creature, or ethereal being fall into the realm of image-magick. They are binding because they transform the intention into a material creation. Most often a poppet is made in the shape of a human figure, a symbolic depiction of yourself. Poppets can be made from clay, straw, corn-husks, any fruit or vegetable, fabric, paper, wood, or any natural material. They can sometimes be filled with straw or herbs.

While creating a poppet, the magickal vibration can be enhanced by binding other items into it or onto it. The written word, numbers, crystals, herbs, and pins will add to the bewitchment. Each item added to the poppet heightens the potency. Poppets can also be painted and decorated. This is a powerful way to bring to life a magickal depiction of an intention. When a human figure is crafted, the poppet also represents the five elements of the pentagram. The head at the place of spirit speaks of magickal thinking. The creation's energetic likeness to yourself brings further potency, so you may add some of your hair or a personal item. During the making of the poppet, imagine weaving threads from your heart's energy to manifest something transformational. It also brings the opportunity for you to go deeper into the magick, your intention, and inner world.

A poppet can also represent any part of the body that is significant. If the purpose of your spell is to clear worry, a depiction of the head may be created to symbolise the mind. If the intention is to change direction in life, a representation of your feet may be crafted to represent the "path of the future."

A symbolic heart is placed into the poppet during the charm making. A piece of copal resin *(Bursera odorata, B. fugaroides)* or something from nature is blessed for this purpose. You then connect with the poppet through the five senses. In your imagination you "see" the heart beating, "hear" its voice, "feel" the energy around it, "smell" its scent, and imagine what "tastes" are associated with the charm. Travel deep into your imagination.

Herbs, talismans, and the written word can be hidden within some poppets or attached to them. They can then be anointed with bewitching scents and purified through smouldering herbs. Poppets are "brought to life" through a charging spell.

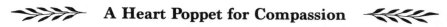 **A Heart Poppet for Compassion**

Purpose: To activate the energy of compassion in you. Compassion can sometimes be hard to connect with because it is easy to judge.

However, once this energy rises within you, connect with a greater purpose and feel free.

When to cast: During the waxing moon. Day or night.

Where to cast: Indoors at your altar or outside under the sky.

You will need: Water in your chalice and your bell. Self-hardening clay to mould. A green and a pink candle of any size. Incense blend of five parts copal (*Bursera odorata, B. fugaroides*), three parts mugwort (*Artemisia vulgaris*), and two parts rosemary (*Rosmarinus officinalis*). Self-igniting charcoal. Salt to sprinkle. A piece of copal (*Bursera odorata, B. fugaroides*). Three pins. Witch's utensils.

Begin with ingredients before you. Become the witch and create magick.

1. Cast a "circle of green and pink light" around you. Imagine the colours from the circle moving into your heart.

2. Light the candles. Light the charcoal and add incense once it's hot.

3. Move your hands near the warmth of the flame, through the smoke. Then touch the water with both hands and sprinkle them with salt. Ring the bell.

4. Create the shape of a heart, a mirror of your own, with the clay. Insert a piece of copal into the heart during the making. Allow your mind to rest and take your time. When you are finished, say:

   "By the power of the moon and sun.
   The trees that grow. The birds that fly.
   I open my heart to the magick of compassion."

5. Insert three pins into the heart to bind your purpose to the poppet. With each pin, fill your heart with green and pink light.

6. Move the poppet through the flame (for fire) and then the incense smoke (for air). Bless it with the power of water. Then sprinkle with salt for earth.

7. Ring the bell.

8. When you are finished, imagine your "circle of green and pink light" disappearing into the heart poppet.

9. Snuff out the candles.

After the spell: Allow your poppet to set. If you wish you can paint it. Place it on your altar or somewhere sacred. Hold it when you need to connect with compassion. If any of the candles remain, relight them, bringing your intention to mind. Pour the water from the chalice and charcoal ash on the Earth.

Binding a Witch's Bottle and Spirit Jar

Witch's bottles and spirit jars are binding charms. They harness, contain, and keep secret magickal energy, and can also be a haven for a spirit. Plants, herbs, oils, crystals, and any natural items can be added to the bottle or jar. The written word can be part of the creation and placed into the bottle. You may also add some of your hair or an animal's tooth if it is significant in the weaving of the magick.

A charging spell is cast on the bottle or jar, and the desired energy or spirit is invited to inhabit it. Scented oils and plants are often added. The scent will always transport you to your intention if the jar is opened. A witch's bottle or spirit jar can also be permanently sealed with wax or any fastening material and remain forever closed.

To energetically protect a house, a witch's bottle may contain a scroll of drawn symbols and significant words, and then be concealed under the floorboards. A bottle or jar can be dedicated to the Goddess and contain drops of lemon oil, moonstones, and a small mirror. This charm could be opened at every full moon and items or wishes added.

Witch's bottles can be used in banishing magick and may contain rusty nails or thorns to symbolically drive away unwanted energy or to banish depleting habits.

A Witch's Bottle to Dispel

Purpose: To be aware of and to eliminate unwanted energy within and around you. To dispel fear and give rise to courage and self-worth. Dispelling and banishing spells never "send back" or reverse energy onto anyone. A spell is always about your own state of being and taking complete responsibility for your life and the creation of your own magickal story. If someone directs negative energy to you, shield yourself and grow in strength.

When to cast: During the waning moon. Begin three nights before the new moon. Then complete on the new moon. At night.

Where to cast: Indoors at your altar or outside under the sky.

You will need: Your witch's tools and water in your chalice. Black candle of any size. Incense blend of seven cloves (*Eugenia caryophyllus, Syzygium aromaticum,* or *Caryophyllus aromaticus*), five juniper berries (*Juniperus communis*), five parts pine resin (*Pinus spp.*), and five parts myrrh (*Commiphora myrrha*). Self-igniting charcoal. A bottle or jar of any size. Nine rusty nails. Square of paper (3 in. x 3 in. or 7 cm x 7 cm) and a pencil. A pin. To anoint: Frankincense essential oil (*Boswellia carterii*). Teaspoon of black salt (refer to The Witch's Cabinet). Sealing wax of any colour. Take all care with the sealing wax. Witch's utensils.

Begin with ingredients before you. Become the witch and create magick.

1. Cast your circle by imagining a "circle of black moons" appearing around you.

2. Breathe into the empty bottle. Imagine your spirit entering it.

3. Draw a pentagram and write your name across it on the paper.

4. Anoint each corner of the paper with the oil. Then with water from your chalice.

5. Roll the paper into a scroll and bind it with the pin.

6. Place the nine rusty nails on the scroll.

7. Sprinkle the scroll and nails with black salt and leave until the night of the new moon.

8. On the night of the new moon, light the candle.

9. Ignite the charcoal and add the incense.

10. Move the scroll and nine nails through the smoke, the flame, and touch them with water.

11. Place all into the bottle and add nine pinches of black salt.

12. Add some of your hair (a strand will do or cut a little).

13. Add some dripping wax from the candle.

13. Close the bottle and seal the top completely with sealing wax.

14. When you are finished, imagine the "circle of black moons" ascending to the new moon.

15. Snuff out the candle.

After the spell: Keep your witch's bottle in a sacred place. If any of the candle remains, relight in the future with the intention to dispel negativity in mind. Pour the water from the chalice on the Earth.

A Binding Jar for Romance

Purpose: To give rise to the energy of romance within you. When you see life as romantic, you imbue the energy of wonder, beauty, and adventure into everything around you. This state of being brings love to you on all levels.

When to cast: During the waxing moon and then add to the jar on full moons. At night.

Where to cast: Indoors at your altar or outside under the sky.

You will need: Your witch's tools, water in your chalice. A jar of any size. A pink candle of any size. An incense blend of five parts copal (*Bursera odorata, B. fugaroides*) and five parts rose resin (*Rosa spp.*). Self-igniting charcoal. A rose quartz crystal (for romance). Container of salt. Three bay leaves (*Laurus nobilis*) and three rose petals. Nine drops of each essential oil of: lavender (*Lavandula officinalis* or *L. vera*), ylang-ylang (*Cananga odorata*), and geranium (*Geranium maculatum* or *P. odoratissimum*). Paper (3 in. x 3 in. or 7 cm x 7 cm). A pencil. Witch's utensils.

Begin with ingredients before you. Become the witch and create magick.

1. Holding your chalice outright, turn and cast a "circle of wild-flowers" around you.

2. Light the candle and charcoal and add a pinch of incense blend.

3. Move the empty jar through the incense so it fills with smoke.

4. Place into the jar the three bay leaves (*Laurus nobilis*), nine drops of each essential oil, and the three rose petals.

5. Draw a circle on the paper. Write your name or sigil inside it. Imagine each letter is emblazoned in silver moonlight. Draw a heart around the circle.

6. Anoint your words with each of the oils and place into the jar.

7. Hold your hands over the jar and imagine stars falling from your palms into it. Say:

   "Three for creation, romance to awake,
   Three for the charm, magick create!"

8. Breathe into the jar, add some dripping wax from the candle, the crystal, and three pinches of salt before closing the lid.

9. Touch the jar three times with water from your chalice.

10. When you are finished, imagine the "circle of wildflowers" dissolving into your heart.

After the spell: If any of the candle remains, relight in the future as you "see" the wildflowers in your heart. Pour the water from your chalice onto the Earth. Keep your witch's jar in a sacred place to conjure the energy of romance. On a full moon, open the jar, inhale the scent, and add any symbolic amulets or talismans you wish—something from nature or the written word. Then leave the jar under the moon.

Binding with Knots

The goddesses Hathor and Isis are sometimes depicted with a knotted head-piece, a talisman of good fortune and protection called a *menat*. Isis wears the *menat* in the front of her dress. It is an amulet similar in design to the ankh and is thought to possess powers of protection.[213]

Knots of cloth, corn, and hair were placed at sacred places in ancient Crete to herald the presence of the Goddess.[214] In Buddhism, the Mystic Knot represents eternity and the "Knot of Vishnu" symbolises immortality.[215]

Knots create powerful binding magick, and can be made with string, cord, ribbon, rope, thread, wool, or any material that ties. The making of a knot symbolically strengthens the intention and creates the energy of closure. When string or any material is tied around a folded written spell or any charm, the binding begins. With each knot made, your commitment and willpower are symbolically strengthened. The number of knots is also symbolic. Words spoken while making the binding knots will enhance the power of the charm. Here is an incantation for your knot magick.

> With each knot, the magick bind,
> With beating heart,
> With words and mind.

The Witch's Ladder

A witch's ladder is a highly personalised magickal necklace that involves knot binding. It is a talisman that you can create yourself. Every aspect of the ladder is significant and will be uniquely yours. Traditionally this amulet is created for protection, to guard your energy, heighten your awareness, and create boundaries.

---

213. Baring and Cashford, *The Myth of the Goddess*, 120, 121.

214. Chevalier and Gheerbrant, *The Penguin Dictionary of Symbols*, trans. Buchanan-Brown. 577.

215. Cooper, *An Illustrated Encyclopedia of Traditional Symbols*, 92.

Everything and everyone emanates energy, an invisible force that influences and seeps into other energy it connects with. Words, actions, sounds, scents, textures, and even tastes hold vitality beyond the physical. They inspire memories as well as desires, they speak of history and personality. They are actual as well as symbolic and as a witch you will learn to read the undercurrent of magick in everything. Energy is contagious. It can be aspirational, but it can also be depleting. If you sit next to an angry person long enough, you may start to feel the same. You feel it in your heart when someone doesn't wish the best for you or is jealous or resentful. Sometimes that person doesn't have to be near you, but when they are the energy becomes stronger and you can feel out of balance, not quite yourself. Sometimes another's feelings toward you can be very harmful energetically and you start to feel that way about yourself without knowing why.

Your fascination with witchcraft most likely means you are very psychic, so you're sensitive to energy. This is important for intuition and any psychic work; however, you need to know boundaries and when to close off your own energy and protect it. The making and wearing of the witch's ladder brings awareness so you are mindful, centred, and resistant.

The creation of this amulet involves finding significant symbols that reflect your magickal story, your ability to read energies, and ways to shield yourself from any negative force. The symbolic charms you chose may be old or new, found or purchased. Nine charms or beads and nine knots on the cord create the ladder (there are other witch's ladders that involve forty beads and forty knots). When you collect your beads or charms, allow them to "speak" to you of the meaning and what they symbolise. With each knot you tie, strengthen your resolve. Use your imagination and intuition to make a truly fascinating necklace.

 ## Witch's Ladder for Protection

Purpose: To invoke the energy of psychic protection and create energetic boundaries. To manifest a protective shield through awareness and intuition.

When to cast: On the full moon. Day or night.

Where to cast: Indoors at your altar or outside under the sky.

You will need: Your witch's tools, water in your chalice. Red, black, or purple cord. Measure it around your neck to the middle of your chest, then double the length of the cord. Nine talismans, amulets, or beads (all your choosing) to be threaded onto the cord. A candle of any size, colour to match the cord. Incense blend of mugwort (*Artemisia vulgaris*), rose petals, and sandalwood (*Santalum album*). Self-igniting charcoal. Container of salt. Witch's utensils.

When you begin to create the necklace, double the cord so the first charm is placed in the middle of the cord's length.

Begin with ingredients before you. Become the witch and create magick.

1. Hold your wand skyward and cast around you a "circle of stars." "See" the stars.

2. Say:

   "I dedicate this amulet to the Goddess."

3. Light the candle and the charcoal. When the charcoal is hot, add a pinch of incense blend.

4. Move the first charm through the smoke and thread onto the cord. Leave around 2 in. (or 5 cm) of cord on either side and tie two knots (so the first charm hangs between them). Continue to cleanse each charm through the smoke and thread. Tie your knots 2 in. apart with the charm or bead in between. The final knot ties the necklace together.

5. For *fire,* touch the ladder with your wand and then move it through the warmth of the flame nine times.

6. For *air,* touch the ladder with your athame and then move it through the incense smoke nine times.

7. For *water,* touch it with water from the chalice nine times.

8. For *earth,* touch it with the pentacle and sprinkle it nine times with salt.

9. Breathe onto your witch's ladder and hold it to your heart to meld your spirit with it.

10. When you are finished, dissolve the "circle of stars" by imagining them entering the ladder.

11. Snuff out the candle.

After the spell: Wear your witch's ladder for energetic protection and always see it as a magical charm. If any of the candle remains, relight in the future in honour of your witch's ladder. Place the water and used salt on the Earth. Use the nine knots and charms with nine incantations for other spells. Cleanse it with incense smoke on the full moon.

Binding with Seals

Seals hold the concentrated power of a magickal force like a planet, number, deity, or creature. They are a binding, unbreakable contract that consecrates, "makes good," and finalizes a purpose. Seals also symbolize a mystical agreement, a binding or mystical promise.

Wax seals bind the charm with the magick of secrecy and will empower the significance of a written spell or charm. Sealing wax can be poured onto a written spell or over a knot. Wax can seal a witch's bottle or spirit jar or enclose the makings of a charm.

The potency of a binding seal can also be enhanced with stamping a symbolic design, or personal sigil, into the liquefied wax before it hardens. This is a mark of your commitment, your pledge. Wax seals remind you that the act of magick is a divine contract. The seal completes the contract and renders it everlasting. The wax seal also symbolizes entering the unknown when opened. A sealed letter or document symbolically brings with it the energy of direct communication and profound importance.

 ## A Spell to Bind a Divine Contract

Purpose: To fasten or bind intent to the contract, both symbolically and actually. To seal your divine agreement or word. This spell also includes the magick of knots.

When to cast: If the intent is to attract, cast during the waxing moon; if to protect or dispel, cast during the waning moon. For new beginnings and mystery, cast on the new moon. To bring ideas and plans to fruition, cast on the full moon. Day or night.

Where to cast: Indoors at your altar or outside under the sky.

You will need: Your athame. Red sealing wax. (Sealing wax is very hot so take care. Have a bowl of water close. Place your hand in the water straight away if it comes into contact with the hot wax.) Paper (7 in. x 7 in. or 18 cm x 18 cm). A pencil. String (9 in. or 22 cm). Witch's utensils.

Begin with ingredients before you. Become the witch and create magick.

1. Stand and raise your arms skyward. Say:

    "Circle of light descend from the heavens and surround me."

    Imagine this "circle of light."

2. Now sit down and write your magickal intention on the paper. Focus on every word, for you are binding your hopes and wishes to a sacred energy.

3. Breathe onto each word.

4. Place your athame on the paper and your hands, palms down, above the athame. Imagine silver light coming from your hands and into the words.

5. Say:

    "By earth and wind, by rain and sun,
    All elements in the wax are one.
    I charge my word with sacred light,
    By morning dawn, by star lit night."

6. Fold the paper three times, then three times again.

7. Tie with string and make six knots.

8. Light the sealing wax and allow it to drip over the fastening until you feel it has made a good seal. Allow the wax to dry.

9. When you are finished, imagine the "circle of light" disappearing into your sacred contract.

After the spell: Keep your contract in a secret place or in your grimoire.

Binding with Talismans, Amulets, and Sigils

A binding talisman is a charm that unites you to a magick belief or intention. The wearing of a creature's feather, tooth, or talon will invoke the energy of the creature and will bind its powers with your spirit. The placing of a written dedication into a pouch of herbs will bind the written word with the magickal energy of the plants. A ring placed into the folds of a flower, a circle drawn in ash, a tear allowed to fall into a shell, and a name written across the pentagram are all binding charms that marry intention with an object.

Binding seals and sigils are also symbolic designs that are carved onto candles; etched into clay, wood, or metal; or drawn on paper. They can be pressed into wax or drawn on fabric or even onto a leaf.

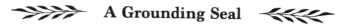 **A Grounding Seal**

Purpose: To bind your journey to stability and steadfastness. To ground you to the magick of earth and bring you into the moment. Sometimes thoughts race and energy scatters. This spell will ground you, bringing you into the present. When you feel grounded, the future unfolds naturally.

When to cast: At the new moon. Day or night.

Where to cast: Indoors at your altar or outside under the sky.

You will need: Your pentacle. Moulding clay (self-hardening is best). A sewing needle or carving tool. Container of salt.

Begin with ingredients before you. Become the witch and create magick.

1. Using the salt, create a small circle on your altar.

2. Say:

   "I connect to the Earth, to the moment,
   to the ground beneath me."

3. Mould the clay into the shape of a coin.

4. Carve a hexagram into the clay. First carve the upward triangle to symbolise the divine. Then on top of it carve the downward triangle to symbolise Earth.

5. Breathe onto the symbol six times. As you do, imagine tree roots growing from your feet and connecting you to Mother Earth.

6. When you are finished, gather the salt and place on the Earth.

After the spell: Allow the clay to harden. Place the seal on your altar or carry in a pouch to connect you to the earth and to invoke stability.

Blending: Earth and Water Element

Tools: Mortar and pestle, containers, bottles, and pouches.
Magickal Process: Unification, infusing, melding.

Blending combines natural items to create a magick vibration. This process often involves the earth and water elements. Natural oils are blended to create powerful scents for anointing, blessing, and to shift energy. Seeds, roots, and plants are infused with water to create mystical concoctions. Blending also brings together plants, resins, and oils to create infusions, herbal charms, incenses, and magickal powders.

A mortar and pestle are used to blend plant material in the creation of these charms. When blended the oils in the plants are released and the resins are powdered so their scent is infused into the mix.

Blending Charm Pouches

Herbs, plants, and oils may be blended together and placed into the pouch. Other significant items can be added to the pouch to enrich it. When worn, carried, or placed somewhere special, the blend in the pouch draws the desired energy to you.

When you blend the following ingredients, cast a circle and with all the power in your heart, keep your intention clear and strong. Place all plants and oils in a mortar and pestle and blend until all combined. You may wish to wait until the plants absorb the oils before placing them in a pouch. Orris powder is good to add to any blend to absorb the oils. As you collect and get to know herbs, resins, and oils, you can create your own blends. Store and label blends in jars. Enjoy creating the blends. You can also add a written spell, an amulet, or talisman to the pouch if you wish.

True Feelings

To connect with the truth within.
Create during the waxing moon.

Plants: Five parts frankincense (*Boswellia carterii*), two parts basil (*Ocimum basilicum*), two parts rose (*Rosa spp.*), one part rue (*Ruta graveolens*).

Philtre/Blend: Three drops of peppermint (*Mentha piperita*) and five drops geranium (*Geranium maculatum* and *P. odoratissimum*) in a half teaspoon of almond oil (*Prunus dulcis*).

True Love

To connect with the path to true love.
Create during the waxing moon.

Plants: Five parts damiana (*Turnera diffusa* or *T. aphrodisiaca*), three parts rose (*Rosa spp.*), one part rue (*Ruta graveolens*), one part thyme (*Thymus vulgaris*), and three pinches of dragon's blood (*Daemonorops draco, D. poppinquos*).

Philtre: Five drops of clary sage (*Salvia sclarea*) and seven drops of patchouli (*Pogostemon cablin* or *P. patchouli*) in a half teaspoon of almond oil (*Prunus dulcis*).

 **Dispel Worry**

To create a magickal thinking.
Create during the waning moon.

Plants: Five parts angelica (*Angelica archangelica*), two parts juniper berries (*Juniperus communis*), two parts St John's Wort (*Hypericum perforatum*), and one part rosemary (*Rosmarinus officinalis*).

Philtre: Three drops rosemary (*Rosmarinus officinalis*), three drops of pine (*Pinus spp.*), and five drops of frankincense oil (*Boswellia carterii*) in a half teaspoon of almond oil (*Prunus dulcis*).

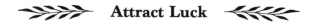 **Attract Luck**

To open your heart and mind to opportunity.
Create on the full moon.

Plants: Three parts rose (*Rosa spp.*), three parts St John's Wort (*Hypericum perforatum*), two parts orris (*Iris germanica var. florentina*), two parts vervain (*Verbena officinalis*), and three pinches of dragon's blood (*Daemonorops draco, D. poppinquos*).

Philtre: Five drops of rose (*Rosa spp.*) and five drops of clary sage (*Salvia sclarea*) in a half teaspoon of almond oil (*Prunus dulcis*).

 **Protection**

For awareness of negative energy and to create boundaries.
Create on the new moon.

Plants: Five parts cinquefoil (*Potentilla canadensis, P. erecta or P. reptans*), two parts hyssop (*Hyssopus officinalis*), three parts mugwort (*Artemisia vulgaris*), and five pieces of frankincense resin (*Boswellia carterii*).

Philtre: Three drops of cypress (*Cupressus sempervirens*), six drops of frankincense (*Boswellia carterii*), and three drops of myrrh (*Commiphora myrrha*) in a half teaspoon of almond oil (*Prunus dulcis*).

 **Prosperity**

To think abundantly.
Create during the waxing moon.

Plants: Four parts cinnamon powder (*Cinnamomum zeylanicum*), five parts patchouli (*Pogostemon cablin* or *P. patchouli*), one part sandalwood (*Santalum album*), and four cloves (*Eugenia caryophyllus, Syzygium aromaticum,* or *Caryophyllus aromaticus*).

Philtre: Two drops of basil (*Ocimum basilicum*), two drops of clove (*Eugenia caryophyllus, Syzygium aromaticum,* or *Caryophyllus aromaticus*), three drops of nutmeg (*Myristica fragrans*) in a half teaspoon of almond oil (*Prunus dulcis*).

 **Psychic Visions**

To heighten psychic abilities.
Create on the new moon.

Plants: Two parts lavender (*Lavandula officinalis* or *L. vera*), two parts damiana (*Turnera diffusa* or *T. aphrodisiaca*), five parts mugwort (*Artemisia vulgaris*), one part sandalwood (*Santalum album*).

Philtre: Five drops of jasmine (*Jasminum grandiflorum, J. officinale,* or *J. odoratissimum*) and three drops of frankincense (*Boswellia carterii*) in a half teaspoon of almond oil (*Prunus dulcis*).

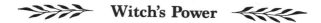 **Witch's Power**

To remind you of choice, of both the
light and the shadow within you.
Create on the full moon.

Plants: Three parts rue (*Ruta graveolens*), three parts wormwood (*Artemisia absinthium*), three parts mugwort (*Artemisia vulgaris*), and one part dragon's blood (*Daemonorops draco, D. poppinquos*).

Philtre: Five drops of hyssop (*Hyssopus officinalis*) and five drops of rosemary (*Rosmarinus officinalis*) in a half teaspoon of almond oil (*Prunus dulcis*).

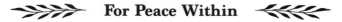

For Peace Within

For stillness and acceptance.
Create on the new moon.

Plants: Two parts lavender (*Lavandula officinalis* or *L. vera*), three parts sandalwood (*Santalum album*), one part orris (*Iris germanica var. florentina*), and four parts rose (*Rosa spp.*).

Philtre: Five drops clary sage (*Salvia sclarea*) and three drops bergamot oil (*Mentha citrata*) in a half teaspoon of almond oil (*Prunus dulcis*).

Blending Sprinkling Powders

Powders are made from ground herbs and plants and are sometimes mixed with liquids like oils. To create powders, talc is sometimes added to absorb any liquid added. Powders are common in the Vodoun magick of the south of North America, and are carried or hung in a house or placed in mojo and gris-gris bags.[216] Sprinkling powers are also placed around the house, on the body, and onto written spells and your witch's tools. Blend both plants and philtre in a mortar and pestle and grind until powdered. Add talc to absorb oils if needed.

Luck Powder

Create during the waxing moon.

Plants: Three parts powdered nutmeg (*Myristica fragrans*), two parts cinquefoil (*Potentilla canadensis, P. erecta,* or *P. reptans*), three parts

---

216. Guiley, *The Encyclopedia of Witches and Witchcraft*, 145, 146.

patchouli (*Pogostemon cablin* or *P. patchouli*), and two parts orris (*Iris germanica var. florentina*).

Oils: Five drops of patchouli (*Pogostemon cablin* or *P. patchouli*), three drops of lime (*Citrus aurantifolia* or *L. Limetta*), and three drops of tuberose (*Polianthes tuberosa*).

Psychic Powder

Create on the new moon.

Plants: Three parts mugwort (*Artemisia vulgaris*), two parts damiana (*Turnera diffusa* or *T. aphrodisiaca*), two parts frankincense (*Boswellia carterii*), two parts sandalwood (*Santalum album*), and one part dragon's blood (*Daemonorops draco, D. poppinquos*).

Oils: Five drops lemongrass (*Cymbopogon citratus*), three drops jasmine (*Jasminum grandiflorum, J. officinale,* or *J. odoratissimum*), and two drops rose (*Rosa spp.*).

Anti-Hex Powder

Create during the waning moon.

Plants: Four parts frankincense (*Boswellia carterii*), four parts myrrh (*Commiphora myrrha*) and two parts angelica (*Angelica archangelica*). Add five juniper berries.

Oils: Five drops of hyssop (*Hyssopus officinalis*) and three drops of bay oil (*Laurus nobilis*).

Love Powder

Create during the waxing moon.

Plants: Three parts rose (*Rosa spp.*), three parts patchouli (*Pogostemon cablin* or *P. patchouli*), two parts rue (*Ruta graveolens*), and two parts orris (*Iris germanica var. florentina*).

Oils: Seven drops of tuberose (*Polianthes tuberosa*), three drops of ylang-ylang (*Cananga odorata*), and two drops of neroli (*Citrus Aurantium*).

Blending Potions and Philtres

A philtre is a blend of liquids created by combining two or more natural ingredients. Ingredients include essential oils, rain, dew, floral water, or purified water. Every essential oil holds the magickal vibration of a plant and is chosen according to the purpose of your spell. All essential oils should be diluted in a base oil like almond oil (*Prunus dulcis*). Some oils, such as citrus and spices, are not to be applied directly on the skin; other oils should never be used during pregnancy. Other diluted oils are beneficial to use directly. Please take all care and research what is right for you. Other natural items, such as roots, berries, seeds, plants, crystals, and stones, can be added to the blend. It is a good practice to label any philtres—invent an intriguing name and add the date.

To render an intention at one with the water element, you can place your written word into water. As the paper turns to pulp, the written word is dissolved into the liquid, merging with the element. This process can be used in banishing spells, dream work, and magick of the heart.

An artist might anoint her hands before her sketching begins. During a love spell a philtre may be used on your heart, and to travel a new path the blend may be placed under your feet. Philtres are used to cleanse and invigorate the chakras, to create a bewitching mood, as well as to dispel energy and to heal.

When anointing written spells, place the blend on each corner of the paper or directly onto a significant word or onto a charm. This act invokes sacredness and aligns the intention to the energy of the philtre. Once anointed, a charm will emit a powerful vibration through its scent and will therefore attract the same energy to it. Blends are used to attract desired energy and to dispel unwanted energy from you, a room, or an object. Blends should always be swirled or stirred to combine, and never shaken.

Magickal philtres have been made throughout history. Even the Bible includes the making of powerful oils. In Exodus 30: 23–33 there is an anointing recipe for protection, a blend of myrrh (*Commiphora myrrha*), cassia (*Cinnamomum cassia*), calamus (*Acorus calamus*), and cinnamon (*Cinnamomum zeylanicum*).

A potion is ingested by the witch and is created with non-poisonous herbs, fruit, and other plants to create a magickal drink. To create a potion, you combine the plants and warm water just like making tea. Sometimes a washed crystal, stone, or other item is added to the blend to infuse the potion with its energy. Any such item should be removed before drinking.

Like a philtre, a potion is created with the intention strong in your mind. Words can be said over it, or the written word placed under the container. You can hold your palms over the potion to symbolically imbue it with your energy and intention. A potion can be left in the sun or under the moon. When you drink the potion, you need to imagine the liquid as an elixir of change. You can visualize the potion as a coloured light moving into your body or merge any other symbol or image with the liquid.

 Blending an Anointing Philtre

Purpose: To use for the anointing, blessing, and consecrating of yourself, others, and magickal objects, charms, and talismans. Use this anointing philtre for all intentions.

When to cast: On the full moon. Day or night.

Where to cast: Indoors at your altar or outside under the sky.

You will need: A bottle or jar. Your witch's tools with water in chalice. Philtre: Five teaspoons of olive oil (*Olea europaea L.*), thirteen drops of frankincense essential oil (*Boswellia carterii*), and five drops of hyssop essential oil (*Hyssopus officinalis*). Three juniper berries (*Juniperus communis*). A green candle of any size. Incense blend of three parts rose resin (*Rosa spp.*), five parts frankincense (*Boswellia carterii*), and two parts lavender (*Lavandula officinalis* or *L. vera*). Self-igniting charcoal. An obsidian crystal, small enough to fit into the container. Witch's utensils.

Begin with ingredients before you. Become the witch and create magick.

1. Hold your chalice in both hands. With your arms extended, turn and cast a "circle of white light."

2. Call the Mother Goddess into the circle. She will rise from your imagination. Say:

> "I invoke the ancient Mother to join me in this circle."

3. Light the candle and imagine light filling the circle.

4. Ignite the charcoal and add a pinch of incense. In the rising smoke, "write" your name using your athame.

5. Breathe onto the crystal. Move it through the smoke then place it into the jar.

6. Add the olive oil to the jar, then the frankincense (*Boswellia carterii*) and hyssop oil (*Hyssopus officinalis*), and then the three juniper berries (*Juniperus communis*).

7. Swirl the blend as you move it through the smoke and over the candle flame.

8. Breath into the jar, binding your lifeforce with the philtre.

9. Say aloud:

> "By moon's own light,
> Owl's midnight flight.
> By stone, breath, and flower,
> This blend empower."

10. Hold the chalice and turn in the opposite direction to dissolve your circle.

11. Snuff out the candle.

After the spell: Use the anointing philtre to anoint the candles and other magick tools. To bless the written word, place some oil on your finger and then dab onto the words or on each corner of the paper. Place the philtre on any part of your body to consecrate, protect, attract, banish, or activate energy. The philtre can be used to activate charms or add to baths or herbal pouches.

Burying: Earth Element

Tools: Containers, boxes, hidden places in
earth or somewhere in Nature.
Magickal Process: Disintegration, elimination,
secrecy, merging, transmutation.

Burying conceals and keeps safe. This magickal process includes keeping spell items secret and hidden away as well as unifying them with the magick of earth, if buried. Powerful energy is created through the concealment of significant items. This process includes hiding objects to render them "invisible." It is also symbolic of removing divine objects from the mundane world. To conceal a love spell or charm symbolises divine reverence, holding the energy "safe" until the change takes place. The hiding of magick spells and tools is an expression of a bond between you and the unseen world.

To bury a written spell in earth unites your intention with the strength and healing of the element. The paper and words will eventually become one with the earth, no longer existing in their original form. A transformation has occurred, a symbolic as well as physical enactment of the change within you.

The burying of coins around a house creates the energy of a prosperous foundation. Four coins buried in the four directions binds the home with the magick of stability and growth. A clay healing charm may be buried in earth, uniting your intention with the nurturing powers of Gaia, the Great Mother.

The ancient Greeks concealed carved amulets of the goddess around the home and the Phoenicians, a maritime civilization (1550 to 332 BC), buried metal charms in tombs with the hope of communicating with the dead.[217] The Assyrians buried charms depicting dogs under their house to ensure protection against evil spirits.[218] Throughout Europe, shoes and other garments have been found concealed under and within houses, churches, hospitals, and schools. European migrants brought this European custom across the seas to Australia. Hidden shoes were thought to be protective and good luck charms, and so were concealed under floors.

During the building of the foundations of ancient Rome, sacred offerings were placed in a central pit called the *mundus*. The builders involved in the

217. González-Wippler, *The Complete Book of Amulets and Talismans*, 44.
218. González-Wippler, *The Complete Book of Amulets and Talismans*, 15.

creation threw earth from their own hometown into the pit, binding a part of themselves to the foundations of the new city.[219]

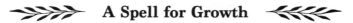

A Spell for Growth

Purpose: To become wiser and connected to your purpose and inner strength. Sometimes it is hard to grow and gain knowledge through experience because a part of us is afraid. We become accustomed to old patterns and reactions and the shadow holds on to what it knows. Create this spell to connect with the strength of Mother Earth.

When to cast: On the new moon. Day or night.

Where to cast: At your altar, then outdoors to bury the charm. If you don't have access to the outdoors, conceal the charm in salt in a secret place indoors.

You will need: Water in your chalice. Five seeds of any kind. Handful of salt. Paper (3 in. x 3 in. or 7 cm x 7 cm) and pencil. Organic cord like hemp (5 in. or 12 cm). Witch's utensils.

Begin with ingredients before you. Become the witch and create magick.

1. Cast your circle by holding your pentagram and imagining a "circle of hills" around you. The hills are Mother Earth.

2. On the paper write: "I plant the seeds of growth." Sign with your witch's sigil.

3. Place the seeds onto your words and fold the paper into a parcel around them.

4. Bind with cord and eight knots.

5. Touch the charm with your wand, your athame, your chalice, and pentacle.

6. When you are finished, imagine your "circle of hills" dissolving.

---

219. Carl Jung, *Man and His Symbols* (London: Picador, 1978), 269.

After the spell: Bury the charm in the Earth or conceal it wrapped in salt indoors. Place the water from the chalice on the earth.

Brewing: All Elements

Tools: Heating containers, cauldron, mortar and pestle, bottles.
Magickal Process: Infusing, releasing, dissolving, magnifying.

Cerridwen, the Celtic goddess of inspiration, brewed a potion for magickal powers in her cauldron. Herbs, including vervain (*Verbena officinalis*) and cress (*Nasturtium*), were added to sea foam and the waters of prophesy. All was created according the movement of the planets.[220]

Brewing is the creation of an infusion that takes time for the essence of the ingredients to melt together. Brewing normally involves natural oils, water, and other liquids as well as plants, natural objects, the written word, and symbolic charms.

A potion is a brew that is ingested. Ensure all plants and herbs included are certified to ingest. A potion can be a tea but must be made with two or more natural ingredients that have been combined with purpose and intent. Stir your brews as you speak incantations.

Plants and oils can be placed into a cauldron and simmered on a flame to create a magickal brew. The fumes, vapours, and scents of the plants are released during the heating. The combined scent produces a magick vibration for clearing, invoking, and dispelling. Oils are also warmed to release scent for a spiritual atmosphere and to raise the heart and mind to the possibilities of magick.

Water combined with crystals, stones, and other natural items can be used for anointing and blessing. A carnelian stone can be left under the sun to absorb the energy of optimism and then placed in warm water. The liquid can then be used to invoke luck. A moonstone placed in water and left overnight under the full moon is a potent psychic brew.

Magickal washes are made with fresh water and herbs; they are used on the body to bless and to also cleanse objects, doorways, and rooms. You create a wash by steeping herbs and other plants in water. Bark and roots can be boiled in water to capture their essence. All other plants should be gently heated and not boiled. Fresh or dried herbs can be used.

---

220. Guiley, *The Encyclopedia of Witches and Witchcraft*, 55.

Witch's Wash for Prosperity

Create during the waxing moon.

Blend for brew: Place three teaspoons of basil (*Ocimum basilicum*) with five teaspoons of patchouli (*Pogostemon cablin* or *P. patchouli*) in two cups of water. Add four drops of bergamot oil (*Mentha citrata*).

Method: Heat gently without boiling the water. Simmer for an hour. Stirring the herbs, say: "Open the gates to the treasures of Earth." Leave the wash overnight, allowing the energies to meld.

Use: Place a clean cloth into the warm blend and use it to anoint your hands and feet. As you do, imagine a coin appearing on each hand and on each foot. Use this wash to also wipe the doorway to your kitchen.

 ## Witch's Wash for Wisdom

Create on the full moon.

Blend for brew: Place four teaspoons of white sage (*Salvia apiana*) and three teaspoons of mullein (*Verbascum thapsus*) in two cups of water. Add three drops of frankincense oil (*Boswellia carterii*).

Method: While creating the wash, imagine the goddess Athena is assisting you. Heat gently without boiling the water. Simmer for an hour. Leave the wash overnight, allowing the energies to meld.

Use: Pour the wash on your hands and place on your belly, heart, and brow. Do this for five days. When you create this magick, do so in a "circle of owls."

Witch's Wash for Romance

Create during the waxing moon.

Blend for brew: Three teaspoons of rose (*Rosa spp.*), three teaspoons of peppermint (*Mentha piperita*), and one teaspoon of thyme (*Thymus vulgaris*). Add three drops of rose oil (*Rosa spp.*)

Method: When creating the wash, imagine the goddess Hathor is assisting you. Heat gently without boiling the water. Simmer for an hour. Leave the wash overnight, allowing the energies to meld.

Use: Bless your heart with the wash for nine days to invoke the truth of love. When you create this magick, do so in a "circle of red roses."

 ## Witch's Wash for Banishment

Create during the waning moon.

Blend for brew: Three teaspoons of rosemary (*Rosmarinus officinalis*) and three teaspoons of mugwort (*Artemisia vulgaris*). Add three drops of myrrh oil (*Commiphora myrrha*).

Method: When creating the wash, imagine the goddess Inanna is assisting you. Heat gently without boiling the water. Simmer for an hour. Leave the wash overnight, allowing the energies to meld.

Use: Wash your hands and the back of your neck with the wash to dispel any unwanted energy. When you create this magick, do so in a "circle of mystic flames."

 ## Iron Water for Protection

Purpose: To energetically protect the home by invigorating it with a magickal vibration.

When to cast: On the new moon. Day or night.

Where to cast: Indoors at your altar or outside under the sky.

You will need: A large jar almost filled with water. White sage leaves (*Salvia apiana*) to burn. A purple candle of any size. Container of salt. Seven nails. Witch's utensils.

Begin with ingredients before you. Become the witch and create magick.

1. Cast a "circle of bubbling cauldrons" around you. See them in your imagination.

2. Light the candle and the sage on the flame.

3. Say:

    "Bless this brew, Hecate. Bring strong magick to my home."

4. Breathe on the four nails to connect your lifeforce to them. Sprinkle with salt for the energy of stability. Place them in the jar of water.

5. Move the other three nails through the flame and smouldering sage. Do this in honour of Hecate. Place the nails into the water.

6. Swirl the jar saying:

    "Goddess bless this home.
    Protect and keep, through wake and sleep."

7. When you are finished, imagine your "circle of bubbling cauldrons" spinning and then dissolving into the jar.

8. Snuff out the candle.

After the spell: The Iron Water is left until the nails have rusted. It is then used to energetically wash floors and doorways. The iron in the nails also invokes the spirit of the planet Mars, conjuring defensive and protective energy. If any of the candle remains, relight in the future, in honour of Hecate.

Four Thieves Vinegar for Protection

Four Thieves Vinegar is a known witch's brew used for protection. It combines cider vinegar, rosemary (*Rosmarinus officinalis*), wormwood (*Artemisia absinthium*), lavender (*Lavandula officinalis* or *L. vera*), common sage (*Salvia officinalis*), rue (*Ruta graveolens*), mint (*Mentham*), and camphor (*Caphura*). The mixture is slowly heated in water and used as a house wash or on magical items. This recipe is old, so use your intuition to decide on the quantity of each plant.

 Fifteenth Century "Fume" to Banish

In the fifteenth century, Cornelius Agrippa referred to a "fume" of calamint (Calamintha), peony (Paeonia), mint (Mentha), and Palma Christi or castor oil (Ricinus communis) to drive away "all evil spirits."221

The magickal processes of *burning, binding, blending, burying, and brewing* takes you into the heart of the spell, uniting you and your charm, amulet, or talisman with the complete force of the element's power.

---

221. Agrippa, *Three Books of Occult Philosophy*, 129.

FIFTEEN
The Witch's Familiar

A Familiar Story ... fall into your imagination.

Hear a wild sound from the darkness. A thump hits the ground. Smell the scent of wet earth. See a shadowy shape hop by the trees. The creature's feet beat a song through the wind. Its ears have heard every word you have spoken, and all your thoughts have echoed in the creature's lively chambers. Smell mushrooms and taste the moon. Round eyes shine in the dark, whiskers wave to you. The moon hare weaves an ancient spell.

Magick is found in the sacred world of animals. The spinning of a web, the building of a nest, the lion's roar, and the creatures of the night. All hold profound power.

The word *"familiar"* comes from the Latin word for family, *"familia,"* and from *"familiaris"* meaning "household servant."[222] Your familiar is an ethereal entity who inspires and protects you. It is often a creature. In ancient Rome, a well-meaning spirit known as *"genii,"* from the Latin word *"genius,"* bestowed natural talents and skills on all babies at birth. The *"genii"* later became associated with the idea of a household guardian.[223]

Your familiar is an embodiment of magickal thinking and is your mystical vehicle of shape shifting. It heeds your spiritual life and always takes you to authenticity. It protects, senses the invisible, and is all knowing. The familiar brings mastery to your journey and energetically merges with your spirit so that you acquire the same instincts, characteristics, and powers.

You and your familiar have an energetically unbreakable bond. The familiar can be a pet, a farm animal or wild creature, alive on this Earth, or can be these same animals in spirit form. The familiar may also appear in dreams and visions bringing messages, from your inner world, as well as from other worlds.

As a household pet in the physical world, a familiar brings love, companionship, protection, joy, and acceptance. Animals teach on many levels; they show you how to relax, to be in the present, and to be true to yourself. Familiars heal; they ground you and communicate energetically. This relationship continues and deepens even after the animal has died.

A magickal familiar from the ethereal realm is invisible to the eyes and comes to you in different ways. Dreams are a portal for familiars to make contact. In dreams an animal symbolises something you need to connect with inside yourself. The dream creature is a symbol or a key to the unravelling of mystery and to a connection with an instinctual force that yearns to be liberated. Dream familiars bring messages that unlock knowledge and offer guidance. They can come and go and are not always a constant companion. From out of the dream you can bring a familiar into your conscious mind to look at your life through the creature's eyes.

All familiars speak of authenticity. It is a muse of the wild and inspires a way of thinking that is free of the mundane. This magickal entity transcends the bounds of earthly existence and takes you into the realms of raw energy, free-

222. "Familiar," Online Etymology Dictionary, accessed August 21, 2020, https://www.etymonline.com/word/familiar.

223. "Genius," Encyclopedia Mythica, Roman Mythology, accessed August 21, 2020. Page created Monday, March 3, 1997. https://pantheon.org/articles/g/genius.html.

dom, intuition, and to the powers of the animal kingdom. Your familiar holds you close and teaches you how to live through truth, courage, playfulness, and wisdom. It is your champion through hardships and challenges. Like all mystical energies, a familiar will always encapsulate mystery and wonder.

Goddess of witchcraft, Hecate, appears with three animal heads, sometimes a horse, a dog, and bear or in other forms as snake, dog, and lion. Each animal brings to the goddess power and attributes.[224] The goddess Artemis, as "Lady of the Animals" in Ephesus, wears a garment adorned with lions, leopards, bulls, griffins, and goats. In her later incarnation, as the youthful huntress, she is the protector as well as hunter of all wild creatures and is able to transform into a bear or deer. Her dual role of protector and hunter unifies the passages of life and death, rendering both sacred and profound.[225]

A "bush soul" refers to a belief system and mystic tradition where a person believes a part of them is mystically entwined with an animal or a tree. "The animal itself is considered as a sort of brother to the man."[226] In animistic cultures, where people believe every creature possesses a soul, totem animals are a vehicle of power and are integral to life and a person's relationship to the divine. The wearing of bones and skins transforms the wearer into the animal and through ceremony and dance the two become one. In cave paintings and ancient totem art a hunter may be depicted as part deer to merge with the physical attributes of the animal and the wearing of a feathered mask may assist a dancer to become a soaring bird.

In Hindu myth, the familiar of the deities is called the "*vahana,*" their vehicle or lifeforce.[227] Children, in shamanic traditions, are often given their medicine animal. The totem is used as a personality to invigorate energy, as a guide, a protector to strengthen the child's passage through life.

Familiar Signs

Through signs, significant appearances, inspiration, and heart-felt connection, your familiar comes to you. Intuitively you may feel a bond or an attraction,

---

224. Monaghan, *The New Book of Goddesses and Heroines*, 147.

225. Baring and Cashford, *The Myth of the Goddess*, 330–332.

226. Jung, *Man and His Symbols*, 7.

227. "Vahana," The Editors of Encyclopaedia Britannica, accessed August 23, 2020, https://www.britannica.com/topic/vahana.

through admiration or a desire to be, or to know, a creature. A kookaburra's call at dawn may bring light and joyful feelings, or the primitive form of a crocodile sinking beneath the muddy waters may incite a yearning to explore the depths of power. A raven's keen intelligence is noticed as the bird turns a container over, looking for food, or its black velvet feathers may be a reminder of the mysteries of life.

Familiars also appear through reoccurring meetings and coincidence. Sometimes a creature appears at a significant time. You might notice a cricket while burying a written spell, see a swan's magnificence as it glides on a lake, or be inspired by the beauty of a giraffe in a painting. In this way a familiar arises from a feeling in your heart, a beautiful attraction of kinship, a mystical fascination. The connection or choosing of a familiar never has to be explained. When a mystical relationship or pact is formed between you and your familiar, it is everlasting.

Shape-Shifting

Your familiar will heighten your instincts, expanding the vision of your life. It will bewitch your imagination, inspire the truth to rise within. It releases you from the mundane. Your familiar is not only a reflection of you; it is an aspect of you liberated into the consciousness. You are both the same story and family. This is when you become a shape-shifter.

Shape-shifting is depicted in myths and fairy tales when the witch transforms physically into her familiar. This transformation is symbolic of the familiar merging with the witch to create a magickal force. By becoming the familiar, by summoning the creature near to you, you disengage from constraints of the mind. You will want to live authentically, for creatures can only live by nature. You will liberate the familiar's attributes within yourself and connect deeply with purpose and meaning. This actualizes when the courage of the bear is activated during a crisis, when the gentleness of the deer wipes a tear from a friend's eye, and when the monkey within you dances. Shape-shifting is experienced when a state of mind is shifted.

To transform into a familiar, you must venture into the realm of the imagination, into mystery, a place where dreams and the divine merge in the creation of a magickal life.

See the creature in your mind's eye and imagine it merging into you. Imagine wings instead of arms, long ears on your head, or a magnificent tail attached to you.

Interpret the message it brings to you through the familiar's position, action, changing colour, or otherworldly voice. Your familiar may curl up to sleep, beckoning you to rest, or may spread its wings, calling you to embrace freedom. The heart is the bridge where you meet your familiar.

Certain creatures have become associated with witchcraft from their partnerships with the ancient gods and goddesses. The myths speak of the sacredness of the animal kingdom, the magnificent powers of creatures, and their spiritual connection to humankind.

All animals offer mystical attributes, and many are found in the myths; however, certain creatures have become associated with the witch. Cats, owls, ravens, wolves, snakes, and frogs are some notable witch's familiars.

The Cat

The witch's black cat may have been born from the wildcat familiars of the ancient deities. Two lionesses flank a Mother Goddess statue from 6000 BC of Çatal Hüyük, whose descendant became The Roman goddess Cybele.[228] They were her guardians and ferocious protectors. The lioness is hunter as well as mother, fertile queen, and majestic commander. The powers of the Greek god, Dionysus, aligned him with the lion and the bear. Dionysus presided over religious ecstasy, a state of being that embodies the wildness and outstanding beauty of his creatures.[229]

The chariot of Freya, the Norse goddess of love and war, is pulled by a clowder of cats. They are her *vahana*, her actual vehicle, her movement and power through the skies.[230] Bast, the Egyptian cat goddess, was originally a solar lion until she became tamer. She is either depicted as feline or a woman with a cat's head. Bast ruled the experience of pleasure, dance, music, and happiness,

---

228. Baring and Cashford, *The Myth of the Goddess*, 82, 83.

229. Willis, ed. *World Mythology: The Illustrated Guide*, 140, 141.

230. Lecouteux, *Encyclopedia of Norse and Germanic Folklore, Mythology, and Magic*, 100.

embodying the sensuality of her familiar and its need for independence and beauty.[231]

The Raven

The messenger ravens, Huginn, meaning "thought," and Muninn, meaning "memory," are the divine familiars of the Norse god, Odin, as are two wolves, his constant companions, named Geri and Freki. Odin hoped humans would learn cooperation and protection from these creatures and actually fathered children who were part wolf.[232] Ravens and crows are the familiars of Morrigan, the Irish war goddess. She conjured charms for her favourite armies and shape-shifted into a crow to feed on the slain in battle.[233] All birds of the corvid family—ravens, crows, magpies, rooks, jackdaws, and jays—are thought to be connected deeply to the witch's spirit and are seen in myths as keenly intelligent, as well as messengers of prophesy.

The Owl

The owl is often depicted as the witch's familiar. Owls are of the Underworld, omens of death and carriers of souls to the Afterlife as well as reincarnation. They symbolise the unity of beginning with ending. Owls bring the magick of wisdom, truth, strategy, and knowledge. Athena's owl sits on her shoulder and illuminates her blind side, enabling her to see truth. Her familiar embodies intellect and enlightenment.[234] The Welsh goddess of the silver wheel, Arianrhod, could shape-shift into her owl, enabling her to also see the truth in the souls of humans.[235]

The Horse

The Goddess rides a thundering horse into the mind of the witch. Magick birds soar above the sacred rider and sing a waking song.

---

231. Monaghan, *The New Book of Goddesses and Heroines*, 66, 67.

232. McCoy, *The Viking Spirit: An Introduction to Norse Mythology and Religion*, 33.

233. Monaghan, *The New Book of Goddesses and Heroines*, 221.

234. Ted Andrews, *Animal Speak: The Spiritual and Magical Powers of Creatures Great and Small* (St. Paul, MN: Llewellyn Publications, 1998), 172, 173.

235. Monaghan, *The New Book of Goddesses and Heroines*, 52, 53.

Epona, the Gallo-Roman goddess, is protector of horses. Her familiar's blood actually runs through her, so she is both goddess and mare.[236] Rhiannon, her Welsh counterpart, rides a magnificent horse through the dreams of humans taking the dreamer to a place where visions are made true. Magickal birds accompany Rhiannon. They have the power to wake the dead and render the living into an enchanted sleep.[237]

The Frog

The frog is a lunar creature at one with water and the dark of night. The frog's relationship with the moon denotes its transformational powers, for the moon is in continuous transition. In fairy tales, the frog transforms into a prince through the kiss of love, an acknowledgement of the frog's fertility powers. The Egyptian goddess Hekat or Heqet is a frog. She is midwife to the sun's own birth. As a Goddess of life, her association with water deems her at one with reproduction and fertility.[238]

The Serpent

The serpent is one of the most mysterious and commanding of animal familiars in magick traditions. This creature is depicted in the universal myths as embodying absolute knowledge of the workings of magick. The snake's medicine and power are a reoccurring theme of healing, transformation, and wisdom. The creature's ability to enter the earth associates it with the Underworld. It also coils like the spiral, symbolising the mystic pathway to the inner world and the shedding of its skin renders the creature at one with the ever-changing moon, the magick of rebirth and re-invention. The serpent embodies the need to liberate the mind from the mundane, for even in physical form this creature defies human convention.

As healing familiar, the serpent is aligned with the Greek god of medicine, Asclepius, and his daughter, Hygieia, goddess of healing. Around their rods of power, the creature depicts oneness with their divine force.[239]

---

236. Monaghan, *The New Book of Goddesses and Heroines*, 114.

237. Monaghan, *The New Book of Goddesses and Heroines*, 266.

238. Monaghan, *The New Book of Goddesses and Heroines*, 148, 149.

239. Farrar, *The Witches' God*, 158.

The serpent as a familiar brings a deep understanding of psychic death intertwined with resurrection, of poison and cure operating together. For what is seen as the cause of hardship can also contain the cure that brings liberation and transformation.

The god Dionysus was aligned with the power of the serpent. As a familiar of the god, this serpent symbolizes liberation from the restriction of the rational mind, through the deity's association with a state of madness.[240] The "madness" expressed in the myth of Dionysus is not the same as madness as defined in the mundane world. It is a state of liberation where the person becomes their animal-self, devoid of society's expectations.

Snakes are coiled at the base of the World Tree and bring the protective powers of the Egyptian cobra goddess Wadjet. They shed their skin and call you to be at one with the renewal through the death of outmoded ways. The snake familiar brings the power of rebirth, wisdom, healing, and deep magick knowledge.[241] Become the serpent, travel into your psyche, into the depths of your thoughts and heart. Own every part of yourself and change what is no longer your truth.

The Pig

The pig and the boar are familiars of the Great Goddess and are symbols of life itself and the powers of fertility. Their ability to grow in size and to store food aligns them with nurture and abundance. The Egyptian sky goddess, Nut, often transformed into a pig and swallowed her piglets, the night stars, every morning.[242] A herd of pigs followed Persephone into the Underworld and became a sacrifice to Demeter to enrich the fertility of the Earth.[243] The magick of abundance is seen in the boar familiar of Freyr, the Norse god. His alignment with the boar speaks of his virility and pleasure seeking. The boar was also the familiar of his divine sister, Freya. She sometimes rode the creature's back, depicting its role as *vahana* and symbol of deep connection with the creature.[244]

---

240. Ronnberg and Martin, eds. *The Book of Symbols: Reflections on Archetypal Images*, 174, 175.

241. Andrews, *Animal Speak: The Spiritual and Magical Powers of Creatures Great and Small*, 360, 361.

242. Lurker, *An Illustrated Dictionary of the Gods and Symbols of Ancient Egypt*, 90.

243. Campbell, *Goddesses: Mysteries of the Feminine Divine*, ed. Saffron Rossi, 41.

244. Monaghan, *The New Book of Goddesses and Heroines*, 127

The Rabbit

Rabbits live in burrows beneath the ground, so they are a symbol of earth, yet their association with rebirth aligns them with the moon, the powers of intuition, so therefore water. Universally rabbits are associated with fertility and abundance. Ostara, the Saxon goddess of spring, was in partnership with a moon-struck hare. Her Teutonic counterpart, Eostre, also had a rabbit as her familiar, as does the youthful form of the Mayan Moon Goddess, Ixchel, and the Chinese Moon Goddess of beauty, Chang'O. All these goddesses are associated with the moon, fertility, youth, beauty, and the rabbit.

The Cow

The divine cow was Hathor herself. This Egyptian goddess was the personification of all aspects of womanhood and was much loved. The life-giving milk associated the cow with abundance and life. It was cow's milk that sustained the Celtic goddess, Brigit, when she was an infant. In the ancient language of India, *Sanskrit,* the words cow and earth have the same meaning, depicting the deep connection of the creature with nurture. Kamadhenu, the sacred cow goddess in Hindu mythology, is the bringer of plenty and earthly fulfilment.[245] Like the pig, the cow embodies the magick of creativity, abundance, home, and Mother.

The Spider

The spider embodies the ability to weave and create so has a profound relationship with the Goddess and therefore witchcraft. The spider is associated with the Indian goddess, Maya, weaver of illusion; the Greek Fates; the Norse Norns; and the great-grandmother of America's First Nation. The spider's web speaks of a life spun through choice and artistry, the need to spiral within and the power of creation.

Imagine silver threads extending from your hands and feet. They spin your own web, creating a unique pattern, the pattern of your life. Weave the life you desire. See the weave in your mind. Create your story.

---

245. Monaghan, *The New Book of Goddesses and Heroines*, 178, 179.

The Dog

Wolves, foxes, and dogs have partnered with the witch because of their power to protect and guard as well as their intelligence and loyalty. The Japanese Kitsune is the intelligent fox often associated with witches because of their ability to shape-shift into human form.[246] Odin gave all the food on his table to his wolf companions Geri and Freki. Symbolically he received his nourishment through them. The great Egyptian god of the Afterlife, Anubis, is a jackal, sometimes depicted as half human. He is both guardian and judge, weighting the hearts of the departed with a feather to see if they are worthy to enter eternity.[247] The Greek Kerberos and Roman Cerberus are three-headed hounds guarding the entrance to the Underworld.

Summoning a Familiar

Binding with a familiar is a way to connect with meaning, to transcend the ordinary and the limitations of the mind. The relationship with a familiar acknowledges the divinity within you, liberating perception, choices, and connection with self and others. Ask your familiar for an answer and you will receive it in your mind. A familiar is a teacher, healer, muse, and guide, a messenger of the divine.

You may have more than one familiar; you may have a mythological familiar. Each take a different role in your life; each bring you their teaching and gifts. Familiars speak of the inner world, the past, present, and future. They rise from the deep mysteries of the unknown, bringing knowledge and liberating what is hidden into the light of the conscious mind.

Your familiar calls you to always be your true self, to remember the Earth is Mother and you are her child.

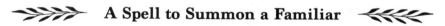

A Spell to Summon a Familiar

Purpose: To invoke a magickal familiar, a guiding force. To rise to your witch's true form, your authenticity and pure nature. To see your life through the familiar's eyes. To transform and become powerful through the art of shape-shifting.

---

246. Willis, ed. *World Mythology: The Illustrated Guide*, 29.

247. Lurker, *An Illustrated Dictionary of the Gods and Symbols of Ancient Egypt*, 28.

When to cast: On the full moon, as the wildness of nature heightens. Day or night.

Where to cast: Indoors at your altar or outside under the sky.

You will need: Your witch's tools. Offerings from Nature to summon your familiar, like a stone or crystal, and a bowl of water. A brown or green candle of any size. Incense blend of three parts sandalwood (*Santalum album*), five parts mugwort (*Artemisia vulgaris*), and two parts patchouli (*Pogostemon cablin* or *P. patchouli*). Self-igniting charcoal. Witch's utensils.

Begin with ingredients before you. Become the witch and create magick.

1. Hold your athame to your brow and imagine a "circle of clouds" around you. The clouds become trees. The trees turn into earth.

2. Light the candle and the charcoal. When the charcoal is hot, place a pinch of incense onto it.

3. Hold each of your witch's tools skyward and say:

   "By the power of my wand I summon you.
   By the magick of this athame I shape-shift.
   Through this chalice of the Goddess I become myself.
   With this token, my pentacle, I enter your world and you mine."

4. Breathe and try not to engage with your thoughts. Simply allow them to move through your mind.

5. Allow your imagination to transport you to a place in nature. Enter a landscape of colours, shapes, scents, sounds, and textures. Whatever comes into your mind is important. Have no expectations.

6. Sense countless creatures living in this landscape. They are too vast to "see" them all. Feel the cold of frost, then the warmth of the sun. See animals moving, smell the scent of

pine, feel the wet grasses, hear rustling. Imagine a tapestry of endless shapes, of rocks and bark, nests, burrows, and flight of birds.

7. Clear your mind and say:

   "Come close to my heart."

8. Listen: What sound do you hear? A howl, a squeak, a call, or the sound of stillness?

9. Smell: What is the scent in the air? Musk, damp, flesh, fur, fertile, pungent?

10. Taste: What do you taste? An apple, moss, shell, meat, vegetable, mud?

11. Feel: Allow your creature to connect with your skin. What does it feel like? Warm, soft, prickly, slippery, furry, wet, or cold like scales?

12. See: Allow your mind's eye to see your familiar. Discover its colour, shape, and size.

13. Speak: Talk to your familiar. Magickal conversation isn't only in words. You can use symbols, actions, feelings, and colours.

14. Bless your familiar by placing your hand on its head, then on the familiar's heart.

15. Now imagine the familiar merging with your body, heart, mind, and spirit.

16. When you are finished, the "circle of clouds" fades.

17. Snuff out the candle.

After the spell: You now have an unbreakable magickal pact. Interface with your familiar and make offerings at significant times. If any of the candle remains, relight in the future in honour of your magickal relationship. Place the water on the Earth. Keep your stone offering by your bed or on your altar.

 ## A Familiar Dream Spell

Purpose: To connect with a dream familiar. For guidance at this time of your life. Like spells, dreams "speak" in the language of symbols. Some dream familiars are not your constant companion, instead they symbolise the magick needed right now and the aspect of yourself you need to liberate. Your familiar will either come to you through a dream or be the first thought upon waking.

When to cast: On the full moon, at night.

Where to cast: In your bedroom.

You will need: Your bell. A dream pouch with a blend of three parts mugwort (*Artemisia vulgaris*), two parts cinquefoil (*Potentilla canadensis, P. erecta,* or *P. reptans*), three parts mullein (*Verbascum thapsus*), and two parts wormwood (*Artemisia absinthium*). Dried mugwort (*Artemisia vulgaris*) to burn. Self-igniting charcoal. A moonstone crystal. A bowl of water. Salt to extinguish burning charcoal. Witch's utensils.

Begin with ingredients before you. Become the witch prepared to invoke your familiar.

1. As an offering to a dream familiar, place the bowl of water next to your bed along with the crystal or stone.

2. Light the charcoal and place some mugwort (*Artemisia vulgaris*) onto it. Holding the censer, turn, casting a "circle of clouds" around you. Imagine the smoke is a pathway to dreams.

3. Move the dream pouch through the incense smoke as you say:

    "By power of heart and mind,
    Creature in a dream to find.
    This magickal rite, my soul to bind,
    By way of will our souls entwine."

4. Place the pouch under your pillow.

5. Ring the bell over your bed. Its sound echoes through the forests of the heavens.

6. Extinguish the charcoal by covering it with salt.

7. When you are finished, close your eyes to the dreamtime world within the "circle of clouds."

8. When you wake, your familiar will be known to you. Either from the dream or within your first thought upon waking.

After the spell: Honour the dream familiar by interfacing with it. Learn its symbolism and transform through it. Keep the crystal in your bedroom. Pour the water on the Earth. Keep the dream pouch close as your sleep to understand the messages of your dreams.

Birds see life from a higher view, a spider reminds us to weave life artfully, and an ant teaches that working with a group can manifest an idea. A silverback gorilla embodies might, a jaguar inspires marvel, and a bee brings riches symbolized in honey. The goddess Cybele was called the Queen Bee, aligned with the creature's essence, and her priestesses were known as "*Melissae.*" Honey was the *Mellisae's* ritual offerings to their goddess.[248]

Over time you learn to understand the ways of your familiars, allowing them to live through you. Forming a bond with a familiar is intimate and requires exploration of the creature's nature, as well as the willingness to allow your imagination to be the landscape of this relationship. Like all creativity and inspiration, the familiar cannot be controlled and must remain free of logic and the mundane. Deeper knowledge of your familiar brings discovery of magick and yourself.

In this same imaginative landscape, you meet the fae and the elementals ...

---

248. Baring and Cashford, *The Myth of the Goddess*, 406.

SIXTEEN
The Fae and
the Elementals

Following is a story of the fae and you. Allow your imagination to take you there ... and meet them.

As you walk a spiral path towards the summit of the hill, your shoes begin to fall apart. They were old shoes, and this was their time to leave you. The ground is warm beneath your feet. You feel the heart of the hill beating with your own heart as you climb. The wind moves your hair in a slow dance through the air. You carry an offering to the hill-folk, the invisible ones. It is a stone etched with one word: "together." This is your gift to the fae, a symbol of your quest to connect with them.

On reaching the top of the hill, you are compelled to lie down on the grass and instantly fall into a deep, irresistible sleep. The hill-folk see the offering in your hand. Having never received such a valuable gift from a human, they instantly begin to weave their silver threads of enchantment around you. The threads promise that forevermore you will find the energy of strength and purpose in the hills of the world. Your heart will be bound to the light and shadow of Mother Earth. The hill-folk place four gold coins in your hand and then they bless your eyelids with drops of rain.

It is only when the moon rises in the sky that you wake. You feel as strong as a tree. Your offering stone is gone. The hill is beautifully silent. The moon's light shows you the path back home.

The Fae

We live in a world where imaginative traditions are fading. Where science excludes mystery and the rational mind diminishes want can't be explained. We have forgotten the power of the invisible realm, the spiritual and creative vision of life it gives us. Science and magick can exist beautifully together; they are not exclusive of each other. When the imagination dwindles, something within us is lost and we become lost. It is hard to always find meaning in the mundane world. It is most often found in a feeling, an experience, or a vision other-worldly and unexplained.

The words "*fairy*" or "*faery*" are thought to come from "*fae*" or "*fay*," from the origin of "*Fatae*," the three Fates in Greek myth.[249] It includes all mythical creatures, nature spirits, and even humans who think in an imaginative, bewitching way. The magick of Nature holds spirits in its embrace, otherworldly entities that personify the power and character of the natural world, as well as live in it. These magickal beings are sometimes known as the *fae*. Every hill, mountain, forest, lake, township, house, and auspicious place is inhabited by the fae and there is a vast variety. They exist everywhere and are found in most cultures and mystical traditions. Legends told about them are intriguing, mysterious, and powerful. They have been given many names and come in many, many forms. They express the magick of nature, artistry, the mind, and the shadow. They live in your psyche, the myths, and the old stories from when your ancestors heard the voice of Mother Earth; they appear in your dreams and may be remembered from your childhood. The fae come from many lands with otherworldly talents, skills, and

---

249. Katharine Briggs, *An Encyclopedia of Fairies: Hobgoblins, Brownies, Bogies, and Other Super-natural Creatures* (London: Penguin Books, 1977), 131.

purpose. They have countless names and myths have been told everywhere about them. Following are some of their stories.

Faery faith is found in Ireland in the tribe of the goddess Danu. Her people are the *Tuatha Dé Danann*. Once thought to be a race of deities, they later become the faeries, inhabiting the hills of their ancient land.[250] Here they were referred to as the "*sidhe*," which is the same name given to a burial mound where they reside, linking their existence to the earth realm and the realm of the dead.[251] There are stories that associate the fae with fallen angels who gifted the good and created havoc for the bad. This is an example of pagan and Christian concepts entwined.

The origins of the winged fae were birthed in the myths and beliefs of Greece, the Renaissance, and the Germanic lands. They also include the winged faeries of the Celts and all universal air spirits.

In general faeries appreciate acknowledgment; a blessing and offerings of milk appease and may incite good luck. Faery festivals are included in the witch's "Wheel of the Year," May Eve or Beltane, Midsummer Eve, and Samhain. At these times "the good people," as they are known, come out in celebration of the season. At Beltane and Midsummer, they are out in force. Bells were rung and protective spells cast to keep their mischief at bay. At Samhain, they came through the "veil" between the worlds, to converse with the spirits, and make magick with both ghost and human.

Faeries include the Irish *leprechaun*, a solitary being who is associated with luck and the making of shoes. Bringer of wealth because of his industrious and skilled work, the leprechaun guards a secret treasure, dresses poorly in drab clothing, and, like many of the fae, is associated with tricks on humans. The Irish leprechaun is akin to the magick of the gnome and brings the energy of good fortune. This magickal being speaks to you of "thinking lucky."

The brownie, like the leprechaun, is an earthy, small human-like figure who wears old clothes and a hat. Brownies bestow a household or a particular member of a household with luck also. They are found in Northern England and Scotland but houses everywhere have a spirit similar to this elf-like creature. Belief in the house brownie opens a portal to the realm of magick and soon enough a small resident will be present. Brownies raise the magickal vibration

---

250. Franklin, *Working With Fairies: Magick, Spells, Potions, and Recipes to Attract and See Them*, 17.

251. Franklin, *Working With Fairies: Magick, Spells, Potions, and Recipes to Attract and See Them*, 17.

of the home, enhancing luck and well-being.[252] Regular offerings are welcomed by this fae; however, it is important not to call in the brownie directly because they value choice and independence. Simply leave an offering of milk, honey, bread, or a piece of string for the brownie to collect. These offerings bring great blessings to your home.[253]

The pixies of the West Country in England are a race of redheaded pranksters who live in the natural world. They are thought to be the creators of "galli-traps" or faery rings, created by riding horses in circles.[254] Any human who steps into rings becomes captive. However, these same creatures are often enticed to grant a wish by an offering of bread.

In the myths of the Norse and Germanic people *elves* are highly skilled intelligent creatures. Frey, the Norse god of virility and sunshine, ruled their realm, *Alfheimr*. Frey was given the land of the elves as a gift when he cut his first tooth. This is one of the stories that may have birthed the legend of the *tooth faery*.[255] Elves and the dwarves of the Norse are devoted to knowledge and mastery of their particular gift and specialise in innovation and the creation of a magickal force in all objects, adornments, and weapons.

Elves, however, are found in many cultures and are usually associated with cleverness, artistic skills, and taking care of plants and trees. In Northern Italy elves are known as "*Gianes.*" These magickal beings could "see" the future on their spinning wheels while weaving spells.[256]

In Japan a race of fox faeries, the "*kitsune*," bestow both luck and mischief on humans. They are highly psychic, very smart, and like their kin from other lands, they live for centuries.[257] In Australian indigenous myth, "*mimis*" are faery-like creatures who inhabit the rocks of Arnhem Land. *Mimis* come out

---

252. Briggs, *An Encyclopedia of Fairies: Hobgoblins, Brownies, Bogies, and Other Supernatural Creatures*, 45.

253. Briggs, *An Encyclopedia of Fairies: Hobgoblins, Brownies, Bogies, and Other Supernatural Creatures*, 45–49.

254. Briggs, *An Encyclopedia of Fairies: Hobgoblins, Brownies, Bogies, and Other Supernatural Creatures*, 328.

255. "Grimnismál - The Ballad of Grimnir," Stanza 5, Völuspá.org, accessed August 21, 2020. http://www.voluspa.org/grimnismal.htm.

256. Conway, *Magical Mythical Mystical Beasts: How to Invite Them into Your Life*, 208.

257. Ronnberg and Martin, eds. *The Book of Symbols: Reflections on Archetypal Images*, 278.

at nightfall and look after the land.[258] *Will-o'-the-wisps* are associated with bogs and appear as strange moving lights in the night.

The fae, as you have read, have a darker side to their nature, just like all of us. Stories tell of their shadow side in the myth of the English changeling, of human babies taken by the faeries, and of an enchanted object or ancient faery left in the child's place.[259] Goblins and boggarts are other creatures that create trouble for humans, and it is said a goblin's smile "curls the blood."[260] Faeries can weave magick energy called "glamour," a strange enchantment that makes a situation appear different to what it truly is. Falling under the spell of faery glamour happens through constant wishful thinking and forgetting the power of choice. Humans find themselves disconnected from what is called reality when under this spell. The darkness and foreboding nature of the *fae* is also shown in the Irish "*pooka*." This trickster creature takes many forms, but in its incarnation as a black horse, it is said to be the cause of people falling over as well as ruined crops before the Celtic winter. However, the *pooka*, in the form of an old man, has been known to help grateful humans.[261]

Water spirits are of other worlds so can be seen as fae. Mermaids, in ancient Greece, were sirens, birds with human heads[262] and in Celtic legend they were giants of the sea luring sailors to their death through their bewitching song.[263] Both were very different from gentle mermaids depicted in modern tales. In Germanic lore mermaids took the form of the "*nixie*," an embodiment of beauty as well as danger.[264] Most fae belonging to the water element have enchanting powers over humans compelling them to fall under their spell of desire and drown in the same element that harbours the potential for true love. Many myths have been told about the "Lady of the Lake," a water spirit in

258. Willis, ed. *World Mythology: The Illustrated Guide*, 285.

259. Briggs, *An Encyclopedia of Fairies: Hobgoblins, Brownies, Bogies, and Other Supernatural Creatures*, 69–72.

260. Conway, *Magical Mythical Mystical Beasts: How to Invite Them into Your Life*, 213.

261. Briggs, *An Encyclopedia of Fairies: Hobgoblins, Brownies, Bogies, and Other Supernatural Creatures*, 327, 327.

262. Cotterell and Storm, *The Ultimate Encyclopedia of Mythology*, 60.

263. Briggs, *An Encyclopedia of Fairies: Hobgoblins, Brownies, Bogies, and Other Supernatural Creatures*, 287.

264. Lecouteux, *Encyclopedia of Norse and Germanic Folklore, Mythology, and Magic*, 211, 212.

Celtic mythology. Some of her names include Nimue, Viviane, and Nivian. She gave King Arthur his sword, Excalibur, and therefore his power.[265] In one of the myths of the Lady of the Lake, the druid wizard, Merlin, is bewitched and becomes a slave of his own desire, handing all his knowledge over to her. However, once the water spirit acquires more magick than him, she binds him to a tree, restricted and under her control. Merlin forgot his own wisdom, mistaking desire for love, and as a result lost his own power.

You meet the fae in curious places: in dreams, the moment before sleep, and in certain places on Earth that emanate an allure, such as ley lines and places of light and dark. These places are gateways to other lands; they include bridges, crossroads, hilltops, swamps, chimneys, wells, abandoned buildings, certain cupboards, holes in the ground, burial mounds, natural circles like faery rings, as well as spirals, labyrinths, and in tree hollows. All these places in Nature hold a powerful magick vibration. Always acknowledge the residing spirits when you feel this change of atmosphere and otherworldly presence.

Children believe in the fae. They are still of their true nature and as the fae are "of Nature," they reflect each other's qualities and are therefore attracted to each other's realms. "Imaginary friends" of childhood often depart when the child grows up and begins to think too much. Children know the secrets of play, of being able to laugh about everything, to hide, and to transform through the imagination. Children will gaze into a mirror bewitched by their own beauty and will have magickal experiences through their ability to become lost in a game. They do things that adults have forgotten and live in their "own world." They explore every part of their psyche and easily experience aspects of themselves through vivid imaginings. By becoming the enchantress, the protector, the trickster, or the thief, they begin to understand the light and the dark within. This aspect of them is enacted, sometimes through costume and play so they "live out" what is within. Their world can be extraordinary, detached from what is thought to be reality, but to them it is very real.

The fae are experienced when you can't stop laughing, when sleep puts you under a spell in strange places, when you feel enchanted and overcome with a dreamy energy or struck by amazing luck or otherworldly insight. The fae are present when you fall in love, at a baby's blessing, and when your feet move in a

---

265. Monaghan, *The New Book of Goddesses and Heroines*, 230.

new dance. They also come to your aid when you are overworked, heartbroken, in despair, and sometimes when you are unwell. Their mischievousness and darkness are present when the threads of authenticity are broken. They may also appear in the form of tricks when gratefulness is forgotten, or self-admiration creates illusion. Their energy is about when you are going somewhere but find yourself back at the same place. This is the "trickster" aspect of the *fae*, akin to the gods Loki, Pan, and Hermes. These deities are reflections of the tricks and traps that are created through inflated self-importance, ignorance, and disconnection with others.

The *fae* speak to you of the complexities of human nature as well as true nature, the energies of other realms, and ways to use Nature's bewitching charms. With the fae, you can venture into other realms to liberate your thoughts as well as meet your shadow. The portal to their magick is the imagination.

Altar for the Fae

In every home there is a resident from the realm of the fae. Create an altar, shrine, or "spirit house" in honour of them. You may want to build a little house out of sticks or simply create a circle of any crystals. You may like to include a mirror, items from Nature, a spiral design, and a small bowl for offerings. Allow your imagination to guide you.

Purpose: This is a place for spells, offerings, and acknowledgement of the fae. The creation of a fae altar will invoke their blessing and favours.

When to cast: Begin to create your altar on the full moon, then continue during any phase of the moon. Day or night.

Where to cast: Create your altar anywhere in your home, garden, or on a porch. Pre-make any structure and bring it to the chosen place.

You will need: You witch's tools. Water in your chalice. Bell ready. Any materials you wish. Four candles of any size to represent the elements: red for fire, yellow for air, blue for water, and green for earth. Incense blend of three parts angelica (*Angelica archangelica*), three parts lavender (*Lavandula officinalis* or *L. vera*), one part basil

(*Ocimum basilicum*), and three parts frankincense (*Boswellia carterii*). Self-igniting charcoal. Any flower petals. An offering of bread or small bowl of milk (vegan milk is also a good offering). Witch's utensils.

Begin with ingredients before you. Become the witch and create magick.

1. Hold your wand in one hand and your athame in the other and turn, casting a "circle of the fae" around you. Look to see who has come to your circle.

2. Light the four candles. Say:

    "I call the fae to the light."

    Ring the bell.

3. Ignite the charcoal and add a pinch or two of the incense. Say:

    "I invoke you by the wind."

    Ring the bell.

4. Move the items for the altar through the smoke.

5. Sprinkle items with water from your chalice. Say:

    "I honour you through the kiss of the Goddess."

    Ring the bell.

6. Sprinkle the items with flower petals. Say:

    "By the magick of Earth I open a portal to this altar for you."

    Ring the bell.

7. Create the altar.

8. When you are finished, say:

    "If it pleases you this is also your home. I welcome you with my heart."

    Ring the bell.

9. Place your offering at the altar and imagine your "circle of the fae" disappearing into the altar.

10. Snuff out the candles.

After the spell: If some of the candles remain, relight in honour of the fae. Place the water on the Earth. Make offerings when guided by your intuition. Place any remaining symbolic offerings on the Earth when needed.

 ## Spell to Attract the Luck of the Fae

Purpose: To invite positive energy into your life, to manifest a new path and opportunity.

When to cast: During the waxing moon. Day or night.

Where to cast: Indoors at your altar or outside under the sky.

You will need: An incense blend of five parts rose resin (*Rosa spp.*), three parts lavender (*Lavandula officinalis* or *L. vera*), and two parts sandalwood (*Santalum album*). Self-igniting charcoal. Two pieces of paper (3 in. x 3 in. or 7 cm x 7 cm). A pencil. The shoes you wear most. Witch's utensils.

Begin with ingredients before you. Become the witch and create magick.

1. To cast your circle, close your eyes and imagine a fork in a path. "Stand" in the middle where the path forks and "see" a "circle of good people" around you.

2. Ignite the charcoal and add a pinch of the incense.

3. On one piece of paper, write "change" and on the other write "luck."

4. Move both pieces of paper through the incense smoke three times.

5. Place the word "change" into the left shoe and "luck" into the right shoe.

6. Move your shoes through the smoke three times. Say three times:

> "Change be born in my mind,
> Shoes to walk, luck to find."

7. When you are finished, imagine the "circle of good people" disappearing.

After the spell: Allow your shoes to invigorate your life with luck and take you where opportunity waits.

The Elementals

Within each of the elements, fire, air, water, and earth, an *elemental* spirit resides, an embodiment of the character and power of the element. The fifteenth century Swiss alchemist and occultist, Paracelsus, expressed the concept of elementals. Each elemental is a manifestation of the element in physical form, though they remain mostly invisible to the human eye. Each inhabits its own element and will die in another.[266] Some of the powers and qualities of the elementals are also found in the realm of the fae, and there are creatures similar in description and purpose. However, the elementals were born from medieval science and live through and within the element itself. The elementals continue to be part of the witch's imagination and the energy and character of the four elements.

The *salamander* is a fire-living creature similar to a lizard. It embodies the magnificence of the element fire as well as its fury. Its magick is mysterious and not to be taken lightly. The *sylph* is a long, human-shaped creature who inhabits the air element. It is light, quick, and sees life always from above. The wind is the sylph's ride and mountaintops are their place of contemplation. The water elemental is the *undine*, a mermaid-like creature, a conjurer of feelings and deep beauty. The *gnome* is the earth elemental, a short, rough figure, keeper of plants, the spirit found in rocks and stones, and the guardian of treasures.

---

266. Manly P. Hall, *The Secret Teachings of All Ages* (New York: Jeremy P. Tarcher/Penguin 2003), 329.

When you engage with the elementals you can also become them and use their powers in different situations. Become the salamander when life becomes mysterious. When you are burdened, when life weighs you down, be inspired by the lightness of the sylph and "see" your story from above. Hold the undine's hand and travel to water's depth to find where forgiveness lies and feel the determination of the gnome when you wish to save money.

The Salamander: Element Fire

A Witch's Practice: Watch for the salamander in the flickering
of a flame and simply bow your head in honour of its power.

By nature, the salamander is dynamic and embodies the energies of will and power. The salamander is the essence of mystery. He reminds you that sometimes mystery needs to be left unsolved. The future is a mystery and other people can be too. Not everything needs to be understood. Sometimes you must wait for the right time. A joyful relationship and acceptance of mystery can be a fascinating experience and a profound state of mind. It is to be in awe and to have faith.

Acceptance is powerful magick in relationships. You can never change another person, that is up to them. However, you can always wish the best for another person, to send them healing, love, and hope they find fulfillment. Acceptance brings a stillness within, peace, and a quiet curiosity and fascination with what is meant to be.

Explanations, answers, and assurances are part of the mundane. Embrace mystery as you weave the threads of magick around your intention. Know that with every spell and magick working, a change will take place, but that change may not be what you thought. However, it will always take you where you need to be and deeper into your inner world to find yourself. To accept the unknown is to accept something extraordinary.

The salamander reminds you to remember that spells are sacred and are never superficial. Always enter your circle with innocence, humbleness, and the intention of enacting your quest for meaning.

This elemental is an enigma living within the flame of a candle as well as in volcanic lava.

Invoking the salamander directly is not advised because its power may be overwhelming. Its magick, however, is found through offerings and acknowledgement. Not everything is always available and to honour the divine brings to you a journey of endless discovery. As a witch you will still experience hardship but you will learn to transform through it. There are times to stop trying; this is when the salamander, at one with the flame, calls you to the light and also to your shadow, to integrate both and surrender.

 ## Offering to the Salamander for Acceptance

Purpose: To surrender and accept what is. Sometimes this is what you need to do. Acceptance takes the courage to let go of trying to control and to freefall with the mystery of the future.

When to cast: On the new moon during the day in honour of the sun.

Where to cast: Indoors at your altar or outside under the sky.

You will need: Your wand. A red candle of any size. Container of salt. Witch's utensils.

Begin with ingredients before you. Become the witch and create magick.

1. Holding your wand outright, turn and in your imagination cast a "circle of lava" around you.

2. Rub salt on your heart and hands to acknowledge your shadow.

3. Light the candle as an offering in honour of the salamander.

4. Imagine the salamander in the flame. Know the elemental is present.

5. Bow your head as a sign of acknowledgement.

6. When you are finished, hold your wand and turn in the opposite direction as you imagine the "circle of lava" and the salamander ascending into the sun.

7. Snuff out the candle.

After the spell: If any of the candle remains, relight in the future in honour of the salamander.

The Sylph: Element Air

"Sound is breath, voice is sound and animated breath; speech is breath pronounced with sound..." Cornelius Agrippa.[267] Breath and sound are of the air element and hold a powerful potential for magick and therefore transformation. Both are part of the story you weave in a spell.

The essence of invisibility, the breath, the magick of speech, and creative freedom can be learnt from the sylph, the elemental of air. Sylphs hear every word you speak; they ride on the winds, communicate with movement, and are extremely intelligent.

The sylph is the wind itself, a gentle breeze, a whirling vortex, and also a hurricane. Imagine these forces within your mind. Allow the sylph to move your thoughts.

This magickal being brings the knowledge of awareness and curiosity of how the mind works. A mind unchecked can become enslaved with doubt, worry, and overthinking. Thoughts need to move and change. When thinking is motionless it loses the breath of life, becoming stuck and eventually poisoned through stagnation. Unlocking the secrets of your mind involves "seeing" an invisible pattern of thoughts or the conversation of your mind.

Watch your thoughts as they seemingly move across your mind. Chose a colour for each one: yellow for genius and invention, grey for old battles and worries, purple for courage, pink for kindness and love, bright red for anger, black for mysterious and strange ideas.

By knowing how your mind works you have the power to transform it. Listen to the whispering sylph and in the realm of your mind inspiration will begin to breathe. The sylph knows when to, and when not to, use the rational path of the mind. At the right time the rational, the logic of the intellect, must be used. This is usually for plans and calculations of how, who, and when; to work out puzzles and strategy; and to sometimes understand problems and challenges. Intelligence is also used to analyse life, to see patterns and progress.

---

267. Agrippa, *Three Books of Occult Philosophy,* 336.

When the emotional world, ruled by water, is flooded with hurt, the intelligence of the air element brings balance, allowing you to "see" that all hardships are temporary. When stuck in the earth element of practicality, the sylph's magick takes you to the mountaintop of freedom, high above everything. And when the fire element creates overreaching and obsessiveness, the sylph's own element brings the ability to understand the need for change.

The sylph brings unworldly vision. A vision may be something mystical or extraordinary, actually seen, or an image or concept of the mind. Visions can't be made to happen or be forced; they rise in the mind from "out of nowhere" magickally. Visions can come to you through the power of the breath. The sylph teaches the art of breathing and its importance as a way of clearing the mind. Concentrating on the breath brings you into the moment and softens the analysing mind. With each breath the winds of change breeze into your life.

The sylphs also embody the movement of play and dance as a way to connect to authenticity. Within this experience mundane thinking is dispelled.

The sylph knows the art of invisibility. Through seeing the unseen, the physical is of no consequence and psychic powers are activated. Invisibility is the art of stillness and the ability to move as a spirit. It is also the power of silence and the wisdom in not trying to work everything out with the mind. It is the ability to also understand what is not seen or heard, to communicate through energy, to sense, to shift perception, and to empty the mind.

The sylph invites you to sit on the summit and surrender to the unknown. These air elementals also teach the art of seeing through another's eyes, the gift of empathy and compassion. This experience always wakes something sacred within and is absolutely transforming.

Creativity comes from a place between thought and dreams, a portal from another world that is not restricted by convention or fear. When thoughts are released, like birds from a cage, the mind surrenders to the creativity of the imagination.

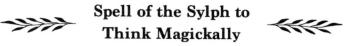

Spell of the Sylph to Think Magickally

Purpose: To clear the mind of the mundane so thinking is aligned with wonder, possibility, and mystical power.

When to cast: On the full moon. Day or night.

Where to cast: Indoors at your altar or outside under the sky.

You will need: Your athame. Yellow candle of any size. Incense blend of five parts white sage (*Salvia apiana*), three parts lavender (*Lavandula officinalis* or *L. vera*), and two parts myrrh (*Commiphora myrrha*).
Self-igniting charcoal. A found feather (if you haven't a feather, use your athame). Witch's utensils.

Begin with ingredients before you. Become the witch and create magick.

1. Holding the athame outward, turn to cast your circle. Imagine sylphs flying from its point.

2. Hold the blade to your brow and imagine your mind filling with light. Allow any thinking to move through your mind without engaging with it.

3. Light the candle.

4. Ignite the charcoal and add a pinch of incense. Imagine the smoke forming dancing sylphs, who move skyward.

5. Move the feather through the smoke. Say:

   "Enchant this feather, so may it be.
   So by its touch my mind is free."

6. Then move your athame through the smoke. Say:

   "Power of my witch's knife, so may it be.
   From a view on high, my thoughts set free."

7. Hold the athame to your brow.

8. Touch your head with the feather three times. Imagine your thoughts transforming into birds.

9. When you are finished, hold your athame and turn in the opposite direction. Imagine the "circle of sylphs" flying skyward, dissolving the circle.

After the spell: The enchanted feather is an amulet for you to use to empty your mind of the mundane and think magickally. When you touch your head with the feather or athame, imagine releasing your thoughts as if they are birds flying from your mind. If any of the candle remains, relight anytime in honour of the sylph.

The Undine: Element Water

A Witch's Practice: At the ocean, a pond, river, or lake,
sing a song in your mind, or aloud, to the undine. This will
connect you to love's truth. Throw a coin, as an offering,
into a fountain to the water spirit and make a wish.

Spellbinding love can be understood through the magick of the undine, the water elemental. Water holds the energy of the heart. It is the realm of feelings and therefore harbours the vibration of love. In Norse and Greek myths, the undine, in the form of a mermaid, bewitched sailors with her song. Unable to resist the allure of her voice, they lost control of their ships and crashed into the rocks. This myth symbolically speaks of the psychic death required in order to connect with new life.

When you truly fall in love, you do "fall" as if magickally compelled to be with that other person. Just like the undine's song. True love is an experience that calls you to a spiritual death because once it happens, life is never the same again.

Love is a state that overwhelms the senses and inspires magnificence of being and presence. Deep love bewitches and transforms, it can be reckless as well as relentless, elated as well as so powerful the heart can break because of it. With true love a mystical energy is birthed as both people experience transformation. This energy has a profound effect on everyone who is near someone in love, compelling them to want the same.

The story of love told in the myth of the undine speaks of the depths of feeling, symbolized by the vast seas, the flow of rivers, and the mirror of still water in ponds and lakes. True love never remains on the surface of experience and is never afraid to venture into the darkness of the ocean, into the raw experience of the heart. Falling in love births a profound journey into the undiscovered parts of the inner world where a deeper level of courage, compassion, and truth await. The undine of the river symbolises the flow and journey of love. In the ponds of prophecy, the undine speaks that true love is destined to those willing to imagine its beauty, to see the magick in another, and to transform.

Residing in wishing wells, the undine is a granter of wishes and a giver of life itself through the water of the Goddess. If you wish for true love, imagine being in love and believe love will find you. Listen for the undine's song and prepare to change within. Raise the essence of true love within you. The one you will love will swim to the depths of the ocean and find you.

Love Spell of the Undine

Purpose: To discover the essence of true love within you and thereby attract this same love to you. To recognise romantic love and allow it to come to you. To open your heart to truth and fall in love completely with someone who feels the same as you do.

When to cast: During the waxing moon. Day or night.

Where to cast: Indoors at your altar or outside under the sky.

You will need: Your chalice filled with water. A shell or a blue crystal, like blue-lace agate (for confidence) or aquamarine (to connect with the water element and for calmness).

Begin with ingredients before you. Become the witch and create magick.

1. Holding your chalice, turn, casting a "circle of water, shells, and fish" around you.

2. Hold the shell/crystal to your heart and say:

   "I ask the Goddess to hold me as I fall into the
   depths of true love's soul."

3. Breathe on the shell/crystal and place it in the chalice of water.

4. Leave the chalice outside under the waxing moon for six nights.

5. On the seventh night, anoint your heart, hands, and bottom of your feet with the water from the chalice.

6. When you are finished, hold your chalice and turn in the opposite direction to the casting of your circle. Imagine your "circle of water, shells, and fish" ascending to the moon. "See" the undine swimming away from you and disappearing into the depths of water.

After the spell: Keep the shell/crystal by your bed. Take the chalice outside the next night and, holding it over the Earth, pour the water over each of your hands until it is empty.

The Gnome: Element Earth

"The sun shines upon all of us equally with its luck. The summer comes to all of us and so does the stormy winter. But while the Sun looks at all of us equally, we look at it unequally" Paracelsus (Selected writings).[268]

These words speak of the connection between the mind and world around you. It speaks of the microcosm, the world within you, and the macrocosm, the greater world, and their reflective relationship. It also encompasses the magick of opportunity and the ability to see and embrace it.

The secrets of money and luck can be learnt. Keep in mind that money and luck are not necessarily entwined or the same. One exists without the other. However, the elemental that rules these concepts is the earth elemental, the gnome, guardian of the mountain treasure. The word gnome comes from the Latin, "*gēnomos*" meaning "earth-dweller."[269]

The element earth holds the energy of foundation, stability, and growth and these elementals are the artful masters of its magick. Money can "slip between your fingers," cause mischief, or disappear quickly. Money is the token of exchange on the Earth plane and holds a unique energy of its own. It is ruled by four, the number that vibrates the energy of steadiness, practicality, and planning.

Money in itself isn't light or dark, right or wrong, useful or draining. These energies are created by how it is used. Money doesn't create fulfilment and happiness either and the lack of it doesn't always create despair. However, money

---

268. Paracelsus. *Selected Writings*. ed. Jolande Jacobi. (New Jersey: Princeton University Press, 1988), 205.

269. Briggs, *An Encyclopedia of Fairies: Hobgoblins, Brownies, Bogies, and Other Supernatural Creatures*, 192, 193.

can bring independence, choice, and experience. If you depend on someone else's money, you tend to lose some of your lifeforce, and if you keep all your money to yourself, you also lose it.

The gnomes bring the message that prosperity is a way of thinking and money is energy. Your money is given a "character" by you. Its character is created by the way you talk about it, think of it, and what to do with it.

Imagine what magickal form your money would take. Would it be a wizard in a green cloak, a gold-winged horse, or wishing well? What would your money move, smell, taste, and feel like as an ethereal personality or a design?

Money Spell of the Gnomes

Purpose: To liberate abundant thinking and allow the energy of prosperity to grow within you. To dispel the energy of "lack" and worry. To invigorate your relationship with money with zest as well as practicality.

When to cast: During the waxing moon. Then on the next new moon. Day or night.

Where to cast: Indoors at your altar or outside under the sky.

You will need: Your pentacle. A handful of salt. Philtre of four drops of basil oil (*Ocimum basilicum*) with eight drops of patchouli oil (*Pogostemon cablin* or *P. patchouli*) in a teaspoon of olive oil (*Olea europaea L.*). A square of paper (4 in. x 4 in. or 8 cm x 8 cm). A pencil. String (9 in. or 22 cm). Four green buttons.

Begin with ingredients before you. Become the witch and create magick.

1. Holding your pentacle, turn to cast a "circle of mountains" around you.

2. Create a small circle before you using the salt. Then, within the circle, create a square with the salt. Imagine this is a portal for the gnomes to enter your world.

3. With the philtre anoint your brow.

4. Draw a square on the paper, and then within it a circle. Within the circle write your witch's sigil or your name.

5. Place the paper on top of your pentacle. Anoint the four corners of the paper with the oil. Place a button on each corner of the paper.

6. Hold your palm downward over the paper and say:

   "I invoke the power of the earth,
   Bewitch my money with true worth.
   Enrich my thoughts and set them free,
   Weave threads of magick, from purse to tree,
   To branches of gold,
   To roots in the ground,
   May prosperity rise.
   Abundance, abound."

7. Put the buttons aside. Fold the paper four times and using the string fasten it with four knots.

8. Leave the written spell and the four buttons on your pentacle.

9. Merge the circle of salt into the square made of salt before you.

10. When you are finished, hold the pentacle and turn in the opposite direction as you imagine the "circle of mountains" and the gnome disappearing.

After the spell: Leave the written spell and the buttons on your pentacle for four days. Then tie the spell to a tree. Sew the four buttons onto a garment. Keep your purse or wallet in an organized way. If you find a button or a key, keep it in your purse/wallet for luck. Place the salt from the spell into the Earth.

The fae are a brilliant aspect of you. They are also beyond you. Their gift is creativity, cleverness, and insight as well as magick boundaries and wisdom. They are the imagination alive, vibrant, and limitless as well as Nature personified.

They hold immense power. When you interface with the fae, when they are a part of the story you weave in a spell, they become muses, guides, healers, and teachers.

Now fall with the fae and the elementals into the beauty of the witch's Wheel of the Year and spin your magick through the seasons.

SEVENTEEN
The Witch's Wheel

The Witch's Wheel of the Year tells the story of the Goddess and the God as personifications of Nature. It speaks of their rise and fall, of birth, growth, of divine power, of their irresistible magnetism, procreation, then retreat, decline, and death. The witch's eight sabbats depicted as a continuous turning wheel is a modern concept. However, the seasonal events highlighted on the "wheel" originated in the agricultural rites of Europe, pagan folklore, the faery faith, as well as spirit communication and beliefs. The times and seasons also coincide with seasonal rituals of the Celtic, Norse, and Saxon people as well as the cult practices of the ancient Greeks, in particular the cult of Dionysus.[270] These same ancient festivals had borrowed myths and mystical concepts from older Sumerian, Babylonian, and Egyptian stories and magickal practice. Worldwide seasonal celebrations hold similar themes from Africa to America, and speak of the same Earth, the same elements, and the continual cycle of birth, death, and then rebirth.

---

270. Grimassi, *The Witch's Craft: The Roots of Witchcraft and Magical Transformation*, 66.

The themes of the witch's sabbats are most likely a combination of these seasonal festivals and pagan beliefs that have evolved through time, to honour the Goddess and the God and to acknowledge human dependence on Nature and also gratitude.

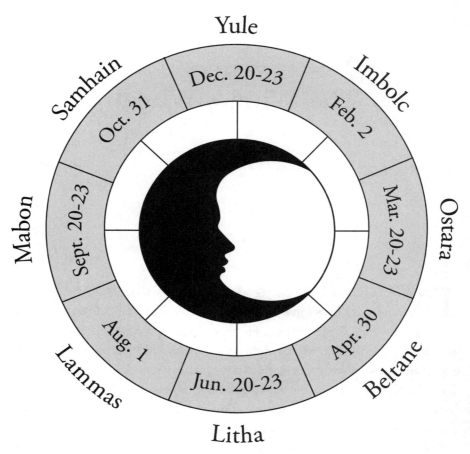

Figure 8: Wheel of the Year

The origin of the word "*sabbat*" is old French, derived from the Hebrew word "*shabbath*" meaning "to rest."[271] Four of these sabbats are the autumn and spring equinox and the winter and summer solstice. The Earth revolves around the sun tilted on its axis. This tilt creates the equinoxes and solstices that define

271. Guiley, *The Encyclopedia of Witches and Witchcraft*, 287.

the length of day and night. Each year the actual date of the equinoxes and solstices varies slightly, within a few days, due to the orbital speed of the Earth. However, the dates of the remaining four sabbats—*Samhain, Imbolc, Beltane, and Lughnasadh*—have a fixed date. All the sabbats dates are mirrored in each hemisphere according to the seasons. The origins of the sabbats are complex and rich in history, however, think of the Wheel of the Year as a spinning wheel, creating the threads of Nature and reminding you of the continuous momentum of change, of beginnings and endings.

The Witch's Sabbats

Samhain

Winter Solstice: Yule

Imbolc

Spring Equinox: Ostara

Beltane

Summer Solstice: Litha

Lammas: Lughnasadh

Autumn Equinox: Mabon

When Europe became Christian, festivals of the new religion replaced seasonal celebrations and deities were renamed as saints. However, many of the new holy days adopted the same theme as the pagan festivals. Easter replaced Ostara at the spring equinox and remained a celebration of new life and resurrection. Christmas was dated at the time of the winter solstice and Yule, a time marking the birth of the sun after the longest night. The myth of the sun's birth was aligned with the birth of Christ, also a solar deity, and like his pagan counterparts he was said to have brought Light to the world. The religious celebrations of All Hallows' Day and All Souls' Day, when the departed are honoured, fall at the same time as Samhain, the ancient pagan festival of dead.

In the Southern Hemisphere the seasons are at the opposite time of the year to the Northern Hemisphere. Many original pagan myths, now holidays in Australia and New Zealand, have remained at their original Northern Hemisphere date. Originally a spring festival in Europe, Easter has stayed at its original date, so it is observed in the Southern Hemisphere autumn. The enduring motif of the Easter egg, a universal symbol of new life was birthed from the creation myths of the Cosmic or World egg.[272] Halloween, originally Samhain, the eve of the Celtic winter, is enacted in the Australian spring and Christmas, originally dated at winter's Yule, is at the height of summer yet the same tree is brought into the home to warm its residing dryad.

Myths and seasonal traditions have been taken to other lands by immigrants and refugees through time and have remained a custom because they hold within their core symbols that speak of meaning. They remind you of your dependence on Nature, the essence of life, and the inevitability of death. Seasonal traditions and myths ask you to stop, to acknowledge, and be in awe of the natural world. Not every day is the same. You are never the same. The myths and stories associated with Nature's events bring mystery into our lives and connect you to the world around you. The symbolism of the myths speaks about you, about your quest for purpose. They were birthed from a universal yearning to be at one with Nature and to merge with it.

The Wheel of the Year takes you into the depth of the psyche to think about your true nature, to acknowledge a power that is beyond your control. It takes you to your spiritual life and reminds you of your home, the Earth. You are not separate from Nature. You are of it. Because of this you are connected to every other human being and creature. We are the one family. You are Gaia's child under the spell of beginnings and endings. The sabbats tell your story.

Creating magick at the sabbats aligns you with the personality of the Earth and the energy of the season. The Wheel turns through a rhythm of light and dark, inward and outward, growth and decay, creation and destruction, beginnings and endings. The myths associated with the sabbats, imagined or enacted, liberate aspects of your own story, the story of your heart, mind, and spirit.

Altars and Spells of the Sabbats

Following each sabbat, there is a description of an altar to be created and a spell for you to weave. Please know that the creation of the altar is a spell in itself. Each altar honours the sabbat and celebrates the seasonal gateway. It is a symbolic expression of your intention to align your life with the transformation of Nature. Your altar will resonate magickal energy through your home and reflect the mystical theme of the season. Each of the eight altars require your witch's

---

272. Cooper, *An Illustrated Encyclopedia of Traditional Symbols*, 60.

tools to be present: wand, athame, chalice, pentacle, cauldron, besom, grimoire, bell, mirror, and mortar and pestle. Some altar creations and spells will focus on a particular tool. Every altar described has the four elements present, a candle or candles for fire, incense for air, salt and plants for earth and water. Each have a different charm or talisman for you to create. Add anything you feel is symbolic to your altar and if you don't have the herbs or oils suggested, you can use what you have available. Your intention, imagination, and creation are the most important ingredients. The spells that follow are cast at your sabbat altar.

During the spell you will venture further into magick using your witch's tools and the items set on your altar. There will be additional items needed for the spell itself. Always place candles in fire-proof holders and self-igniting incense in a censer or fire-proof container.

The Wheel of the Year begins at Samhain...

Samhain

Also known as Halloween
Season: Autumn
Northern Hemisphere: October 31
Southern Hemisphere: April 30

On the Wheel of the Year

The Crone Goddess rises and rules the night.
Remembers the departed and your ancestors.
The shadow is liberated.
The worlds meet.

A Samhain Story...

Lanterns flicker light on the trees bringing to birth ghosts and apparitions. You walk with others towards the graves where loved ones lie carrying apples for the dead and burning frankincense to welcome them to the Earth. Children rush by with carved pumpkin lights and baskets of treats. They are dressed as the fae tonight, wearing wings and ghostly garbs. Horns protrude through matted hair and eyes shine through their pixie masks. Some children are adorned with crowns and others wear the snouts and ears of wild creatures.

There is no moon tonight. As you move through the mist the veil opens between the worlds. Tears fall from your eyes. You hear the whispering voices of spirits. You feel their presence as they join you in the walk. Shoulder to shoulder, the dead and the living stride together. Above in a starless sky an ancient hag reigns as queen, astride her broom. She watches as the veil fades.

Halloween derives from the ancient pagan festival of Samhain, a time that neither belonged to the past or present. Falling between the autumn equinox and the winter solstice, Samhain was called the Festival of the Dead and was the eve of the Celtic New Year.[273] On the Wheel of the Year, the young Goddess has entered the Underworld of autumn. The old God dies, the Crone Goddess rises in full splendour as winter itself: barren, cold, and powerful.

At Samhain, the veil between the world of the living and the spirit realm was at its finest and neither human nor ghost needed a password to enter each other's worlds. Departed friends and relatives made contact with their living kin. Offerings of food and drink were left out for the ghosts moving west in the direction of the dying Sun. Samhain is rooted in a past when life was not taken for granted, when ancestors were revered, and when an afterlife was deemed to be true.

Samhain was the beginning of winter for the ancient Celts, a time of dread, for survival was not guaranteed. Before the night of Samhain farmers slaughter their stock and preserved the meat in preparation for the months ahead. Crops were gathered quickly before the Pooka, a shape-shifting goblin, often in the form of a black horse, could contaminate the harvest. The line between life and death weakened and both realms merged.

Fires were lit on the hillsides, calling the spirits home. Stones were cast into the flames to see if death was likely during the following year and the ash was spread over the surrounding fields to ensure fertility.

As the veil between the worlds opened, faeries and darker creatures like demons and goblins rose under the spell of the night. In Ireland the faeries of Tuatha Dé Danann emerged from burial mounds where oracles took place at the entrances.

---

273. Franklin, *Working With Fairies: Magick, Spells, Potions, and Recipes to Attract and See Them*, 93.

The crone witch, as embodiment of the ancient goddess, was queen of the night. Her old age spoke of death itself, however her cackling howls echoed defiance at death's door. Now was the time for the crone queen to stir her magnificent cauldron, a reminder of the passage of death as well as the promise of new life. Now was the time for witches to take up their besoms and ride the night skies.

The custom of trick-or-treat at Halloween derives from the offerings made to appease the wandering ghosts and entities. The costumes not only mimic, they assist you with merging with the shadow creature within. During this enactment, an aspect of the psyche is experienced, the hidden, the mystical, and with that comes greater depth of self-realization.

Samhain was also a time to embrace atonement and it was customary to write down weaknesses on parchment and then burn for purification.

It was also a night of mischief and the beginning of the "Lord of Misrule." As winter began the coming hardship, the hope of survival, and the dread of death was challenged by human unruliness. Such enactments were a proclamation of faith in divine protection. So, while the fires blazed on the hillsides merry-making, love and fertility rites were enacted in defiance of the darkest hour of the year.[274]

Love spells were created and mirrors were used to conjure visions of the future. Girls washed their nightdresses and hung them at the fires to attract a husband. Apples, as symbols of the dead, and nuts representing fertility and sexual freedom, were used for divination. Fortunes were told and intentions were made for the year ahead, a tradition that is still enacted through New Year's resolutions.

The Mexican Day of the Dead is also celebrated around this same time, from the 31st of October to the 2nd of November, although the preparation of altars and grave decorations would in general begin prior due to their elaborations and embellishments. Offerings of fruit, marigold flowers, and food are placed by ceramic skulls, religious statues, and photos of the departed creating altars, inviting the dead home again. Sugar skulls are sold for the living to write their names on, a reminder that no one can evade death. Cemeteries become places for party and offerings.

---

274. Frazer, *The Golden Bough: A Study in Magic and Religion*, 634, 635.

All Souls' Day is still commemorated in the Catholic tradition on the 2nd of November, the eve of which was All Hallows'. The word *hallows* derives from Old English, German, and Old Norse words meaning "holy" and is the origin of the word Halloween.[275]

Samhain is a time to remember loved ones and to explore magickal aspects within you by enacting myth. It is a celebration uniting the community, a time to mask, veil, and costume for fun and defiance as well as for freedom and mysticism. On this sabbat the living and the dead converse. They are given this moment to experience each other's worlds. Allow the spirit world to rise in your mind, for it is a realm unbound by the mundane. Samhain is a moment to look at life from the perceptive of the dead, to liberate new creative vision, acknowledge the shadow within, and imbue a dream-like quality to your life. And through this you will awake. To acknowledge death is also to acknowledge life.

October 31: The Enactment Halloween in the Southern Hemisphere
Season: Spring

Traditionally, the 31st of October is Beltane Eve according the Wheel of the Year in the Southern Hemisphere. However, in recent times the enactment of Halloween, with all its symbolism, remains at is original date in Australia and New Zealand.

Halloween is intriguing and rich with play and has been resurrected in distant lands because children want to experience magick. To become a faery, witch, ghost, or demon for a night, the thrill of knocking on a stranger's door, masked and costumed, is a way to experience myth and mysticism and to connect to a universal consciousness. It isn't the eve of winter in the Southern Hemisphere and we no longer live in fear of food running out, goblins ruining the crops, or evil spirits visiting our homes. But this forgotten world may remind our children that they are of nature and part of the cycle of birth and death, part of our ever-evolving myths.

Allow your imagination to create a magickal night. Keep the ancient myth of Samhain alive by losing yourself in the art of make-believe and costume. Have treats for trick-or-treaters as a symbolic offering to the spirit world. Hold

---

275. McCoy, *Sabbats: A Witch's Approach to Living the Old Ways*, 24.

a ghost gathering and talk about loved ones passed. Delve deeply into your relationships with others by exploring the experience of grief and loss together. Set a symbolic place at your table for the spirits. Set a plate with offering food and an empty chair.

Symbols, Charms, and Plants of Samhain/Halloween

Apples: They are potent symbols of the realm of the dead and can be used as offerings as well as games. An Irish custom of placing apples in water and trying to catch one in the mouth was played around Halloween. Peeling an apple to divine future love is also an old Samhain tradition. Peel the apple allowing the skin to fall on a surface. Scry the pattern the apple peel has made.

Basil *(Ocimum basilicum)*: To honour the ancestors. Burn in an incense blend, eat on food, or use in a dream pillow to connect with the departed.

Besom: Symbol of fertility and freedom.

Cauldron: The passage of life and death. The Roman occupation of the Celtic lands may have entwined Samhain with the celebration of their goddess Pomona,[276] whose name is the origin of the word "apple" with Samhain. The Welsh called their realm of the dead Avalon, meaning "apple land."[277]

Elder *(Sambucus Nigra)*: The tree of the dead. Leave a stone as an offering to the dryad, the spirit of the tree.

Faeries and Shadow Creatures: The fae also move through the veil along with the spirits.

Fire or candle flames: Burnt to hold the energy of the dead God as waning Sun, to illuminate the darkness and ward off unwanted spirits, and to purify the home.

Frankincense *(Boswellia carterii)*: To honour the dead and connect with the spirit realm. Burn as incense or add to a psychic charm pouch for energetic protection. Use the oil to anoint yourself and magickal objects, for protection, purification, and otherworldly connections.

---

276. McCoy, *Sabbats: A Witch's Approach to Living the Old Ways,* 27.
277. McCoy, *Sabbats: A Witch's Approach to Living the Old Ways,* 41.

Jack-o'-Lantern: Represents the wandering spirit and protection. Originally these lanterns were carved from huge turnips before pumpkins replaced them in America.

Mirror: To scry past, present, and future.

Mullein *(Verbascum thapsus)*: Used to substitute graveyard dust in spells and can be placed in charm pouches to dream of the dead.

Myrrh *(Commiphora myrrha)*: Traditionally used for embalming in ancient Egypt, myrrh reminds us mortality brings a divine energy with anointing and burning as incense.

Nuts: Symbols of fertility and life.

Offerings: Gifts to honour the dead.

Rosemary *(Rosmarinus officinalis)*: To remember the dead. Use the fresh plant on your altar or burn the dried leaves as an incense. Wear the oil to enhance memory and for spiritual awakening.

Veil: The barrier between the worlds of the living and the dead.

Samhain Altar

During the creation of your altar, you will open a portal to the spirit world and enchant a jack-o'-lantern. You may wish to prepare a few days before Samhain. The altar will manifest within the circle of the spell.

Purpose: Your altar is to be dedicated to the Crone Goddesses, to the passage between the worlds and eternal life. It will express love and the sacred relationship you have with loved ones and your ancestors. During the creation of the altar, you will open a portal of communication with spirits and invite them into your home. Samhain is a time of wonder, a time to "see the invisible" both within yourself and around you.

When to create your altar: In the time leading up to Samhain so the altar is complete before the sabbat. The sabbat begins at moonrise on the eve.

You will need: Your witch's tools. Cauldron containing water. A black candle and an orange candle of any size. Container of salt. Incense blend of five parts rosemary (*Rosmarinus officinalis*), three parts mullein (*Verbascum thapsus*), and one part myrrh (*Commiphora myrrha*). Self-igniting charcoal. You will burn this blend again during the Samhain spell. Philtre of seven drops of rosemary (*Rosmarinus officinalis*), three drops of pine (*Pinus spp.*), and five drops of frankincense essential oil (*Boswellia carterii*) in a teaspoon of almond oil (*Prunus dulcis*). Place in a small bowl or container and swirl. Apples as offerings, as well as nuts, fresh rosemary (*Rosmarinus officinalis*), mugwort (*Artemisia vulgaris*), and flowers of the season. A jack-o'-lantern. Carving tools. You may wish to carve the pumpkin in your kitchen or at a table. If so, imagine the circle expanding as you leave the altar with the pumpkin and then contracting as you return with the carved jack-o'-lantern. A new charm or ribbon to embellish your broom.

Photos of loved ones and other symbols of the spirit world, such as clay or crystal skulls. Witch's utensils. Position your witch's tools, candles, censer and incense blend, philtre, plants, and symbolic items creatively on the altar.

Begin with ingredients before you. Become the witch and create the magick of Samhain.

1. Raise your cauldron as you say:

   "I invoke the grandmother goddess, show me the way
   to the ancestors as I cast a circle of light. This circle is
   a portal for the wandering spirits of Samhain."
   Imagine the circle.

2. Carve your jack-o'-lantern (where you wish) and then return to the altar.

3. Light the two candle flames. Say:

   "Be guided to the light."

4. Ignite the charcoal and add a pinch or two of incense. Say:

   "My message in the smoke."

5. Touch the water in the cauldron. Say:

   "To the waters of love."

6. Place a grain or two of salt on your tongue. Say:

   "For our journey on Earth."

7. Move the jack-o'-lantern over the candles, through the two flames. Then sprinkle with water and salt.

8. Ring your bell over the altar.

9. With flowers, leaves, herbs, nuts, and apples, create a circle around the pumpkin.

10. Add a charm, ribbon, or amulet to your besom and position it close to the altar.

11. When you are finished, move your cauldron over the altar to dissolve your circle.

12. Snuff out the candles to relight at your spell.

On the night of the sabbat of Samhain, you will create a spirit jar at your altar. You may wish to dedicate the spirit jar to one or many loved ones.

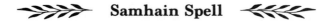 **Samhain Spell**

To Connect with Loved Ones

Purpose: This is an offering spell to those in spirit. The spirit jar you create is an expression of love, acknowledgment, and connection. During the making of the spirit jar, your psychic channels will open, you may receive messages, resolve mysteries, and feel a comforting spiritual presence. The spirit jar becomes a memorial, encapsulating grief, devotion, and memories.

When to cast: At Samhain/Halloween. At night.

Where to cast: Indoors at your altar or outside under the sky.

You will need: Altar items and ingredients as prepared. A white candle to place inside your jack-o'-lantern. A jar or container. Small pieces of paper (1 in. x 1 in. or 3 cm x 3 cm), the number depends on how many loved ones are in the spirit realm. Pencil. A stone, a rose quartz crystal for love, and an amethyst crystal for transformation.

As you create this spell, gaze into your scrying mirror from time to time to catch a glance or see a spirit.

Create the spell at your altar. As the witch, prepare to connect with loved ones.

1. Holding your athame outright, turn and cast a circle around you. Imagine this circle is an entryway to the spirit realm, like a portal. Say:

   "I call my loved ones through the circle."

2. Ring the bell.

3. Anoint your heart, brow, and the bottom of your feet with the philtre.

4. Light the candle flames and the incense blend. Sprinkle some water and salt around the jack-o'-lantern.

5. Say:

   "The spirits sing. I hear your song. Let's hold each
   other's pain. We are bones. We are heart. We all
   return to Mother, our Earth. We are one story,
   threads to flesh, myth, love, shadow, knowledge,
   moon, sun, wind, and tree. We are one."

6. Begin to write the names of loved ones passed on the pieces of paper. Write onto the paper any words or symbolics that are significant. Anoint each piece of paper with the philtre.

7. Place into the jar the stone, love quartz, and amethyst as offerings. Add flowers, leaves, and any significant items you wish.

8. Move the jar through the candle flame three times, through the incense smoke, and with your fingers add some water from the cauldron and a pinch of salt.

9. Breathe into the jar, connecting the breath of your life to your loved ones. Ring the bell over the opened jar.

10. Close the lid.

11. When you are finished, hold your athame outright and turn in the opposite direction to dissolve the circle and close the portal.

12. When you leave the room, snuff out the candles.

After the spell: Keep the spirit jar in a sacred place and add names of the departed. Open the spirit jar every Samhain. Allow your jack-o'-lantern to begin to decompose to remind you of endings, then place the remains in compost to return to earth. If any candles remain, relight over the following days in honour of your loved ones. Anoint your heart every day with the remaining philtre until it is gone. Place water and any used salt on the Earth. Compost the flowers when it is time.

The sun's light wanes, taking you deeper into stillness and the stagnation of winter.

Winter Solstice: Yule

Also known as Midwinter
Season: Winter
Northern Hemisphere: December 21–23
Southern Hemisphere: June 21–23

On the Wheel of the Year

The reign of the Crone Goddess comes to an end.
The Virgin Goddess awakes from her sleep to find she is
pregnant, then at the solstice she gives birth to the Sun God.
Remember light always follows darkness.
A beginning follows an ending. Rebirth follows a death.
Embrace hope.

A Winter Solstice Story...

The chill of winter takes you deep into your shadow, into the loss and pain of life, the disappointment and fear. You have visited the Underworld, met with the lost, with the dead, with the tricksters, and the hopeless.

You light a flame as you travel into the longest night holding a dying god in your heart. You see his divine light wane and you fall with him into sacred darkness. You surrender. You fall further. Then, a distant echo of hope, a star appears in your mind. At first it is far away then grows brilliant. Dawn arrives with a newborn's cry of bright tomorrows.

At the winter solstice in the Northern Hemisphere, the North Pole is tilted farthest from the sun. The South Pole tilts its maximum distance away from the Sun six months later, creating the longest night in the Southern Hemisphere.

Since ancient times, myths associated with the solstice speak of a Virgin Goddess giving birth to the sun. Symbolically the sun's journey at the solstice is the story of our own endurance through hardship and calls us to never give in. Through the darkest night of the year the sun is reborn at dawn, reminding us that a beginning always follows an ending. The inward journey through winter now turns outward with the waxing sun and the days become longer.

Gods as victors over darkness were birthed at the winter solstice. In the mythology of the Norse, the goddess Frigg laboured through the longest night to birth Baldur, the beautiful god of Light. Baldur is associated with the mistletoe, still a traditional Christmas symbol. According to myth, the mistletoe was the only thing on Earth able to kill this magnificent god and did so in the form of a mistletoe branch.[278]

Like the sun itself, Baldur brought brilliance wherever he went and was adored by all the deities. The evergreen mistletoe growing on the barren oak of winter may have inspired the myth of Baldur's birth.

The Egyptian goddess, Isis, also gave birth to Horus at the winter solstice. His symbol is the winged sun. The solar deity Osiris was also born. Tammuz

---

278. Farrar, *The Witches' God*, 117.

and Dumuzi were resurrected in Mesopotamia. In Persia, Mithras, the Unconquered Sun and god of light, rose at this time, also bringing truth into the world.[279]

The pine tree (*Pinus spp.*) associated with the Roman god Attis was a symbol of the death of winter. He wounded himself under a pine tree, died, and became the tree itself. Attis resurrected through the new growth of spring and the pine remained a traditional Yule symbol and favoured Christmas tree.[280] However the pine, like the solstice and the god himself, embodies the concept of rebirth as well as death in its incarnation as a maypole in spring. In Rome the festival of Saturnalia celebrated Saturn, god of agriculture and plenty. Homes were decorated with lights and holly became a gift of good wishes. Akin with the tradition of misrule during magickal festivals, Saturnalia was a time to defy normality. Social norms were reversed, the rich served the poor, and the fool became king.

In the Celtic lands, two nature entities, the Holly King and the Oak King, battled for power at both the winter and summer solstices. These mythical beings symbolized the seasonal interplay of dark and light. Their battle speaks of the perpetual struggle of energies within us as well as the movement of the Earth. At the winter solstice the Oak King defeats the Holly King and remains the paramount energy until the summer solstice.[281]

At the winter solstice the magick of fire was present in burning the Yule Log, later called a "Christmas block."[282] In some traditions the log, often from the slow-burning oak tree, was placed under the house fire to glow throughout the year. Remaining ashes from the log were scattered in the fields to promote growth.

In other traditions, the Yule log was burnt over the twelve days after Christmas Eve and then placed in the house for protection. Yule logs and large candles were used as charms to assist the sun through the darkest night, to illuminate the home, and to protect it from lightning and fire itself.

---

279. Baring and Cashford, *The Myth of the Goddess*, 561.

280. Alexander S. Murray, *Who's Who in Mythology: A Classic Guide to the Ancient World* (London: Bracken Books, 1994), 34.

281. McCoy, *Sabbats: A Witch's Approach to Living the Old Ways*, 63.

282. Frazer, *The Golden Bough: A Study in Magic and Religion*, 638.

In many traditions, animals were moved through the smoke of the burning log or over the coals to purify and banish illness. It was also custom for people to jump over the fire to promote fertility and become invigorated with the magick of the element.

In Germanic lands, Yule was a celebration of fertility as well as a festival of the dead and, in many ways, was similar to the themes of Samhain. Stags and goats were associated with the time and pigs were sacrificed to the Norse god, Freyr, whose army of spirits flew through the air lead by Odin on his magickal horse. Odin distributed gifts at this time as symbols of hope. Another gift-giver associated with the season was the Germanic agricultural witch goddess Frau Holle,[283] another weaver deity. She rode the skies in a wagon giving gifts to the good and bathing in a fountain from which children were born.

The new religion, Christianity, dated the birth of their solar god Christ at Yule to coincide with pagan celebrations. Christmas customs adapted pagan symbolism to present day with the tree lights that were once candles, the virgin birth, the wreath, bells, the Druid's sacred mistletoe, holly, and the tree.

Symbolically the winter solstice speaks of wonder and hope, the light, the dark, and the rebirth that always follows the pain of an ending. It is a time of rebirth, marking a turning point of the seasons.

The solar god's power is now on the rise, bringing light and promise of warmth. The seeds within the Earth feel the force of his magick and begin to stir.

Symbols, Charms, and Plants of the Winter Solstice

Apple: Associated with winter solstice deities Baldur and Frigg. Apple trees grow next to the sacred oak on which the mistletoe grows.

Candle and Lights: Symbol of the sun and the Solar God.

Firs *(Abies)*, **Pines** *(Pinus spp.)*, **Spruces** *(Picea)*: Symbols of new growth.

Gifts: Symbol of hope. Offerings.

Holly *(Ilex aquifolium)*: Home for nature spirits and for wishes.

Mistletoe *(Viscum album)*: Symbol of fertility. The druids believed that mistletoe should be gathered in white cloth and should never touch the Earth.

Pinecones: Symbol of regeneration.

---

283. Monaghan, *The New Book of Goddesses and Heroines*, 127.

Tree: The connection between the three realms: Sky, Earth, and the Underworld.

Wreath: Symbol of the Wheel of the Year.

Yew *(Taxus baccata)*: The "tree of death" dedicated to the death of the Sun on the 23rd of December in Irish folklore.

Yule Log: The fire of purification and protection. The log is an imitational sun charm, an enactment of sympathetic magick assisting the Sun through the longest night.

Winter Solstice Altar

During the creation of your altar, you will make a sun charm and wreath. You may wish to prepare a few days before the solstice. The altar will manifest within the circle of spell.

Purpose: Your altar is to be dedicated to the birth of the Sun God; radiant, life-affirming, and powerful. It is a celebration of the sun's rebirth, the waxing light and warmth. It expresses waking from sleep, rising from hardship, and "seeing" the light in the dark. The creation and energy of your altar calls you to endure, believe, and embrace hope.

When to create your altar: In the time leading up to the winter solstice so the altar is complete before the sabbat.

You will need: Your witch's tools. Water in your chalice. A red candle, of any size for the charm-making. An orange candle, of any size, for the spell to come. Container of salt.

Incense blend of five parts frankincense (*Boswellia carterii*), three parts clove (*Eugenia caryophyllus, Syzygium aromaticum,* or *Caryophyllus aromaticus*), and two parts dried orange peel (*Citrus sinensis*). Self-igniting charcoal. You will burn this blend again during the winter solstice spell.

Philtre of eight drops of bergamot (*Mentha citrata*), five of frankincense (*Boswellia carterii*), and three of pine essential oils (*Pinus spp.*) in a teaspoon of almond oil (*Prunus dulcis*). Place in a small bowl or container and swirl. Winter plants and branches to create a wreath. A ball of string, bells, or ribbons to create the wreath.

A symbolic yule log. This can be a piece of natural wood or a branch. Pinecones.

Self-hardening clay to create a sun-charm. Watercolour paints of red, yellow, and orange. Small paint brush. Toothpicks or pins to represent the sun's rays are optional. Witch's utensils.

Position your witch's tools, candles, censer and incense blend, philtre, plants, and symbolic items creatively on the altar.

Begin with ingredients before you. Become the witch and create the magick of the winter solstice.

1. Raise your wand as you say:

   "I invoke the gods of the sun, shine strong in my
   heart as I cast a circle of light."
   Imagine the circle.

2. Light the candle and the charcoal. Add the incense blend.

3. With the branches and plants, fashion a circle using the string to fasten it together. Decorate with ribbon and bells.

4. Make a ball with clay by rolling it between your palms. Paint it with the colours of the sun. If you wish, push pins or toothpicks partially into it to create symbolic rays. Paint the toothpicks if you wish. You may need to wait for the paint to dry. If so, re-cast your circle when you return to the altar.

5. To charge the wreath and sun-charm, move them both through the candle flame and incense smoke three times. Then sprinkle with water and salt three times.

6. Rub the philtre into the wood of your yule log and on the pinecones.

7. Place the wreath, pinecone, yule log, and sun charm in the centre of the altar.

8. Decorate with flowers, plants, and any symbolic items.

9. When you are finished, move your wand over the altar to dissolve your circle.

On the night of the sabbat of the winter solstice, you will anoint your solstice candle at your altar. You will also leave a written charm outside.

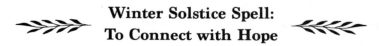

Winter Solstice Spell: To Connect with Hope

Purpose: This candle-anointing spell will give rise to a deep understanding that any hardship can be transformed. Bring to the spell any unwanted energy you wish to change. As you create the magick, a mystical vision of the future will birth. When you see the flame, fill your mind with its light and embrace hope.

When to cast: On the night of the winter solstice.

Where to cast: Indoors at your altar or outside under the sky.

You will need: Altar items and ingredients as prepared. Two small pieces of paper (3 in. x 3 in. or 7c m x 7 cm). String (9 in. or 22 cm). Three pins.

Create the spell at your altar. As the witch, prepare to connect with the dying sun.

1. Hold your wand outright and turn, casting a "circle of golden light" around you.

2. Ignite the charcoal and add a pinch of incense.

3. Dedicate the candle to the illumination of Light within you and to symbolically assist the sun through the longest night. Carve the word LIGHT into the wax.

4. Anoint the candle with the philtre. Starting in the middle, circle the candle with oil then cover it from middle to the top. Then cover the bottom half of the candle with the philtre.

5. Insert the three pins into the middle of the candle. Each time you do, say:

   "From dark to light."

6. Set the unlit candle in its holder.

7. Write your hardships and worries on one of the pieces of paper. Then write your hopes on the other piece of paper. Roll the two papers with string and fastened with eight knots. With the philtre on your finger, anoint the paper three times.

8. Light the candle and imagine light filling your heart.

9. Move your written charm of hardships and hope through the elements: the flame, incense smoke, water, and over the plants of the wreath.

10. Leave your written charm outside under the darkness of night to gather the morning dew of the sun's rebirth at dawn.

11. When you are finished, dissolve your "circle of golden light" into your heart.

12. When you leave the room, snuff out the candle.

After the spell: Bring your written charm inside the next day and leave on your altar. The following night relight any remaining candle and then every night until it is finished. The night following the solstice, burn the written spell on the flame (use another candle if needed). Place water and any used salt on the Earth. Anoint your heart every day with the remaining philtre until it is gone. Compost the flowers when it is time. Keep your yule log for next year or burn on a fire.

The sun's light is now waxing, taking you towards the energy of promise and cleansing.

Imbolc

Meaning "in the belly" or "in milk"
Also known as Candlemas and Imbolg
Season: Winter
Northern Hemisphere: Eve of Imbolc,
February 1 at moonrise until February 2

Southern Hemisphere: Eve of Imbolc,
August 1 at moonrise until August 2

On the Wheel of the Year
The young God sees the Goddess for the first time.
The stirring of passion ignites.
Connect with the Light.
Creativity and passion are liberated.
Renewal is promised.

An Imbolc Story...

By candlelight and with great precision, you fold, loop, and twist a corn-husk to form a splendid poppet. Your poppet represents the young Goddess, found in the new life of spring.

As you weave away, your mind is filled with a memory of yesterday when you saw someone who you can't stop thinking about. This someone makes you feel as warm as the sun. You only saw this person once, but everything changed from that moment. You breathe this memory onto the poppet, then move it over the warmth of a candle flame and then through smouldering rose petals and copal. You sprinkle the poppet with water, then with salt. With milk, you anoint the poppet's head. And then your own.

Suddenly the poppet wakes. It jumps out of your hand and dashes through an open window. You chase the charm of corn through the city streets to a park. The moon begins to rise. The poppet runs towards a fountain and then, as if bewitched, it dives straight into the water and disappears through a door of silver coins.

You follow into the water and through the door. Once inside you are dressed as a bride. Fruit grows in your belly, vines are where your clothes once were, and a spider's web is a shimmering veil over your head.

You call goodbye to what was dying within you as you travel into a state of falling in love.

Imbolc marks the first signs of spring as new growth emerges from the Earth. In ancient Europe this time was a celebration of light, acknowledging the return of the sun and promise of abundance. To lure the warmth of the sun, circles of candles called sun-wheels were lit. This charm represented the Wheel of the Year, the return of the sun, and the enduring power of light.

In the Celtic world, Imbolc honoured Brigid whose name means "bright one." She was a tri-fold deity, but unlike other Triple Goddesses she wasn't depicted as embodiments of the three stages of age. Instead, she was the divine embodiment of the arts of poetry, smithcraft, and healing. This ancient Irish goddess was later renamed Saint Brigid under the new religion.[284] The origins of Brigid are thought to go back to 3000 BCE where she was spring goddess in association with Cailleach, the ancient pre-Celtic hag goddess of the winter solstice.[285]

Brigid as divine artist gives rise to the creativity within. She brings illumination to ignite the divine spark that initiates all artistic projects. She shows the way with spiritual light to "see" truth and to gain awareness of self.

Express the art within your soul and never judge it. Notice the signs of prophesy in the everyday. Hear messages in the songs of birds, scry the weather and the cloud formations in the sky.

As goddess of smithcraft, Brigid is the forger of spiritual weapons, directional tools, arrows, and spears. She presides over the binding and restoring of things. The cauldron of Brigid is the vessel of alchemy where metals are liquefied and manifested into objects both practical and magickal.

Feel the yearning in your spirit to manifest ideas and conjure magick to protect your own energy. Remain centred and strong and know you create your life through every choice and action. Restore what is broken and design a spiritual weapon of protection. Create each step in the imagination and it will awake in the greater world. Past experience and old energy can transform at Imbolc. It is true, the past has brought you to where you are. The past is part of you, belonging to your story and may never be forgotten; however, there is a time when it needs to evolve and move from the shadows into the light.

Brigid raises the power to heal through the purification of the fire element. She embodies the magick of new growth, fertility, and conception. A sheaf of oats was dressed as a woman and placed in a "Brigid's bed" alongside a block

---

284. Farrar, *The Witches' Goddess*, 32, 33.
285. Monaghan, *The New Book of Goddesses and Heroines*, 74.

of wood.[286] With incantations to Brigid during this ancient ritual, the god was invoked to "impregnate the doll" that was symbolic of the fertile earth and the Goddess herself. Similarly corn and grain poppets were created in Northern Europe as fertility charms and dressed as a waiting bride at Imbolc. They symbolize her eventual union with the God and divine conception.

At Imbolc, a cross, created out of rushes, was dedicated to Brigid. This charm invoked her protection and was hung in the home. The cross from the previous year was never thrown away. Instead, it was burnt to unite it with the energy of purification.

The witch's besom symbolically sweeps away the old at Imbolc. With the coming of warmth and light, it is time to purify the home and unburden the mind of the past. As the home is a reflection of the mind, it accumulates energy in the physical and stores experience. With the coming of spring, "sweeping" your home energetically prepares your mind for a new way of thinking.

Imbolc calls you from the retreat of winter and asks you to replenish and banish the outmoded and all that hinders your creativity. It is a celebration of light and aligns you with the start of Nature's rise towards the sun. It is a time to open the mind to inspiration, to be creative, romantic, and to purify, cleanse, and banish the old.

Symbols, Charms, and Plants of Imbolc

Besom: Symbolic of "sweeping out" old energy.

Brigid's Cross: A charm to protect the home.

Corn Dollies or Poppets: Represents the fertile young Goddess representing growth and the future and the old Goddess representing decline and the past.

Milk: Symbolising the nurture of life.

Sun Wheels: Representing the return of the Sun.

---

286. Frazer, *The Golden Bough: A Study in Magic and Religion*, 134.

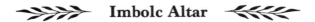 **Imbolc Altar**

During the creation of your altar you will make two corn dollies. You may wish to prepare a few days before Imbolc. The altar will manifest within the circle of spell.

Purpose: Your altar is to be dedicated to the Goddess Brigid—to restoration, artistry, and growth. It will reflect the vision and inspiration needed for a fulfilling, creative life. Your altar will remind you that, like the Goddess Brigid, you are able to unite all aspects of yourself and shine brightly.

When to create your altar: In the time leading to Imbolc, so the altar is complete before the sabbat. The sabbat begins at moonrise on the eve.

You will need: Your witch's tools. Water in your chalice. Eight yellow candles (free-standing, approximately 1.5 in. x 1.5 in. or 4 cm x 4 cm). The candles need to be positioned in a circle, so consider standing them on a large plate. Container of salt. Incense blend of five parts copal (*Bursera odorata, B. fugaroides*), three parts rose resin (*Rosa spp.*), and two parts lavender (*Lavandula officinalis* or *L. vera*). Self-igniting charcoal. You will burn this blend again during the Imbolc spell. Philtre of five drops of clary sage oil (*Salvia sclarea*) in a teaspoon of almond oil (*Prunus dulcis*). Place in a small bowl or container and swirl. Flowers, fruits, and herbs of the season. Two corncobs with husks. A ball of string. A small bowl of any type of seeds. Witch's utensils.

On the day of Imbolc, a bowl of milk (vegan milk can be used). This is an offering to the Goddess and a symbol of life. Position your witch's tools, candles, censer and incense blend, philtre, plants, and symbolic items creatively on the altar.

Begin with ingredients before you. Become the witch and create the magick of Imbolc.

1. Raise your chalice as you say:

   "I invoke the Goddess Brigid to heal and restore
   what is broken, whisper my life's poem, as I cast a
   circle of light." Imagine the circle.

2. Remove the husks from the corncobs. Using your imagination and the husk, begin to fashion a figure representing
   the Crone Goddess of winter. Start by folding the husk to
   make a head. Tie string around the husk to create the head
   and body. Gather some husks together and create the arms
   by positioning the husk horizontally below the "neck" of the
   dolly. Create a dress beneath the arms and hold together with
   string. You can use any part of the corn in the creation.

3. Next create a figure of the Young Goddess using the same
   method.

4. Place the two corn dollies in a circle of leaves and fruit.

5. When you are finished, move your chalice over the altar to
   dissolve your circle.

On the day or night of the sabbat of Imbolc, you will create a spell at your altar.
The sabbat begins at moonrise on the eve.

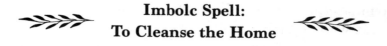

Imbolc Spell: To Cleanse the Home

Purpose: When you create this spell, you will refresh your home
and your spirit with new energy. You will dispel old energy, invigorate your home with a magickal vibration, renew, and heal it. Your
home reflects your own energy. It also influences, seeps, and holds
on to the past. When you cleanse the energy in your home, you set
the foundation for the future.

When to cast: On Imbolc. During the day.

Where to cast: Begin at your altar and then through every room of your home.

You will need: Altar items and ingredients as prepared.

Create the spell at your altar. As the witch, prepare to connect with the energy of home and cleansing.

1. Hold your pentacle to your heart and imagine your home is surrounded by a "circle of flowers" that reach to the sky.

2. Anoint your heart and the bottom of your feet with the philtre.

3. Light the charcoal and add incense. Carry the incense into every room. Imagine the old energy leaving with the scent of the incense.

4. Move your besom through the incense smoke. Then, ringing the bell, go into every room with the incense. Speak this incantation in each room:

   "By the power of my witch's broom and bell, the old is taken by the wind and the new comes in."

5. Return to the altar and light the eight candles.

6. Move the crone corn dolly through the incense smoke and over the warmth of the eight flames. Sprinkle with water from your chalice and then salt. Say:

   "The past is blessed."

7. Repeat the same blessing with the young corn dolly, except instead of using salt sprinkle her with seeds. Say:

   "The future is blessed."

8. When you are finished, hold your pentacle to your heart and see your "circle of flowers" fading.

9. When you leave the room, snuff the candles.

Figure 9: Corn Dolly

After the spell: Leave the corn dollies on the altar until the spring equinox. Relight any remaining candles over the following days in honour of the Goddess Brigid. Place the milk, water, any used salt, and charcoal ash on the Earth. Anoint your heart every day with the remaining philtre until it is gone. Compost the flowers when it is time. Cook and eat the corn as you imagine your body, heart, and mind healing.

The foundation for growth and renewal has been created. Now what is new is seen and begins to take form. From beneath the surface of incubation, ideas and new energy appear, turning the wheel of change.

Spring Equinox: Ostara
Also known as Vernal Equinox
Season: Spring
Northern Hemisphere: March 21–23
Southern Hemisphere: September 21–23

On the Wheel of the Year
The young Goddess and God are in the raptures of desire and attraction.
Contemplate beginnings and renewal.
True beauty and desire are liberated.

A Spring Equinox Story …

You wake in the burrow, deep in the Earth. A dream familiar, a doe rabbit has been guarding you while you were asleep. You shake the dirt from your hair and follow the doe to her litter of baby kits. They have no fur and smell like sweet earth and blood. The waxing moon has spun her spell over the kits. They will soon rise with the dawn, eyes like saucers, ears moving with the wild, hearts forever beating with the Great Mother.

At the spring equinox, day and night are equal. It is a time when light and dark are balanced. Now the theme of fertility that began at Imbolc becomes divine resurrection as waking seedlings appear on the surface of the Earth.

Life flourishes and is encapsulated in the symbol of the Egg, the motif of the equinox. The story of the World Egg or Cosmic Egg is primordial. In many myths, the Great Mother took the form of an egg. Leto, the Greek Mother

Goddess, birthed the moon and sun from the Egg.[287] In Egypt, a celestial goose laid an egg containing a solar bird whose heat manifested the world.[288] In Greek mythology, the Orphic Egg hatched Phanes, the deity of new life, and creator of other gods.[289] This is a universal story. Did our ancestors hear the whispering wind speak of the stories of other lands or did the story well within the human psyche, the one myth connecting humanity as one family? So too the story tells of a waterbird in Africa, as well as the Arctic lands, that laid an egg from which all life came.

The spring equinox is known by the modern witch as the festival of Ostara, though there is no definite knowledge as to whether this goddess was celebrated at this time in ancient Europe. However, this goddess embodies the magick of spring and has come to personify the season. So the sabbat of the spring equinox has been named Ostara, after the Germanic goddess of spring and fertility. Her name means "movement towards the rising sun"[290] so she is also a deity of the dawn and therefore beginnings. Her name is also connected to and may have originated from the eastern goddesses Astarte and Ishtar,[291] deities associated, like Ostara, with sexuality and therefore fertility.

Ostara's Anglo-Saxon name is Eostre, the origin of the word Easter, another celebration of resurrection. Easter shows its pagan roots and remains dated, according to the lunar calendar, as the first Sunday after the full moon following the equinox. Ostara's familiar was the hare, a creature spellbound by the moon's bewitching powers. According to the myth, Ostara's hare laid eggs and painted them to impress the goddess.[292] This magick familiar lives on through the incarnation of the Easter Bunny. At the spring equinox, eggs were planted in the fields to encourage the growth of the crops and were eaten to connect with the magick of fertility.

Painted eggs, as symbols of life, precedes this myth into antiquity and are found in the worship of the Bird Goddess. From the Palaeolithic period, depictions of the goddess as a bird, sometimes half-human with a bird's long neck or

---

287. Monaghan, *The New Book of Goddesses and Heroines*, 194.

288. Cooper, *An Illustrated Encyclopedia of Traditional Symbols*, 75.

289. Willis, ed. *World Mythology: The Illustrated Guide*, 128.

290. Monaghan, *The New Book of Goddesses and Heroines*, 241.

291. Farrar, *The Witches' Goddess*, 218.

292. McCoy, *Sabbats: A Witch's Approach to Living the Old Ways*, 111.

beak, or depicted with an egg in the womb, have endured and speak of life originating from the goddess and encapsulated in the form of an egg. This symbol comes to you from a time 25,000 years ago.[293] It has prevailed through distant Sumeria, Egypt, and Crete and the ancient lands of Europe to this day and reminds you that life is a divine creation and is sacred.

So the symbol of the egg, now waiting in the womb of the young Goddess, returns at Ostara as the Wheel of the Year brings in spring. From their first glance at Imbolc, the God and Goddess now meet as equals at the spring equinox. Their unrelenting desire stirs. Both youthful and vibrant, their passion and beauty are expressed in nature's movement and rise from the earth. At the equinox, fertility, the moon, and life entwine, reminding you of perpetual change, the need to connect with lost-youth, and to hold the dawn of each day close to the heart as a new beginning.

Symbols, Charms, and Plants of the Spring Equinox

Egg: Symbol of life and beginnings.

Flowers of the Season: The embodiment of growth and beauty.

Lily of the Valley *(Convallaria majalis)*: The flower dedicated to Ostara. It was customary to throw lily of the valley into the bonfire as an offering in Germanic tradition.

Rabbit: Symbol of fertility and moon magick.

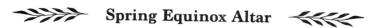 **Spring Equinox Altar**

During the creation of your altar you will decorate an egg as an offering to spring and new beginnings. You may wish to prepare a few days before the equinox. The altar will manifest within the circle of spell.

Purpose: Your altar is to be dedicated to the goddess, Ostara, to new life, opportunity, and the ever-changing moon. The altar will express the beauty and fertility of the Earth. After your Imbolc cleansing, call into your home the energy of newness and manifestation. Your

---

293. Baring and Cashford, *The Myth of the Goddess*, 59.

altar celebrates growth, the birth of creation around and within you. It will inspire the dawn of potential.

When to create your altar: In the time leading to the spring equinox, so the altar is complete before the sabbat.

You will need: Your witch's tools. Water in the chalice. White, yellow, and green candles of any size. Container of salt. Incense blend of five parts mugwort (*Artemisia vulgaris*), three parts benzoin (genus *Styrax*), and two parts sandalwood (*Santalum album*). Self-igniting charcoal. You will burn this blend again during the Ostara spell. Philtre of eight drops of jasmine (*Jasminum grandiflorum, J. officinale,* or *J. odoratissimum*) and three drops of lime essential oil (*Citrus aurantifolia* or *L. Limetta*) in a teaspoon of almond oil (*Prunus dulcis*). Place in a small bowl or container and swirl. Flowers, fruits, and herbs of the season. An egg (if vegan you can make a clay egg or draw an egg on paper). Watercolour paints of all colours and a small brush (you may need a rag and some extra water). Moonstone, selenite, and rose quartz crystals to connect with moon magick and the heart. Your Imbolc corn dollies. Witch's utensils. Position your witch's tools, candles, censer and incense blend, philtre, plants, and symbolic items creatively on the altar.

Begin with ingredients before you. Become the witch and create the magick of Ostara.

1. Raise your pentacle as you say:

    "I invoke Ostara and her familiar hare. Bless my life with true beauty and moon-struck wonder as I cast a circle of light."

    Imagine the circle.

2. Ignite the charcoal and add a pinch or two of incense blend.

3. Anoint your heart with the philtre.

4. Move the egg three times through the incense smoke. Begin to paint it, creating an offering to Ostara.

5. With the crystals, flowers, plants, and fruit, create a circle and place the egg inside it.

6. When you are finished, move your pentacle over the altar to dissolve your circle.

On the day of the sabbat of Ostara, you will create a spell at your altar.

 ## Spring Equinox Spell: To Invoke Abundance and Potential

Purpose: This spell will invoke newness and fertility of body, mind, and heart. Fertility expands beyond procreation. It is expansive thinking, an open heart, and a free spirit. The magick you create will align you with the energy of creativity, purpose, and authenticity, and with this power comes a new beginning.

When to cast: At the spring equinox. During the day.

Where to cast: Indoors at your altar or outside under the sky.

You will need: Altar items and ingredients as prepared. A sewing needle to carve the candles.

Create the spell at your altar. As the witch prepare to connect with new beginnings.

1. Hold your chalice skyward and imagine a "circle of moons" descending from the sky. The moons surround you.

2. Anoint your heart and hands with the philtre.

3. Ignite the charcoal and add a pinch or two of incense blend.

4. On the white candle carve three 3's for *creation*.

5. On the yellow candle carve the four triangle symbols of the elements for *life*.

6. On the green candle carve a circle for *spirit*.

7. Place the candles in their holders and light.

8. Hold the egg to your heart. Imagine it cracking open. What do you see?

9. Move the egg through the three candle flames and the incense smoke three times. Sprinkle it with water and then touch it with a flower.

10. Now breathe onto the egg and say:

> "By Ostara, the moon, dawn and the rabbit,
> Bless thoughts, my heart on the eve of the sabbat.
> By growth in the earth.
> By all creature's birth.
> I pray to the trees.
> The sun and the seas."

11. Ring the bell over your circle altar.

12. When you are finished, imagine your "circle of moons" fading into the dark of night.

13. When you leave the room, snuff out the candles.

After the spell: Three days after Ostara, bury your egg in the Earth. If any of the candles remain, relight over the following days until they are finished. Place water and any used salt on the Earth. Anoint your heart every day with the remaining philtre until it is gone. Compost the flowers when it is time. Keep your corn dollies for Lammas or remove the string and compost or bury.

The energy of renewal and change heightens you towards a reckoning of magickal energies at Beltane.

Beltane
Name meaning: Bel-fire
Also known as Walpurgis Night
Season: Spring
Northern Hemisphere: Eve of Beltane at moonrise on April 30
Southern Hemisphere: Eve of Beltane at moonrise on October 31

On the Wheel of the Year
The God and Goddess become lovers.
Manifests your dreams and passions.
See love and romance in all things.

A Beltane Story…

As you climb out of the burrow you notice a shadow moving through the trees in the distance. The night wind is warm and dries the dirt on your skin. Will-o'-the-wisps beckon you to enter a nearby forest. Owls talk to the moon through their silent flight. You feel your heart move in your chest, feel the moss on the forest floor. You smell pine and animals.

Ahead a figure dances with the shadows of the trees. You see him in the clearing, moving in his circle. The trees whisper to him, "She has arrived." They whisper to you, "He has arrived."

You enter the circle to dance with him on this warm, warm night.

On the eve of Beltane, Druidic fires burnt on hillsides followed by great ceremony. In Germanic folklore it was *Walpurgis* Night when witches took to their broomsticks to congregate and feast on a high mountain peak called Mount Brocken. In Norway, old brooms were burnt in bonfires and new ones were brought into the home. In Slavic countries, healing wreaths were thrown into fires as a purification rite.

Beltane was a celebration of sexuality and pleasure. Now the God and Goddess finally consummate desire. Their divine conception embodied in the fertility of the future harvest. So, at the height of Earth's beauty and abundance the theme of the season became love, sensuality, and joy.

In Rome, and then in Britain, the ancient goddess, Flora, was celebrated with garlands and dancing on the 1st of May. She was the patron of the flowering Earth so embodied the procreation power of plants and also of humans. In her myth, Flora brought flowers to the world through her love with the wind Zephyrus.[294] Her festival preceded the Celtic Beltane and celebrated the female body as well as sexual promiscuity. At Floralia, people adorned themselves, their

294. Murray, *Who's Who in Mythology: A Classic Guide to the Ancient World*, 131.

homes, and even their animals with flowers. There was dancing and an atmosphere of sensuality.

Celebrations on the 1ˢᵗ of May throughout Northern Europe depicted the union of the Goddess and the God with representatives called the May Queen and King. The couple lead processions wearing crowns of flowers and carrying symbols of the earth. The May King was the personification of Nature and was known as Jack-in-the-Green or Green Man, an entity that may have descended from the ancient vegetation gods of Mesopotamia, Dumuzi and Tammuz, and the Greek god, Attis.[295]

A maypole, often a pine, the tree of Attis, was erected to symbolise the sexual power embodied in these fertility gods and was a central motif of Beltane. This phallic shape planted into Mother Earth was crowned with red ribbons for the Goddess and white for the God. Erected in Celtic and Germanic villages, it represented the thrust of the season. Men and women held the ribbons and danced, interweaving as an enactment of the divine union.

The Phoenician vegetation god Baal[296] and the Norse god, Baldur, were also associated with Beltane as they brought healing and fertility to the land. The Nature god Cerenunnos personified the magick of the wilds. This Celtic Horned God also incarnated into the Green Man, as a personification of the forest. All these nature spirits are associated with the sexual readiness and play of Beltane and exemplify the rapture of the young God for the Goddess.

The Norse goddess, Freya, inspired the procession of a naked "holy bride" on horseback through the streets on May Day. This goddess of spring was the feminine counterpart to the fertile Green Man and represented the goddess Goda, an ancient deity who inspired the story of Lady Godiva.[297] In May Day processions, the Godiva followed the black hag, Annis, representing the passing of winter.[298]

It was customary to visit holy wells and leave offerings of coins at Beltane. The water from the wells, along with morning dew, was thought to enhance beauty and young girls washed their faces with it.

---

295. Baring and Cashford, *The Myth of the Goddess*, 411.

296. Frazer, *The Golden Bough: A Study in Magic and Religion*, 619.

297. Barbara G. Walker, *The Woman's Encyclopedia of Myths and Secrets* (San Francisco: Harper-Collins, 1985), 347.

298. Farrar, *The Witches' Goddess*, 224.

With the rise of nature's power, the faery folk were out in force and bells were rung to deter the fae from meddling with the human world. Like Samhain, the proximity of the human and divine world grew closer at Beltane. According to Celtic legend, ghosts could be seen on May Day and English fishermen refused to look into the sea in case they saw the dead.

The Celtic faery queen Rhiannon also presided over Beltane and rode her magnificent horse through the night, bewitching humans and luring them into the land of the fae. Rowan and larch trees were used as protective charms against the heightened magick of the faeries. Primroses were also made into charms and hung over the threshold and in Ireland the plant was tied to cow's tails to deflect mischievous magick.

The sabbat of Beltane is a time to be free from worry and to embrace romance, mischief, and love. Light and growth return to the planet and to your heart and mind.

Symbols, Charms, and Plants of Beltane

Bells: Rung for protection and purification.

Faeries: The boundary between the two worlds blurs.

Larch *(Larix)* **and Rowan Trees** *(Sorbus subg. Sorbus)*: To protect against faeries.

Maypole: Symbol of fertility. The phallic shape and the fertile earth are unified.

Morning Dew: For inner beauty.

Primrose *(Primula vulgaris)*: Dispels the mischief of the fae.

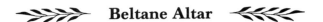 ## Beltane Altar

During the creation of your altar, you will deem two candles symbolic of the Goddess and the God. You will also make a faery pouch. You may wish to prepare a few days before Beltane. The altar will manifest within the circle of spell.

Purpose: Your altar is to be dedicated to the young Goddess and God, to pleasure, sensuality, and the faery realm. It is an expression of passion, union, and creation. The altar acknowledges that pleasure and play are magickal energies needed within you and in your home. The altar is a shrine to the invisible forces of attraction that create life, the god and goddess aspects of yourself, and the power of desire found between people, invention, and the arts. The faery pouch is an invitation to the fae into your home.

When to create your altar: In the time leading to Beltane so the altar is complete before the sabbat. The sabbat begins at moonrise on the eve.

You will need: Your witch's tools. Water in your chalice. One red candle and one pink candle wide enough to stand alone (approximately 2–3 in. or 5–8 cm wide). The candles represent the god and goddess (it is up to you which colour you chose for each deity). Container of salt. An incense blend of three parts frankincense (*Boswellia carterii*), two parts rose petals (*Rosa spp.*), two parts patchouli (*Pogostemon cablin* or *P. patchouli*), one part orris (*Iris germanica var. florentina*), one part sandalwood (*Santalum album*), and one part thyme (*Thymus vulgaris*). Self-igniting charcoal. You will burn this blend again during the Beltane spell. Philtre of ten drops of patchouli (*Pogostemon cablin* or *P. patchouli*), five drops of rose (*Rosa spp.*), and three drops of clary sage (*Salvia sclarea*) essential oils in a teaspoon of almond oil (*Prunus dulcis*). Place in a small bowl or container and swirl. Gather for charm pouch: three parts Rue (*Ruta graveolens*), three parts rose (*Rosa spp.*), two parts sandalwood (*Santalum album*), and two parts vervain (*Verbena officinalis*). Gather a flower for each deity. Red thread. A cloth pouch (around 3 in. x 5 in. or 7 cm x 12 cm, though the size is up to you). Witch's utensils. Position your witch's tools, candles, censer and incense blend, philtre, plants, and symbolic items creatively on the altar.

Begin with ingredients before you. Become the witch and create the magick of Beltane.

1. Ring your bell as you say:

   "I invoke the deities of love and delight. Let me feel your kiss as I cast a circle of light."

   Imagine the circle. Say:

   "Beauty and love from the heavens bind."

2. Place the herbs and most of the philtre into the mortar. Leave a little of the philtre for heart anointing. Breathe onto the blend. Then ring the bell over the mortar and say:

"By all the dreams that children make,
Good faeries of Beltane awake!"

3. Using the pestle, spend time grinding the mix together.

4. Place the blend into the pouch and fasten.

5. Position the two candles on the plate. With the thread create a figure 8 around them so each candle stands in one of the loops.

6. Position your chalice by the goddess candle and your athame by the god candle.

7. Place each flower in front of each candle and place your faery pouch in front of the plate.

8. Decorate the altar with flowers and any symbols of love you wish to add.

9. When you are finished, ring your bell over the altar to dissolve your circle.

On the day of the sabbat of Beltane you will create a spell at your altar.

Beltane Spell: To Activate Deep Love

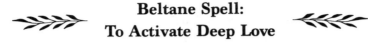

Purpose: This spell invokes the powerful energies of creativity and action within you. It will activate love in you and therefore attract it to you. It will imbue your energy field with true beauty. This spell is not about forcing energy; it is an act of surrendering to self-worth, wildness, and love for life itself. This spell can be created for romantic love, self-love, and activating any attraction magick for creative purposes.

When to cast: At Beltane. Day or night.

Where to cast: Indoors at your altar or outside under the sky.

You will need: Altar items and ingredients as prepared. Also bring two pins to the spell.

Create the spell at your altar. As the witch prepare to connect with deep passion for life.

1. Ignite the charcoal. Add a pinch of the incense blend.

2. Holding the censer, turn, allowing the incense smoke to cast your circle. Say:

   "I hear the voice of the divine in the wind."

3. Breathe onto each candle.

4. Insert a pin into the centre of the god candle as you imagine the sun in your mind.

5. Insert a pin into the centre of the goddess candle as you imagine the moon in your heart.

6. Hold the candles together and from bottom to top weave the thread around both so they hold together. When you are finished, stand them in place on the plate.

7. Light each flame as you say:

   "I surrender to the power of love and passion within.
   To become both god and goddess, both sun and moon."

8. Ring the bell over the altar, hold your love pouch, and inhale the scent as you feel the presence of the deities near.

9. Hold your athame and place the blade into the chalice to enact the union of the god and goddess. Repeat this three times.

10. When you are finished, hold the athame and chalice skyward and say:

    "I return my circle to the realm of the divine."

11. Snuff out the candles when you leave the room.

After the spell: If any of the candles remain, relight in the future in honour of the god and goddess. Keep the fallen pins for other charms to carry with them the energy of love. Place water and any used salt on the Earth. Anoint your heart every day with the remaining philtre until it is gone. Compost the flowers when it is time. Place the pouch in your bed to invoke love and divine dreaming.

The power of the sun rises, the days become longer as light guides you towards the summer solstice.

Summer Solstice: Litha
Also known as Midsummer
Season: Summer
Northern Hemisphere: Begins on Midsummer's Eve, June 21–23
Southern Hemisphere: Begins on Midsummer's Eve, December 21–23

On the Wheel of the Year
The Goddess is pregnant and the God is in his prime.
Open your mind to magickal illumination.
The passage of rebirth waits in the heart and mind.

A Midsummer Story…

Wheels of fire roll, sparkling and roaring with might towards a distant river. You are running with them. The sun is magnificent today. The colours of the landscape rich. The scent of Nature exhilarating. You feel the warm earth under your feet. You are in love and every part of you is alive, light, and radiant.

The summer solstice marks the longest day of the year and is both a fire and a water festival. It is a turning point of the season. The solstice celebrates the sun's magnificence before its light begins to wane. *Litha* is a modern name given to this sabbat and may have come from the Anglo-Saxon name *"lida"* meaning moon.[299]

As a celebration of Light, the God was honoured throughout Europe with magickal enactments involving fire. To imitate the sun and invoke the element's power, bonfires were lit on the high peaks. Blazing discs of wood were hurled through the air and torches were carried into the fields. Huge fire-wheels rolled down hillsides into waterways over Europe.[300] This mirrored the heightened force of the sun before its decline towards autumn.

In Germany, crowns of mugwort (*Artemisia vulgaris*) and vervain (*Verbena officinalis*) were worn and then thrown into a fire to invoke good fortune.[301] Ash and wood from the Midsummer fires was used to rekindle the hearth and invigorate homes with the sun's magick. Ash was spread through the fields as a fertility rite, mirroring the same ritual at the winter solstice.

Midsummer fires were jumped over for good luck, and animals and people moved through the smoke for purification. This same practice took place in North Africa at the solstice where fires were scented with fennel, rue, chervil-seed, chamomile, geranium, and pennyroyal and were also burnt to promote fertility, good fortune, and healing.[302]

As Midwinter heralds the birth of the sun, Midsummer speaks of the Sun's decline. The story of Midsummer was often told through the mock sacrifice of a god or nature spirit. In myth, Hercules was sacrificed at this seasonal gateway and his blood scattered to fertilise the earth. In Norway, the Midsummer fires were called "Baldur's Fires" and renamed "St. John's Fires" by the new religion.[303] An effigy of Baldur was set ablaze, symbolising the dying Sun to be reborn at the winter solstice. Huge human-like figures called *wickermen, tatermanns, lotters, and angelmen* were set alight throughout Europe.[304] These effigies represented nature entities like the Green Man and the now-defeated Oak King conquered by the victorious Holly King. Their sacrifice marked the waning of light and the death of the sun.

---

299. Grimassi. *Encyclopedia of Wicca and Witchcraft*, 354.

300. Frazer, *The Golden Bough: A Study in Magic and Religion*, 622.

301. Frazer, *The Golden Bough: A Study in Magic and Religion*, 623.

302. Frazer, *The Golden Bough: A Study in Magic and Religion*, 631.

303. Frazer, *The Golden Bough: A Study in Magic and Religion*, 625.

304. Frazer, *The Golden Bough: A Study in Magic and Religion*, 624, 625.

Midsummer fires were also used for love divination and to invoke luck. Girls would throw garlands into the flames for future husbands to retrieve. Special magickal powers were given to the night and it was celebrated with ritual of romance, dream interpretation, more faery banishing, and dancing.

Although the summer solstice foreshadowed the death of the sun, it also held strong to the promise of rebirth. This promise is represented by the Goddess's cauldron, another motif of the sabbat and sacred vessel of the water element.

The cauldron is a symbolic passage of death and rebirth. The same water held in the womb is also held in the cauldron, hence the power of water is akin to new life, healing, and renewal. So at the solstice, morning dew and springs were believed to hold significant enchantment and healing powers.

The summer solstice is a glorious ending to the waxing Sun and the beginning of a magick descent towards deep transformation.

Symbols, Charms, and Plants of the Summer Solstice

Ash Tree *(Fraxinus)*: For protection

Birch *(Betula)*: For predictions of love.

Candles: Element of the Sun.

Cauldron: Symbol of the passage of life and death. The promise of the future.

Chamomile *(Chamaemelum nobile, Anthemis nobilis)*: Dedicated to Baldur. This plant is used for energetic protection.

Daisy *(Bellis perennis)*: Known as "Baldur's brow" for the joy of the Sun.

Fir *(Abies)*: Symbol of fertility. Once was decorated with eggs at the solstice and danced around.

Four Leaf Clover *(Trifolium)*: Gathered for love at the solstice.

God's Eye Amulet: A traditional indigenous Mexican protective charm.

Hawthorn Tree *(Crataegus)*: Meeting place for faeries at Midsummer, Beltane, and Samhain.

Hazel *(Corylus)*: A divining rod was cut from the hazel tree at the solstice to find buried treasure.

Mistletoe *(Viscum album)*: Mistletoe was cut from the tree at midsummer and used in ritual.

Mugwort *(Artemisia vulgaris)*: Used with vervain *(Verbena officinalis)* to create garlands and burnt for protection, wishes, and prophetic dreams.

Poppy *(Papaver)*: Associated with St. John's flowers for protection.

Protective Amulets: Eyes, hands, and the pentagram.

St. John's Wort *(Hypericum perforatum)*: Hang in the home for protection. Use for predictions and dream magick.

Sun-Wheels: Symbol of the waxing and waning Sun.

Vervain *(Verbena officinalis)*: Traditionally used for Litha garlands and burnt for wishes and protection.

Yew *(Taxus baccata)*: The day of the death of the sun was dedicated to the yew tree.

Summer Solstice Altar

During the creation of your altar you will draw protective talismans on paper. You may wish to prepare a few days before the solstice. The altar will manifest within the circle of spell.

Purpose: Your altar is to be dedicated to both the ultimate power of the solar god as well as his decline. It speaks of energetic protection for the seed of promise, present in the womb of the goddess. Creating a midsummer altar invokes the magick of illumination into your home and heart, urging you to embrace this experience before the light wanes.

When to create your altar: In the time leading up to the summer solstice so the altar is complete before the sabbat.

You will need: Your witch's tools and cauldron of water. Three yellow candles of any size. Container of salt. Incense blend of seven parts mugwort *(Artemisia vulgaris)* and three parts vervain *(Verbena officinalis)*. Self-igniting charcoal. You will burn this blend again during the summer solstice spell. Philtre of ten drops of chamomile *(Chamaemelum nobile, Anthemis nobilis)* and three drops of jasmine essential oil *(Jasminum grandiflorum, J. officinale,* or *J. odoratissimum)* in a teaspoon of olive oil *(Olea europaea L.)*. Place in a small bowl or container and swirl. Flowers, fruits, and herbs of the season. Ten coins, five gold for the sun and five silver for the moon (old coins are good to use). Ten small pieces of paper (3 in. x 3 in. or 7 cm x 7 cm). Watercolour paint or pencils. Witch's utensils.

You will create paper talismans for your altar on or before the sabbat of Litha. Position your witch's tools, candles, censer and incense blend, philtre, plants, and symbolic items creatively on the altar.

Begin with ingredients before you. Become the witch and create the magick of the summer solstice.

1. Raise both your chalice and wand as you say:

    "I invoke the god and the goddess of midsummer.
    Bless my hands and eyes as I cast a circle of light."

    Imagine the circle.

2. Ignite the charcoal and add a pinch or two of incense blend.

3. Place your cauldron of water in the centre of the altar and position the three candles in a triangle space around it. The point of the triangle should be pointing away from you to represent the element fire.

4. With the fruit and the flowers, create a circle around the cauldron and candles.

5. Place three flowers into the cauldron to symbolize life in the womb of the Goddess.

6. With art materials and paper, draw or paint a protective hand or an eye on each. Write a hope or dream on the back of each or a person's name to send love to. Place the drawings around the cauldron and place a coin on each.

7. Move the incense around the altar to purify and bless.

8. When you are finished, move your chalice and your wand over the altar to dissolve your circle.

On the day of the sabbat of the summer solstice you will create a spell at your altar.

Summer Solstice Spell: To Invoke Lightness of Being

Purpose: This spell will help you to embrace a lightness of being and then reflect this light into the world. This midsummer spell is a way to master a brighter outlook and to see all aspects of life as a magickal experience that can take you to a higher perspective of yourself and all around you. This spell also celebrates the promise of tomorrow.

When to cast: At the summer solstice. During the day.

Where to cast: Indoors at your altar or outside under the sky.

You will need: Altar items and ingredients as prepared. A sewing needle for carving.

Create the spell at your altar. As the witch prepare to connect with light and promise.

1. Hold your wand to your heart and imagine a circle of white light around you. Imagine this light fills the circle and like a mystical tunnel it extends into the heavens. In your mind go to where the tunnel ends and "see" what is there. Seek the meaning of what you see.

2. Ignite the charcoal. Add a pinch or two of the incense blend.

3. Move the needle through the incense smoke, then with it carve a sun and your name on each candle. With the philtre on your finger, anoint each candle with a line from middle to top, then middle to the bottom of each.

4. Anoint your heart and back of the neck with the philtre to connect with the energy of the sun.

5. Say:

    "By sunlight bright,
    At one with light.
    By moon glow rise,
    By midnight skies.
    To see my life through witch's eyes."

6. Move each candle through the incense smoke.

7. Light each candle in turn as you imagine light seeping into any doubt or fear within you.

8. When you are finished, breathe into your spirit, the "circle of light."

9. Before you leave the room, snuff out the candles.

After the spell: If any of the candles remain, relight them over the following days in honour of the sun and the pregnant Goddess. After three days, empty the water from the cauldron onto the earth and place the ten coins in your kitchen to attract prosperity. Place any used salt on the Earth. Compost the flowers when it is time.

The sun has reached its full power and is beginning to wane. The pregnant Goddess holds the life of the future in her belly, reminding you of your relationship to earth. She is Mother and you are her child.

Lammas
Also known as Lughnasadh
Season: Summer
Northern Hemisphere: Eve of Lammas,
August 1 at moonrise until August 2
Southern Hemisphere: Eve of Lammas,
February 1 at moonrise until February 2

On the Wheel of the Year
The Mother Goddess still holds life in her womb.
The God enters the Underworld.
Connects with Mother Earth.
All gifts of life are acknowledged.

A Lammas Story...
You light candles and holy incense of frankincense. You hold two fresh cobs of corn. One represents the Goddess of the past. The other is the Goddess of

the future. You whisper to one, "Thank you, Mother." And to the other, "Welcome Sister."

The fae arrive with offerings from their cauldron: a key to a poet's heart, a bewitched hag stone, and an enchanted candle. Together with heavenly weavers, you and the fae bind old mother corn and sister corn together with cobweb threads. As you weave, you thank Mother Earth for your life.

Lammas is a Saxon word meaning "the feast of bread"[305] and was the beginning of the harvest festivals of the Northern Hemisphere, a Christian/pagan merged tradition when bread was offered, often in churches, to petition a blessing of the harvest. Lammas is the name most commonly used for this sabbat. Lughnasadh, another name associated with the sabbat, finds its origins in Lugh, the Celtic sun god who also presided over the arts, poetry, magick, and truth. Lugh lived with the Tuatha Dé Danann, the Irish faery race, and was a consort of the harvest goddess Danu.[306] He is associated with the first sheaf of grain harvested, and his name is thought to be the origin of the word Leprechaun.[307] His festival involved dance, athletic competition, and feasting. Like all the sabbats, the origins of Lammas are complex and a marriage of borrowed seasonal celebrations. However, at Lammas, life, symbolised by the grain, is about blessings, gratitude, and Earth's bounty.

Again, at this sabbat the relationship of beginnings and endings merged in a play of sacred opposites. The bounty of Lammas was entwined again with the symbolic sacrifice of a king, or god, called the Corn King or Corn Spirit. The deity Lugh played this role with his entry into the Underworld. In Egypt, Osiris was a corn god[308] whose dismembered body was scattered over the land to promote fertility. In the ancient Middle East, the sacrificed vegetation gods Tammuz and Dumuzi were mourned for a month after the corn and other crops had been harvested.

---

305. Grimassi, *Encyclopedia of Wicca and Witchcraft*, 227.

306. McCoy, *Sabbats: A Witch's Approach to Living the Old Ways*, 174.

307. Cotterell and Storm, *The Ultimate Encyclopedia of Mythology*, 145.

308. Baring and Cashford, *The Myth of the Goddess*, 389.

Grain and fruits are honoured at Lammas as symbols of life and as gifts from the Corn Mother because life was still in the womb of the Goddess. Her Celtic names were Danu, Mother of the Tuatha Dé Danann, and Bride, a spring/summer goddess, thought to be an earlier version of Brigid. In Greece, she was Demeter, her Great Mysteries, held in August[309] involved offerings of corn and wheat. She was named Grain Mother or Corn Mother and in Rome she was Ceres. In the August solar festivals of America's First Nations, Grand-mother Corn is celebrated.[310]

In Europe, the last sheaf of the harvest at Lammas was invested with powerful magick and was cut ritualistically. Charms called "corn-mothers" represented the old Goddess[311] of the past, and "corn-maidens" were symbolic of the future young Goddess. It was common to drench these corn-charms in water to invoke rain. Sometimes they were fed to livestock for fertility. In spring, they were buried in the field or burnt, and their ashes scattered as a fertility rite.

In Scotland the "corn-maiden" was dressed as a bride and a "corn-groom" accompanied her. Sometimes "corn-mother" and "corn-maiden" were made and bound together unifying the old with the new. These charms were sometimes made from other crops and called "Wheat-Mother" or "Barley-Mother." In Peru, "Maize-Mother" (Zara-Mama) was adorned with clothing as the embodiment of the crop's spirit. The poppet was asked questions as to how she was feeling throughout the year. In the East Indies a soul was believed to reside in rice. "Mother-Rice" was chosen from the crop and seven "rice-children" are cut from her and ceremoniously cared for. In Bali, "husband and wife" grains were bound together from the first cutting of the crop to invoke abundance.[312]

Universal myths speak of this Corn or Grain Goddess. These ancient stories were told when your ancestors were at one with the heartbeat of the Earth and totally dependent on the harvest for survival. Nothing has changed, and like your ancestors, you are still dependant on Mother Earth.

The sabbat of Lammas is a time to acknowledge the gift of food. It is a time of surrender, to let go of what was, and to welcome the shadow of the waning sun.

---

309. Baring and Cashford, *The Myth of the Goddess*, 378.

310. McCoy, *Sabbats: A Witch's Approach to Living the Old Ways*, 175.

311. Frazer, *The Golden Bough: A Study in Magic and Religion*, 143.

312. Frazer, *The Golden Bough: A Study in Magic and Religion*, 415–424.

Symbols, Charms, and Plants of Lammas

Bread: The holy grain, a symbol of life.

Corn Dollies: Representing the pregnant Goddess of the future and the old Goddess of the past. The corn dollies appear again at this sabbat. Now the young Goddess is becoming a mother, holding life in her womb, and again with the final harvest the old Goddess speaks of what was as the Earth moves towards dormancy.

Cornucopia: A horn-shaped vessel holding the harvest. It is a symbol of the Mother Goddess because it is receptive and represents the abundant Earth. This motif is also used at Mabon in some traditions.

Fruit of the Season: Symbolic of Earth's gifts.

Grains: Offering to the grain deities.

Rowan *(Sorbus subg. Sorbus)*: Crosses were made from Rowan in Scotland on Lammas Eve and placed above doors for protection.

Lammas Altar

During the creation of your altar you will bind a corn charm representing the past and the future. You may wish to prepare a few days before Lammas. The altar will manifest within the circle of spell.

Purpose: Your altar is to be dedicated to the Mother Goddess of the harvest, to the magick of the Earth, and to the food that gives you life. It is an expression of abundance, festivity, and hope for renewal of the soil. Your altar brings awareness of the health of your body, the comfort of your home, and the planet. It brings nature and its magick into your home.

When to create your altar: In the time leading up to Lammas, so the altar is complete before the sabbat. The sabbat begins at moonrise on the eve.

You will need: Your witch's tools. Water in your chalice. A purple and a green candle of any size. Container of salt. Incense blend of five parts frankincense (*Boswellia carterii*), three parts patchouli (*Pogostemon cablin* or *P. patchouli*), and two parts lavender (*Lavan-*

dula officinalis or *L. vera*). Self-igniting charcoal. You will burn this blend again during the Lammas spell. Philtre of three drops lime (*Citrus aurantifolia* or *L. Limetta*), five drops ylang-ylang (*Cananga odorata*), and two drops sandalwood (*Santalum album*) in a teaspoon of olive oil (*Olea europaea*). Place in a small bowl or container and swirl. A plate of fruit and vegetables or a cornucopia. Two corncobs with husks. A ball of string. Two pins. Witch's utensils.

Position your witch's tools, candles, censer and incense blend, philtre, plants, and symbolic items creatively on the altar.

Begin with ingredients before you. Become the witch and create the magick of Lammas.

1. Raise your pentacle as you say:

   "I invoke the Mother Goddess, hold me in your
   arms as I cast a circle of light."

   Imagine the circle.

2. Ignite the incense.

3. Move the two corncobs through the smoke. Move the cornucopia or the plate of fruit and vegetables through the smoke. Place the corn in the cornucopia or on the plate.

4. Position the candle and the two pins near your wand. Place salt next to the pentacle and the incense censer next to your athame.

5. Decorate the altar with plants and flowers.

6. When you are finished, move your pentacle over the altar to dissolve your circle.

On the sabbat of Lammas you will create your spell. The sabbat begins at moonrise on the eve.

Lammas Spell:
To Acknowledge Life

Purpose: This spell is to acknowledge life, to show appreciation and honour Mother Earth. This is a powerful magickal intention. To appreciate and to accept without wanting brings rest and peace of mind. Sometimes when you are still and not expecting, the best things happen. This spell also acknowledges that the past, present, and future are interdependent and are created through your choices.

When to cast: At Lammas. The sabbat begins at moonrise on the eve. Day or night.

Where to cast: Indoors at your altar or outside under the sky.

You will need: Altar items and ingredients as prepared. Also bring to the spell: A loaf of bread or cake. Seeds of any kind.

Create the spell at your altar. As the witch prepare to connect with the Earth Goddess.

1. Holding the two corncobs to your heart, cast your circle by imagining you are surrounded by goddesses. They are from all parts of the Earth, they are young, they are mothers, they are also ancient. They hold fruit, grains, and vegetables of their lands. Take your time. Look around the circle and greet them. Place the corn back on the altar.

2. Light the two candles.

3. Anoint your heart with the philtre.

4. Ignite the charcoal and add a pinch or two of incense.

5. Move the two pins through the incense smoke. Say:

   "With all endings, a beginning. With all beginnings, an ending."

6. Holding the candle, insert a pin into the wax and say:

   "To end with gratitude."

   Then in the same place, insert the other pin as you say:

   "To begin with gratitude."

7. Move the candle through the incense smoke. Then light it.

8. Hold one corncob to your heart and say:

   "Grandmother."

   Hold the other corncob also to your heart and say:

   "Mother."

   Place a seed inside the Mother's husk to represent new life in her "belly."

9. Bind the two corncobs together with the string and fasten with three knots. Say:

   "Yesterday, today, and tomorrow are one."

10. Bless this corn-charm by moving it through the candle flame and then the incense smoke.

11. Sprinkle it with water and then with salt.

12. Breathe onto the corn to connect with the Earth.

13. When you are finished, imagine your "circle of goddesses" walking away and disappearing.

14. Before you leave the room, snuff out the candle.

After the spell: A day or so after Lammas, eat the corn, bread, and vegetables. If any of the candle remains, relight in honour of the Earth Goddess. Place the water and any used salt on the Earth. Anoint your heart every day with the remaining philtre until it is gone. Compost flowers when it is time. Keep the string for future poppet making.

From the harvest of the Earth and the nurture of your body, the Mother Goddess directs you to a place of retrospection, inward to find yourself again or maybe re-invent, as Nature transforms.

Autumn Equinox

Also known as Mabon
Northern Hemisphere: September 21–23
Southern Hemisphere: March 21–23

On the Wheel of the Year

The Goddess enters the Underworld.
Go into your inner world.
The shadow of the psyche is acknowledged.

An Autumn Equinox Story…

The wind whips up and fills the air with brown, red, and yellow leaves. You are dressed for a meeting with the fae—lavish, exquisite, and refined. Your hair is entwined with yellow, brown, and orange vines and crowned with a ring of jade and emerald.

Your elven-spun shoes, made from the mosses of last winter, begin to become a part of the land again as you walk head on into a gust of wind. The fae rise from the Earth and take your hands. The ancient Crone Witch holds a ripe apple and calls you towards a passage in the hill. Your clothes fall from you as you venture into the darkness, then through the gates into a hidden world.

Here clothes of velvet red lichen grow over you. Your crown of jade and emerald becomes a gold and obsidian wreath. Your transformation to Queen of the Underworld has begun.

The autumn equinox is a time when day and night are of equal length. When light and dark energies are of equal power. It is a seasonal gateway, a time between beginnings and endings. With the concept of the Wheel of the Year, modern witches adopted Mabon as a name for this equinox. Mabon is a Welsh god, a male counterpart of Persephone. Like her, he was abducted and taken to the Underworld. After his rescue, Mabon ascended to the surface of Earth. From that time, he was thought to be both the oldest creature on Earth, as well as the youngest. So, he came to embody the ages of growth as well as decline.

His symbolic death in the Underworld associates him with the dying god at the autumn equinox to be reborn at the winter solstice. This may be the reason for the naming of the sabbat.

The story of the equinox tells also of the descent of the young goddess, Persephone, into the Underworld. Her mother Demeter is the embodiment of the fertility of the harvest. But after the harvest, she loses her daughter to the realm of the dead. With her absence, the surface of the Earth transforms into bareness and stillness. Demeter then embarks on a journey to find her daughter and, when she does, life returns to the world with the flowering and growth of spring.

This myth was ritualised in the Eleusinian Mysteries,[313] sacred rites that were held in autumn after the harvest was stored. These rites involved elaborate purification rituals, the sacrifice of pigs and initiation ceremony. It was a festival of renewal and life affirmation. Initiates enacted the pain and rage of Demeter's loss and torches were carried into the darkness, symbolizing her search into the Underworld.

The decent of the goddess is also told in the stories of the Sumerian goddess, Inanna, and her Babylonian sister goddess, Ishtar. Both goddesses entered the Underworld to rescue their lover/son, a vegetation god. Both undergo a death of self for they must meet and integrate with their darker aspect, embodied by Ereshkigal, ruler of the realm. Like Persephone, both goddesses needed to sacrifice who they thought they were. They needed to meet their shadow, what lies beneath the surface of consciousness in order to find their true power.

There are many versions of both myths. In one version of Ishtar's descent, her lover Tammuz, wounded by a boar, falls into an enchanted sleep in the Underworld. Everyone and everything on the surface of the Earth also sleeps and all fertility diminishes. In both myths the son/lover of the goddess is sacrificed to the Underworld and once rescued, their return to Earth brings life to the surface again. This Sumerian/Babylonian myth is similar to the myth of the Egyptian goddess, Isis, who after restoring the dismembered god, Osiris, brings growth back to the land.

---

313. Baring and Cashford, *The Myth of the Goddess*, 374.

Autumn may ask you to retreat and discover yourself fully. What is on the surface of your life is not complete unless you understand what lies hidden within you. Inanna's journey into the Underworld brings the two sides of life together as interconnected and essential for understanding the self. This journey is hard and sometimes seems impossible because we never want to sacrifice the familiar within. However, fulfillment and completion await in the shadow. Remember all that is stored there is powerful and can be directed towards your transformation.

Inanna's journey was told in an epic poem dated around 1750 BC. "Inanna from the 'great above' set her mind toward the 'great below.'"[314] Take Inanna's hand and journey within and you will ignite an adventure into your own mysterious story.

Like all sabbats, Mabon unites opposites to create dynamic reinvention. A death is required, and a sacrifice needed in order to birth growth and abundance. An inward journey waits.

Baba Yaga is the crone witch of autumn in Slavic tradition. It is she who lives in the last sheaf of grain cut and rides her mortar and pestle through the sky. Baba Yaga could scare a person to death by her sudden appearance or decide to assist instead. This magickal character is aligned with the Underworld Goddesses who take you deep into yourself as the leaves begin to fall.[315]

Symbols, Charms, and Plants of the Autumn Equinox

Autumn Leaves: Symbol of change.

Cornucopia, Horn of Plenty: Symbol of the harvest and emblem of the goddesses Demeter and Ceres.

Grain and Corn: Motif of Demeter.

Pomegranate *(Punica granatum)*: Fruit of the Underworld.

Wine: The Mabon "sacrifice." Also associated with Dionysus of the Eleusinian Mysteries.

---

314. Campbell, *Goddesses: Mysteries of the Feminine Divine*, ed. Saffron Rossi, 83.

315. Guiley, *The Encyclopedia of Witches and Witchcraft*, 20.

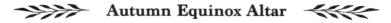 ## Autumn Equinox Altar

During the creation of your altar you will make a clay seal. The seal is a talisman dedicated to the magick of knowledge as well as mystery. A binding seal to self-discovery. It is a token to enter the symbolic realm of the Underworld.

Purpose: Your altar is to be dedicated to the Goddess of the Underworld, newfound knowledge, and reinvention of self. It is a symbolic expression of the unknown, your dreams, and the subconscious, for in these places you will find truth, healing, and profound change. Your altar is a creativity that represents the shadow of your psyche, bringing it into form and thereby opening a passage to explore the hidden within.

When to create your altar: In the time leading up to the autumn equinox so the altar is complete before the sabbat.

You will need: Your witch's tools. Red wine in your chalice. Five black candles (wide enough to stand, approximately 2 in. x 2 in. or 5 cm x 5 cm). Container of black salt. Incense blend of five parts mugwort (*Artemisia vulgaris*), four parts frankincense (*Boswellia carterii*), and one part myrrh (*Commiphora myrrha*). You will burn this blend again during the autumn equinox spell. Philtre of nine drops of cypress essential oil (*Cupressus sempervirens*) in a teaspoon of olive oil (*Olea europaea L.*). Place in a small bowl or container and swirl. Branches with autumn leaves or bare. Deep red and purple flowers. Seven fallen leaves. A pomegranate (or red apple, if unavailable). Three obsidian crystals in honour of the Underworld. Self-hardening clay. A sewing needle. Position your witch's tools, candles, censer and incense blend, plants, and symbolic items creatively on the altar.

Begin with ingredients before you. Become the witch and create the magick of the autumn equinox.

1. Raise the chalice of wine as you say:

   "I invoke the goddesses of the Underworld. Breathe
   your breath into me as I cast a circle of light."

   Imagine the circle.

2. Place the wine and pomegranate together at the centre of the
   altar.

3. Position the five candles at the points of the pentagram
   around them.

4. With the black salt, create the lines of the pentagram from
   point to point.

5. Place the leaves in a circle around the black salt pentagram.

6. Position your wand, athame, chalice, and pentacle around the
   circle.

7. With the clay, begin to fashion a disk shape (like a large
   coin). The size of the disk is up to you. Take your time and
   allow your imagination to guide you.

8. When you are ready, begin to carve a pentagram on one side
   of the seal and your witch's sigil on the other side. With the
   philtre on your finger, place nine dabs onto the seal and then
   allow the clay to harden.

9. Place your scrying mirror on the altar.

10. Decorate with plants and flowers.

11. When you are finished, move the glass of wine over the altar
    to dissolve your circle.

On the sabbat of Mabon, you will create your spell. The sabbat begins at moonrise on the eve.

Autumn Equinox Spell:
Enter the Underworld

Purpose: This spell is a rite of passage into the symbolic Underworld. Your intention is to know yourself deeply, discover hidden energies, and maybe to reinvent yourself. As leaves fall, you too need to fall into the unknown and travel with the young goddesses Persephone, Inanna, and Ishtar into the Underworld of the psyche. During the spell, allow your imagination to guide you. Take note of images, feelings, and symbols that arise.

When to cast: At the autumn equinox. Day or night.

Where to cast: Indoors at your altar or outside under the sky.

You will need: Altar items and ingredients as prepared.

Create the spell at your altar. As the witch prepare to connect with the Underworld.

1. To cast your circle, become the pentagram by standing with both arms extended to the sides and legs apart. Say:

   "By the power of the Goddess, I cast a circle at the gates to the Underworld. By love and courage, I transform."

2. Ignite the charcoal and add a pinch or two of incense blend.

3. Move your mirror through the smoke.

4. One by one, light each candle flame and with each one, say one of these Goddesses' names:

   "Hecate, Persephone, Iannna, Ishtar, Ereshkigal."

5. Take a sip of the wine or place some on your lips.

6. Hold the pomegranate and the seal and say:

   "This fruit is an offering. This seal is my token to enter."

   Note what you see in your mind.

7. Sit down. Hold the fruit and token in each hand. Close your eyes and breathe. Imagine the gates of the Underworld. What do they look like? Imagine stepping inside. What do you see? When you are ready, ask for a guide. Ask your guide to show you what you need to know about yourself to transform.

8. When you are ready, open your eyes and look into your scrying mirror. Note what is shown in the mirror, what you see in your mind, feel in your body, hear, or taste.

9. When you are ready, go back to the gates of the Underworld in your mind and "place" the circle into your heart.

10. Before you leave the room, snuff out the candles.

After the spell: Pour the wine on the Earth as the symbolic sacrifice of an aspect of yourself. Eat the pomegranate with the intention of seeking knowledge. If any of the candles remain, relight them in honour of the five goddesses. Place water, any used salt, and charcoal ash on the Earth. Anoint your heart every day with the remaining philtre until it is gone. Compost flowers when it is time.

You can repeat this spell whenever you wish to discover your shadow. Keep the seal in a sacred place.

From the shadows of the Underworld, new knowledge and a deeper sense of yourself is found. With the coming of winter, the crone witch asks you to ride your broom into the hallowed realm of the dead at Samhain.

As the Earth moves around the sun and the moon moves around the Earth, light and dark create a marriage of beginnings and endings. The oceans, rivers, plants, and creatures of the Earth move as one with the seasons under the spell of something mysterious and divine.

Feel the weather, smell the Earth, see the colours around you, and listen to the bird's songs. Remind yourself where you are: on a spinning sphere in an endless Universe. Create your story. The Wheel of the Year turns, and your path rises and falls, inward and outward, through longing and hope, darkness and light.

Mother Earth watches, the fae conjure dreams, dawn breaks into colour, and the night creatures remain bewitched by the moon. Look to the night sky. Hear the voice of the wind in the trees. Weave your heart to the season. See the gateway of endings and beginnings.

Thank Mother Earth.

EIGHTEEN

A Witch's Story

Nyx was the primordial goddess of night. She birthed the first Light, the Hesperides, the evening stars. Nyx also birthed the fates, age, and also death.

Remember the first light you saw. Imagine the moment you entered this world. Darkness was Mother, safe and warm, then change…you entered a place of beauty as well as pain, of joy as well as loss, a world of endless stories and countless stars. You came to a place of mystery. And above everything, you wanted love.

Witchcraft is a way of thinking. It is creative, innovative, and heartfelt. It is a way to explore your story beneath what is seen, beneath the world's expectations and values. It encapsulates a deeply complex interweave of who you are spiritually, your dreams, your longings, and your search for purpose and meaning. Becoming the witch means becoming yourself, living authentically, and thinking magickally.

The first book I bought with my own money was a tiny book of spells from a shop that sold newspapers. The first spell I did from the book was one to make freckles disappear. I was excited because, at thirteen, freckles were the cause of all my problems. According to the instructions, I gathered morning dew to mix in a teaspoon of olive oil. I applied the blend to my face every day as prescribed. It turned out I was meant to have freckles for awhile. However, I will never forget the thrill of getting up at dawn and going into the garden to gather the dew. It was my secret with Nature.

When I first began reading about witchcraft, I thought I needed to be a perfect witch and be happy all the time. This was impossible. Then over time spells taught me that experiencing my shadow was also part of my story and therefore magickal. I learnt that fear, doubt, disappointment, and anger are also part of being a witch; so are mistakes. Every spell changed me in some way, and I got to know myself a little more each time. Each spell took me to a place of meaning and I was always amazed how the lighting of a candle could be so powerful. Each spell reminded me that I created my own life, that I always had a choice of who I want to be in every situation. Just like the two-sided coin, witchcraft taught me that when challenged, my shadow-self rises along with my strength. It taught me that along with the Light within me—the wiser, kinder aspects of myself—I sometimes needed to be in the shadow. To fully realise my own destructive abilities was also a part of me. I learnt that to disconnect from the shadow is a denial of my humanness and the discovery of how these feelings within came about. Witchcraft has taught me that the shadow is a powerful energy and, through understanding, it could be transformed into growth.

For a long time, through my twenties and early thirties, I wanted to find true love and I wished so hard I thought I had found it a few times. But nothing felt that deep within me. I created a love spell with three bay leaves wrapped in a written spell. During the spell, I realised that I thought of true love as something that existed outside of myself. Something I needed from someone else to make me feel complete. At that moment I let every wish go. I hid the love spell and forgot about it. I felt free, no longer searching for love. Time moved on. Then one night, at a party, I was in the middle of an interesting conversation with a friend of a friend. He, the person I was speaking to, seemed kind, open, and clever. I found myself thinking, "What a beautiful partner you would be for someone." Then I heard a whisper from a spirit, "Why can't it be you?"

This is when I realised I was ready for true love because it had found me. That person was my future husband. A few days later my bay leaf spell fell out of a book I had taken off the shelf.

So, as above so below. How you think will create your world. Each spell takes you on a journey to transform something inside of you so you come closer to yourself and to fulfillment. Each spell I have done has manifested in its own way, sometimes surprising, sometimes better than I imagined, and sometimes what manifested has been deeply challenging and also difficult.

Because I loved magick and wanted to live in this world, I began a business called SpellBox with two friends. I thought wow, now I really am a witch! I imagined I would be talking about magick all day and floating around making spells. Despite all my magick-making, nothing was what I hoped it would be. I knew nothing about the foundations of business or how to be when one of the friendships I had was falling apart. I felt like I was pushing a mountain and learnt how my determination could also be destructive. A great friendship was lost for awhile, and I had also lost a part of myself because I was consumed with my own sense of justice.

To keep my dream of SpellBox, I had to sacrifice and learn. After many, many years of hard work, SpellBox has become very successful and has shown people the ways of the witch for more than twenty years. My idea to create and sell spells was innovative and genuine, but in the beginning, there was no other clever plan supporting it, just desire. There always needs to be more than desire. Dreams can also need dedication, endurance, and hard work to manifest. This is what a true spell will show you.

I learnt that magick is also found in the depths of disappointment and grief. We wanted a child and I did many spells to align our wish with the divine. But all that came was sadness and loss. Then years later, a son came to us, but not in the usual way. He was five when we met him. He brought with him the magick of a love deeper that I could have ever imagined. He taught me that real love endures. He showed me that I can't do everything, I can just try my best. Spells work in unexpected ways. They weave hearts together. My wish came true. And yours will too.

Through history the witch has been demeaned and persecuted, considered mad, dangerous, and an outsider. Maybe she is still seen this way. Embrace it, and live it in defiance of oppression, dogma, and the mundane. Create your own vision of life, your own religion, spiritual beauty, and sacred haven. Despite all opposition, the Witch never went away. You are here.

Spin your sacred threads through your feelings, thinking, and your body and connect them to the moon, the sun, the wind, and the trees. When you truly connect, you will become them, become a goddess and a god, an oracle, sage, magician, enchanter, and divine weaver. Know that you are in an ever-changing world and that you are also always changing. With every situation, easy or hard, there is a choice you make, and this choice creates life. So, own your life completely and live your truth with kindness. Enter your imagination every day and play, speak to ghosts, shape-shift, meet your ancestors, divine the future, heal the past, and create your own art. Cast your circles and be amazed at becoming the witch.

A Witch's Incantation

Mother is the moon,
Her glow is blessed with wishes.
Mother is the Earth,
Meet her in the temple of trees.
Mother is the mystery of the sea,
The power in the storm.
She is the warm heart,
The tears of love,
Kindness.
Light candle bright,
With ancient Goddess weave threads tonight.
Hold dreams in thoughts of wonder,
As Gaia's cauldron swirls.
Wish upon a charm,
By flame, By rain.
Weaving threads to breeze,
With light. With shadow.
With moon and sun.
In Gaia's arms.

Your Story…

At the crossroads, a place of singing ghosts and ancient prayers, you wait and weave your magick. Above a sky of light and dark. It is a realm where birds carry souls to other worlds, a place where suns die and are also born. The sky spirits call your name. You weave a message to the Goddess with threads bound to the wind.

Rabbits gather. They watch the setting sun. They ask you to feel the Earth beneath your feet, to connect with Mother, to your home.

You hear the heartbeat of the Goddess, feel the rush of love in a growing flower, and the loss in the crashing sea of the heart. Hear the wind calling you to change, see the labyrinth rise. Then a door opens. The unknown. Hold Hecate's hand. Your familiar is with you and so are your ancestors. Enter the Underworld. Create your story.

By the power of fire, air, water, and earth, by way of the Goddess, you become the witch.

NINETEEN
The Witch's Cabinet

A Magick Room Story...

The scent of flowers, herbs, and incense lingers like the praying spirit of air that stays after their conjuring in your spells. The fragrance of the mountain wind swirls with flowers in a field, with essence of rose, wax, myrrh, and honey. A bundle of rosemary, sage, and mugwort hang to dry. Poppets on a shelf speak of past desires, a hope for love, a hurt to heal, a birth to bless. Made from husks tied with string, fashioned from old cloth and button, from straw and wood. Within each a beating copal heart tells the story of a time threaded to the moon and sun, your journey as Witch. Jars of herbal blends and perfumes of earth release their spells as you open each bottle. Charms, stones, and crystal treasures, a feather found, a whisker in a jar, pins in a bottle, a bowl of buttons, a hanging key, a star, half-burnt wax seals, a loved one's brooch, a pouch tied with seven knots, a drum, your Book of Shadows, the face of a goddess, a crescent moon, your witch's tools.

Rain pours into your chalice and through a shell you hear the Goddess whisper, "Feel your heart." The sunlight through your wand calls, "Find the way…" The cauldron bubbles, Hecate's willow twig stirs the brew. Your witch's knife calls in the wind, it makes silent words, "Know your mind." Holding your pentacle, you enter the invisible realm through your circle…you hear, "Find your purpose…"

Over time you may gather any ingredient or tool you deeply connect with; sometimes they come to you as a gift or you find them unexpectedly. There is no need to have every herb or oil or even a large collection. You may simply select all-purpose oils and herbs. Every witch stores their materials in different ways—in a cabinet, on a shelf, or as part of an altar. Information on colours, numbers, and metals is sometimes added to your Book of Shadows. I have included a simplified list of witch's tools and practical items needed to make charms and cast spells. You will always add your own unique items. Be imaginative and create a story with your witch's materials…

Ethics and Care

Essential Oils

All essential oils should be diluted in a base oil like almond oil (*Prunus dulcis*). Some oils, such as citrus and spices, are not to be applied directly on the skin. Other diluted oils are beneficial to use directly. Please take all care and research what is right for you. Essential oils, such as cinnamon (*Cinnamomum zeylanicum*), clove (*Eugenia caryophyllus, Syzygium aromaticum,* or *Caryophyllus aromaticus*), lemongrass (*Cymbopogon citratus*), orange (*Citrus sinensis*), and black pepper (*Piper nigrum*), can irritate the skin. Please ensure you avoid most essential oils during pregnancy. Oils listed in this book to avoid while pregnant include: basil (*Ocimum basilicum*), clove (*Eugenia caryophyllus, Syzygium aromaticum,* or *Caryophyllus aromaticus*), cinnamon (*Cinnamomum zeylanicum*), clary sage (*Salvia sclarea*), hyssop (*Hyssopus officinalis*), mugwort (*Artemisia vulgaris*), peppermint (*Mentha piperita*), rosemary (*Rosmarinus officinalis*), common sage (*Salvia officinalis*), thyme (*Thymus vulgaris*), and wormwood (*Artemisia absinthium*). However, there are oils that are safe to use, so please research any oil before you use it. It is important to always read labels carefully before purchasing any products.

White Sage *(Salvia apiana)* and Palo Santo *(Bursera graveolens)*

Always choose organically grown white sage and avoid wild harvested. Ask your supplier where the white sage was sourced before you buy it. In America, there are First Nations suppliers of sage and in Australia and other places there are some organic growers. There are also ethical considerations regarding white sage smudges, including cultural appropriation.

The wood of the palo santo, used commonly for incense, should also be ethically sourced and used.

Candles

Try always to use environmentally friendly candles that don't contain toxins. Avoid petroleum-based paraffin candles. Always attempt to recycle wax and dispose of ethically. Never leave a candle unattended and take care when burning a written spell. Always have a bowl of water nearby when burning paper or using sealing wax. Melted sealing wax is very hot and can burn the skin.

Feathers and Animal Amulets

In some countries, the United States in particular, laws strictly prohibit collecting and buying feathers of native birds and it is important to respect this. Research which feathers you are able to collect. If you find a feather in the wild and you are unsure whether you can collect it, simply give honour to the bird and make a wish. Then leave the feather where it was found.

Any part of an animal used in a spell should be ethically and legally sourced or collected. Your health and safety and the honouring of the creature should also be a priority if you use animal amulets.

Witch's Tools

Athame: Tool of the Element Air. Usually double-bladed. Any knife or purpose-made object.

Bell: Tool of the Element Air. Any size bell, chimes, or singing bowl.

Besom: Tool of the Elements Air, Fire, and Earth. A broom of any type, purchased or created.

Chalice and Cauldron: Tool of the Element Water. Any receptive vessel or traditional design.

Grimoire: Tool of the Element Air. A book or journal of any kind.

Mirror: Tool of the Element Water: Any size mirror, created black mirror, or obsidian mirror.

Mortar and Pestle: Tool of the Element Earth. Any kind.

Pentacle: Tool of the Element Earth. Draw on paper, a coin, or purpose-made object.

Wand: Tool of the Element Fire. Stick, pointer, or purpose-made object.

Witch's Utensils

As a witch you need to be practical and safe while using the elements so you will require utensils. You will need fire-proof holders and containers, made of metal or ceramic, for candles and incense. A metal censer can be used for the burning of charcoal. Take all care burning candles, incense, charcoal, and sealing wax. Never leave a burning candle unattended and cover hot charcoal with salt when you have finished using it. A spell may not require every element; however, it is good to have utensils for all purposes.

Candleholders or plates: Sometimes when multiple candles are used, you may position them on a plate. A hint: If the candle isn't self-standing, melt wax onto the plate and stand the candle in it before it sets.

Incense censer or holders: For burning charcoal, place a bed of salt in the censer of container. This allows some air to move under the charcoal.

Container for salt.

Blending vessel for oils: Swirl oils in a small container.

Bowl for water: Keep nearby when using sealing wax or for burning spells.

Self-igniting charcoal: To ignite the charcoal, hold it to a flame using tongs. It will begin to spark. Place it on a bed of salt in the censer. Wait for the charcoal to turn ash white and then add resin or incense. Place a pinch of incense to begin and add more if required.

Candle snuffer and charcoal tongs.

Matches and taper candles.

Witch's Accessories

For Written Magick: Inks, chalk, quill, charcoal sticks, paper, and pencils. Any art material you like to use. Needles and carving tools to carve onto candles and other objects.

For Binding Magick: Binding items include items that fix or join, such as sealing wax, pins, string, ribbon, buttons, coloured cottons, cloth, pouches, and natural twine or cord.

Poppet and Image Magick: Cloth, clay, straw, wood, corn husks, needle, and threads. Straw is an important ingredient for the witch's cabinet as it is a home for the faeries as well as an amulet for luck and protection. Also use straw to fill cloth poppets.

Natural Amulets: Anything for nature as long as it is sourced ethically and safely. Amulets include leaves, stones, crystals, shells, feathers, and branches.

Jars, Bottles, and Bowls: For herbs, philtres, spells, and spirit jars.

Witch's Herbs, Resins, and Plants

Every plant, herb, and flower is associated with an element and resonates magickal energy. Keep a selection of dried herbs and plants, oils, salts and resins for incense blends, powders, potions, and charms. I have invented my own "folk name" for each to enhance the quality of the plant's personality and powers. You may like to invent your own.

Angelica *(Angelica archangelica)*: Plant and Essential Oil. *Fae's Brew.*

The scent of angelica transports you to a faery realm, yet it has a deep tone that brings calmness as well as grounding. The plant provides energetic protection and breaks hexes. It is associated with Archangel Michael, so is a powerful banishing plant.

Carry in a charm pouch as an amulet for protection. Combine with frankincense and mugwort to break unwanted habits. Angelica is burnt as incense for healing and to invoke luck. Use in poppet magick to manifest change. Raise the warrior of courage within you with Angelica.

Basil *(Ocimum basilicum)*: Plant and Essential Oil. *Herb of Vishnu.*

Basil calls on courage and bravery. Inhaling its scent may bring awareness of any weakness or fears. It also promotes empathy. The herb clears the head and settles worries. It also enhances dream and love magick. Basil is also used to attract money and for business expansion.

Use basil oil to anoint candles in strength spells. Combine with rose, patchouli, and sandalwood to create a love-attracting charm pouch. Add to incense mixes and sprinkles for abundance. Combine with rue and juniper to attract luck. Create an infusion and add to purification baths. As a gift it brings good luck to any home. Make a dream pillow with a blend with rose, wood betony, wormwood, and lavender, add a few drops of basil oil.

Grow basil as an offering to the gnomes.

Bay Leaves *(Laurus nobilis)*: Plant and Essential Oil. *Wishing Leaf.*

Apollo's own crown was made from bay leaves. Since ancient times it has been considered a purification and reconciliation plant. It is a protective herb and is carried for this purpose. Pythia, the priestess at Delphi, was said to chew the leaf before her oracle. Hence it is thought to enhance insight and psychic vision. Bay is healing for the spirit and is also a wish-granting herb.

Wish on three bay leaves and place under your pillow or add to cooking. Burn alone to purify a circle or combine with myrrh and dragon's blood. Create a protective charm pouch with bay, frankincense, and blessed thistle to hang over your front door. Make a psychic charm pouch with bay, damiana, lady's mantle, and add rose oil. Place a bay leaf into a gift for a wish to be made. Use the scent to enhance psychic readings.

Benzoin *(genus Styrax)* **Resin and Essential Oil:** *Winged Perfume.*

As an incense, benzoin clears and purifies a space of any low energies. Add sandalwood and copal to create a high spiritual vibration in your home. Benzoin also has money-drawing powers. Move your purse or wallet through the smoke of benzoin for this purpose. Use the incense in a place of business to attract prosperity. Add clove, orris, and patchouli to the blend for potency.

Cinquefoil or "Five Finger Grass" *(Potentilla canadensis, P. erecta, or P. reptans)*: Plant and Essential Oil. *Protective Hand.*

Cinquefoil is said to invoke abundance, protection, and wisdom because it strengthens the powers of spells and charms. It is also associated with restful sleep and attracting favours. Prophetic dreams also come under its mystical influence.

Carry cinquefoil in a charm pouch or hang by your bed or door for protection. Combine with rosemary and frankincense oil and hold while making important decisions. As a protective infusion, anoint your brow and hands to dispel negative energy. Add to purification bath sachets with lavender and rose oil. Carry for luck in legal matters. Create a dream pillow with it and add mugwort and straw.

Cloves *(Eugenia caryophyllus, Syzygium aromaticum,* or *Caryophyllus aromaticus)*: Plant and Essential Oil. *Jupiter's Spice.*

The strong scent of cloves creates the energy of banishing magick. The oil itself is very dark in colour so aligns with dispelling hues and draws love as well as abundance.

Burn alone as incense or combine with patchouli and benzoin to invoke a change in your prosperity. Anoint candles and charms to banish unwanted energy. Combine with mullein and copal to create purifying incense. Add the oil to poppet fillings or combine with orange essential oil for fire-magick charms.

Copal *(Bursera odorata, B. fugaroides)*: Resin. *Moving Sylphs.*

Copal resin has a sweet scent and can create a joyful, energetic atmosphere. It is used for love on every level. Because of this it raises the vibration of a location, so it is used for purification and cleansing.

Burn copal to create the energy of joy and celebration before a gathering. Combine with rose petals and mugwort to induce dreams of true love and with rosemary and pine to clear a space of negativity. Add copal to love powders and combine with lavender and sandalwood in a calming charm. A piece of copal represents the "heart" in a poppet. Bless the heart with the four elements before placing into the poppet.

Send your message to the mountaintop of the sylph through the smoke of copal incenses.

Damiana *(Turnera diffusa* or *T. aphrodisiaca)*: Plant and Essential Oil. *Visions of the Heart.*

Damiana is potent for any dream and psychic work, taking you through a mystical portal into the spirit realm. The plant combines love with psychic vision, offering a way for the witch to communicate with ghosts, understand dreams, and raise the heart vibration.

Powder damiana to create a love sprinkle for written spells and love letters. Burn to conjure insight and visions. A potent dream pillow ingredient combined with mugwort, wood betony, lavender, and wormwood.

Journey into otherworldly dimensions with this mystical plant.

Dragon's Blood *(Daemonorops draco, D. poppinquos)*: Resin and oil. *Fire Breath.*

Dragon's Blood is the red sap produced from the Socotra dragon tree, native to Yemen.

This resin is highly effective for any magickal intent. Dragon's Blood amplifies the witch's intention for it mirrors her/his own lifeforce within the spell.

Powder Dragon's Blood resin in a mortar and pestle and add to any incense or charm to amplify the magick. Combine with frankincense for powerful fire element incense. Add rose petals and patchouli for love or mugwort and sandalwood for a potent psychic blend. Dragon's Blood is true to its name and like the creature itself will banish negativity as well as protect your energy. Dragon's Blood is also available as ink for mystical writing and as oil for banishing and anointing.

While using Dragon's Blood, invoke to the mythical dragon to assist your magick work.

Frankincense *(Boswellia carterii)*: Resin and Essential Oil. *Call to the Angels.*

Frankincense calls in the divine and is the resin every witch should have. The spiritual vibration of frankincense aligns the witch with otherworldly notions and opens the realm of future possibilities through magickal thinking.

Burn frankincense as an incense to lift the spiritual vibration and to drive away negativity. The incense will also enhance visions and meditation. Combine with myrrh to create a truly hallowed space. Add to charm pouches and magick powders to align your intention with divine aspirations. Frankincense oil is a magnificent anointing oil to bless yourself and others. Traditionally frankincense incense and oil have been used as an offering to the departed.

Allow the beauty of frankincense to introduce you to the angels.

Hyssop *(Hyssopus officinalis)*: Plant and Essential Oil. *Sprinkle of Sacrifice.*

Hyssop has been used since ancient times in purification rituals and is mentioned in the Bible for this use. The plant belongs to the mint family and has a fresh, strong perfume.

Place a charm pouch of hyssop in the home for purification. During difficult times this magickal plant will help you to understand the benefits of sacrifice. Create an infusion for the bath to cleanse your aura and to dispel negative thinking. Add hyssop to sprinkles and charm pouches for protection. Anoint your chakras with the essential oil to spiritually cleanse.

Journey to ancient mysticism through the wonder of hyssop.

Juniper Berries *(Juniperus communis)*: Plant and Essential Oil. *For the Good Folk.*

Juniper berries have traditionally been used to attract good people and friends. Because of this the berries are also used in love magick spells and charms. Juniper is also a powerful hex-breaking ingredient due to the high spiritual vibration it creates.

Grind in a mortar and pestle and add to any incense mix to invoke positive energy or to enhance any celebration. Add to love charm pouches and sprinkles. Anoint juniper oil on the body to dispel negative energy. Combine the oil with orange or bergamot to create a candle blessing blend for vitality and luck.

Experience a shift in energy with the magickal juniper berry.

Lavender *(Lavandula officinalis* or *L. vera)*: Plant and Essential Oil. *Dust of the Fae.*

Lavender conjures serenity, healing, and comfort. It is also a flower associated with the fae and will attract happy energy. This flower is a basic addition to the witch's cabinet because it adds a sweet scent to any incense or herbal mix. It is also an all-purpose magickal ingredient invoking love, peace, and psychic vision. Lavender heals because it connects thinking to dreams and rests the mind.

Combine lavender with sandalwood in an incense to awaken the third eye; add rose petals to the mix for moon magick. Add lavender to dream pillows by combining with mugwort, basil, and rose. Add a few drops of lavender oil to the blend. Create a sprinkle and rub on love letters and written spells. Add lavender oil to a bath for rest and combine with rose and clary sage oils to invoke the love Goddess.

Connect with the peaceful scent of lavender and give rise to happiness.

Mugwort *(Artemisia vulgaris)*: Plant and Oil. *Herb of Artemis.*

Mugwort is a magnificent addition to the witch's cabinet and I would recommend it highly. This plant is extremely powerful and emits a magickally charged aroma when fresh and when burnt. This all-purpose plant can be used in countless ways. It is highly effective when trying to achieve altered states of consciousness. When burnt it has a dreamlike result and takes the witch away from mundane thinking.

Mugwort is essential for the witch who scries with mirrors and crystal spheres. To cleanse these psychic tools, move scrying tools through the smoke of mugwort incense or make an infusion and wash the reflective surface. An infusion is like making a tea. Place a teaspoon of mugwort in hot water (not quite boiling) and seep.

This plant helps in the understanding of dreams, so burn in your bedroom before sleep or make a dream pillow and add wormwood, lavender, and wood betony. Like all dried plants it can be made into a smudge stick or burnt on self-igniting charcoal. Mugwort incense is beneficial before any psychic work, Tarot reading, or channelling. Its magickal effect is amazing and helps the psychic reader achieve a trance-like state.

Open the door to other realms with the witch's mugwort.

Myrrh *(Commiphora myrrha)*: Resin and Essential Oil. *Perfume of Anubis.*

Myrrh is one of the oldest perfumes. The Egyptian jackal god Anubis used myrrh to consecrate the dead. Since ancient times it has been associated with the spirit world and the divine.

The scent of myrrh is warm and unusual compared to modern perfumes. Therefore, its woody fragrance transports you back in time. Myrrh is the perfume of the Underworld so is potent during hardship, grief, and disappointment. Myrrh heals because it connects you to spiritual purpose.

Combine powdered myrrh with any incense mix to heighten the magickal vibration. Mix with frankincense oil, or resin to connect the realms of the living and the spirit. Anoint candles with myrrh oil as an offering to the dead.

Connect with this ancient plant to open a portal to the spirit world.

Mullein *(Verbascum thapsus)*: Plant and Essential Oil. *Of Ghosts and Visions.*

Mullein is connected to spirits and the dreamworld, making it a divination plant. It is thought to also draw love and liberate courage. The dried leaves were once dipped in oil and used as ceremonial torches. Hence the plant brings vision in the dark and therefore insight.

Use to fill poppets and dream pillows combined with mugwort and wormwood. To communicate with spirits, blend mullein, frankincense, and orris in a pouch and add cypress oil. Hang in sachets in the home for protection. Mullein is a substitute for graveyard dust. Because of this, it can be placed in a bottle or pouch and be used to connect with the spirit world.

Orris Powder *(Iris germanica var. florentina)*: Plant. *Magnetic Dust.*

Orris powder is from the iris flower and has a violet scent. It has been used as a religious herb in ceremonies for the departed. Its fragrance brings peace to their souls. Iris is the goddess of the rainbow, a symbol of beginnings and hope. Orris is used for love, attraction, and divination. It is also protective, guarding your energy against negativity.

Add orris powder to incense mixes. Combine with pine and mugwort to cleanse wands with the air element. Orris absorbs oils so is good to add to any charm pouches. It is added to magick sprinkles to attract energy to you. As a divination incense, either burn alone or combine with sandalwood, rose, and lavender. Make an orris charm pouch and carry or place in your home for protection. Combine with Epsom salt for a protection wash.

Pine *(Pinus spp.)*: Resin and Essential Oil. *Banishing Darkness.*

Pine is highly potent in banishing and cleansing spells. The god, Attis, was said to be a pine tree so its magick is associated with rebirth and resurrection. It is a winter solstice resin but can be used any time.

Powder in a mortar and pestle and burn as incense to purify magickal objects. Add copal and white sage for a powerful banishing blend. Use pine oil to bless and raise hope. Combine oil with lemon or lime to invigorate the chakras and bring balance.

Call on the power of transformation with the magick of pine.

Rose *(Rosa spp.)*: Plant, Resin, and Essential Oil. *The Goddess Rises.*

Rose is the flower of Aphrodite and symbolizes beauty and the power of love. It embodies happiness and perfection. The flower is also linked to predictions and the spirit world. It can be the scent indicating a ghostly presence as well as a mystical experience. Rose is found in the myths and its image used in art, emblems, and alchemy. The word rosary comes from "rose garden," so roses are also seen as protective and healing. The flower brings a quality of mysticism to all intentions and can also be used in psychic work and to invoke success.

Rose has endless uses: fresh, dried, and as an oil. Use the oil for anointing your body, especially the heart. Wear to liberate the beauty of your spirit and to conjure the energy of romance. Blend with ylang-ylang and jasmine for a philtre to invoke the Moon Goddess. Anoint poppets and charms used for spirit communication and add to love charm pouches. Dried rose petals are added to incense mixes and sprinkles, bringing to them a heavenly scent.

Rosemary *(Rosmarinus officinalis)*: Plant and Essential Oil. *Spirit Visions.*

Rosemary can be easily grown and is a substitute for frankincense. It is a plant associated with birth as well as death, so is potent for initiation and transformation. It has been associated with marriage, attracting love, and also memory. It is a banishing herb. It is healing and protective.

Like rose, rosemary is a foundation ingredient in your witch's cabinet because it is powerful and can be used for any intentions. Burn dried rosemary as a purifying incense to dispel negativity and as an offering to the dead. Combine with rose resin and frankincense for spirit communication and with orris and copal to purify your home. Add herb and oil to bath sachets, charm pouches, and sprinkles for all intentions. Use for poppet magick and place fresh rosemary by your bed for protection. Use the essential oil for anointing the chakras and tools with spiritual energy. Wear through your hair to heighten memory and connect the mind to divine thoughts.

Rue *(Ruta graveolens)*: Plant and Essential Oil. *Witch's Herb.*

Rue is used for protection, dispelling, and hex-breaking. Hex-breaking means energetic cleansing and centring and the dispelling of fear and constant worry. It is also used to remove energy you may have absorbed from others so you are completely contained and yourself. It is a bath herb and has been associated with "grace," a sacred state of being. Rue has also been used in love magick.

Carry rue in a charm pouch to ward off negative energy. Create a cleansing wash and anointing water for magickal objects and to use on your body. Grind into a powder for a dispelling sprinkle and combine with orris, vervain, and rose oil. Place on the written word during hex-breaking spells and add to a protective poppet. Fresh rue can be used to sprinkle magick washes around your home.

Sandalwood White *(Santalum album)*: Plant and Essential Oil. *Third Eye Opens.*

Sandalwood brings the power of protection, love, and healing. It is an essential herb or oil in your cabinet because of its all-purpose qualities and unique scent. It has been used in Eastern mysticism for meditation and trance-work because it transports the senses into dream-like realms. It protects, dispels low vibrations, and is used for spirit communication and to imbue any intention with a lucky vibration. Sandalwood is also used as a wish-granting plant.

Use sandalwood in psychic and dispelling incense blends. Mix powder with lavender and rose and burn to speak with the departed. Use the oil as a full moon anointing philtre and mix with lemon oil to enhance intuition. Use to fill a wishing poppet in combination with rue, witch hazel, and straw. To enhance creativity, create a sandalwood pouch and add patchouli oil. Sprinkle on a written wish and on a letter dedication. Rub oil on your hands and move through your aura to dispel unwanted energy.

St. John's Wort *(Hypericum perforatum)*: (Poisonous) Plant. *Baldur's Light.*

St. John's Wort is associated with dispelling energy and banishing harmful spirits. It lifts the spirits out of depression, bringing with it the vibration of courage as well as happiness. Its powers align with strength, love, and divination. It is associated with the Norse god of light, Baldur, who emanated brightness and joy.

Use the plant to create a circle and as a happiness sprinkle. Combine with vervain and copal in a charm to lighten the mind. Fill a protective poppet to invoke love. Carry a pouch of St. John's Wort when courage and confidence are needed.

Vervain *(Verbena officinalis)*: Plant and Essential Oil. *Peaceful Shrine.*

Vervain is another all-purpose witch's plant emanating the spirit of purification, peace, and love. It consecrates and imbues the energy of peace when in contact. Vervain draws romance in your life and is considered a plant of artists.

Carry vervain when creating art or during a performance of any kind. Burn or use as a wash to enchant and cleanse your witch's tools. Sprinkle a vervain infusion in your circle to create a hallowed vibration and infuse with rose and rosemary to attract true and lasting love. Create a magick powder for peace and harmony with vervain, white sage, and juniper. Place in a pouch and carry or sprinkle over written spells and candles.

Wormwood *(Artemisia absinthium)*: (Poisonous) Plant and Essential Oil. *Caller of Spirits.*

Wormwood is a potent protective herb and a conjurer for spirit communication. It is the patron plant of herbalists and was sacred to Artemis. Wormwood banishes anger by directing it into creative and peaceful expression. It is a visionary plant that calls in spirits. Contact with it increases your psychic abilities and everyday intuition.

Create an incense blend of wormwood and mugwort for psychic powers and the understanding of dreams. This blend expands the imagination, so it will enhance creativity and vision. Use wormwood in protective pouches and in sprinkles for protective charms and poppets. To transform anger, carry and inhale the plant's scent. You can also place the pouch on your brow and heart.

Smudges and Bundles

Herb bundles and wood are burnt to clear a place of unwanted energy and to invoke a sacred vibration.

Cedar *(Cedrus libani or C. spp.)*: *Prayer to the Sky.*

Cedar provides harmony, protection, and clarity. Incense of cedar is often used to carry prayers to the Divine; its fragrance expands and clarifies the mind.

Common Sage *(Salvia officinalis)*

Gallic Druids used common sage for divination[316] and in fifteenth-century Italy, wishes were written on the leaves and eaten.[317] The ancient Egyptians used it to promote fertility.[318] When burnt, the smoke dispels unwanted energy; it purifies and creates a sacred atmosphere.

---

316. De Cleene and Lejeune, *Compendium of Symbolic and Ritual Plants in Europe, Vol 1*, 669.

317. De Cleene and Lejeune, *Compendium of Symbolic and Ritual Plants in Europe, Vol 1*, 669.

318. De Cleene and Lejeune, *Compendium of Symbolic and Ritual Plants in Europe, Vol 1*, 669.

Eucalyptus Leaves *(Eucalyptus spp. globulus)*: *Leaf of Ceremony.*
Dry leaves are used to purify a space and to invoke sacred intervention. Also use as essential oil.

Palo Santo *(Bursera graveolens)*: *Holy Wood.*
Palo Santo comes from a holy tree in South America that is related to frankincense. The wood is burnt to invoke the sacred, to dispel unwanted energy, and to attract good fortune.

Sweetgrass *(Hierochloe odorata)*: *Spirit Smoke.*
Sweetgrass is burnt to invoke positive energy and to call on Mother Earth. It is also used to call in spirits.

White Sage *(Salvia apiana)*: *Grandfather.*
First Nations people of America have used white sage bundles for generations. In this tradition, smudging with white sage is deeply connected to spiritual aspirations, ceremony, and knowledge. The sacred smoke from a smouldering smudge stick is used in purification and blessing rituals and for prayer. (See Ethics and Care).

Bewitching Oils

A philtre is a blend of natural oils that creates an enchanting scent and magickal vibration. Roots, berries, crystals, or other objects can be added to the blend for potency.

The witch uses specific oils and philtres to anoint herself, others, or sacred items. Oils and philtres are used in the creation of charms, to anoint written spells and candles, and to charge ritual objects. To anoint is to acknowledge and activate the sacredness of a person or object. Anointing also dispels unwanted energy. Charging invigorates the object with a magickal vibration. Refer to Ethics and Care before choosing essential oils.

Base Oils

Olive oil (*Olea europaea L.*) is often used in spells or combined with essential oil. Olive oil is symbolic of the mystical light as it was originally used to light lamps. Almond base oil (*Prunus dulcis*) holds the energy of fertility and growth.

Essential Oils

Basil *(Ocimum basilicum)*: Love, Wealth, Faeries Magick.

Bay *(Laurus nobilis)*: Magnetic, Healing, Psychic, Wishes.

Bergamot *(Mentha citrata)*: Prosperity, Hex-Breaking, Luck.

Black Pepper *(Piper nigrum)*: Dispelling, Banishing, Purifying.

Borage *(Borago officinalis)*: Bravery, Psychic Powers, Intuition.

Cedar *(Cedrus libani or C. spp.)*: Healing, Protection, Purification, Money.

Chamomile, Roman *(Chamaemelum nobile, Anthemis nobilis)*: Meditation, Sleep, Purification.

Cinnamon *(Cinnamomum zeylanicum)*: Spirituality, Success, Healing.

Clary Sage *(Salvia sclarea)*: Love, Protection, Calming.

Clove *(Eugenia caryophyllus, Syzygium aromaticum, or Caryophyllus aromaticus)*: Abundance, Love, Protection, Exorcism.

Cypress *(Cupressus sempervirens)*: Healing, Grief, Protection.

Eucalyptus *(Eucalyptus spp. globulus)*: Banishing, Protection, Purification.

Frankincense *(Boswellia carterii)*: Protection, Exorcism, Spirituality.

Galangal *(Alpinia officinarum or A. galanga)*: Psychic Powers, Hex-Breaking.

Geranium *(Geranium maculatum or P. odoratissimum)*: Love, Protection, Growth.

Ginger *(Zingiber officinale)*: Love, Wealth, Luck, Confidence.

Hyssop *(Hyssopus officinalis)*: Purification, Banishing, Protection.

Jasmine *(Jasminum grandiflorum, J. officinale, or J. odoratissimum)*: Love, Prophetic Dreams, Moon Magick.

Juniper *(Juniperus communis)*: Protection, Exorcism, Friendship.

Lavender *(Lavandula officinalis or L. vera)*: Love, Protection, Happiness, Peace.

Lemon *(Citrus limon)*: Psychic Energy, Moon Magick, Love.

Lemongrass *(Cymbopogon citratus)*: Psychic Powers, Intuition, Passion.

Lemon Verbena *(Lippia citriodora)*: Love, Purification, Attraction.

Lime *(Citrus aurantifolia or L. Limetta)*: Anti-Hex, Creativity, Confidence.

Neroli *(Citrus aurantium)*: Spirituality, Calming, Balance.

Nutmeg *(Myristica fragrans)*: Prosperity, Success, Vitality.

Orange *(Citrus sinensis)*: Luck, Love, Prosperity, Divination.

Palmarosa *(Cymbopogon martini)*: Sensuality, Love, Healing.

Patchouli *(Pogostemon cablin or P. patchouli)*: Money, Fertility, Passion, Attraction.

Pine *(Pinus spp.)*: Healing, Fertility, Protection, Exorcism.

Peppermint *(Mentha piperita)*: Purification, Healing, Psychic Powers.

Rose *(Rosa spp.)*: Goddess Magick, Love, Peace, Divinity.

Rosemary *(Rosmarinus officinalis)*: Protection, Dispelling, Spirituality.

Sage Oil *(Salvia officinalis)*: Wisdom, Spirituality, Purification.

Tea Tree *(Melaleuca alternifolia)*: Banishing, Healing, Protection.

Thyme *(Thymus vulgaris)*: Healing, Psychic Powers, Courage.

Tuberose *(Polianthes tuberosa)*: Romance, Joy, Dreams.

Ylang-Ylang *(Cananga odorata)*: Sensuality, Inner Beauty, Love.

Salts

Common Salt: Represents the earth element in spells. Salt is used for purifying, dispelling, and protection. The witch can create the spell circle with salt or create other symbols with it, such as a pentagram. Essential oils can be added to salt for a charm pouch or a healing bath. Sacred objects can be placed into salt for cleansing, as can some crystals.

Black Salt: Black salt is created from the cauldron's ash and iron mixed with salt. Adding black pepper *(Piper nigrum)* to white salt can also create witch's black salt. It is highly protective and dispelling. There is another black salt that can be ingested. It is a volcanic rock salt with a high sulphur content. This can be used for any Underworld or fire magick.

Epsom Salt: Used for purification and aura cleansing. Add desired essential oils, herbs, and colour for a magickal bath or use alone to cleanse your aura.

Rock Salt: Used to line the bottom of a censer when using charcoal disks; this allows air to move under the disk for easier burning. Incense sticks can also be stood up in rock salt.

APPENDIX
Correspondence

The Magick of Colours

Colours resonate with a mystical vibration. You select the colour of a candle, ink, or material according to the intention of the spell.

Red: *Fire Element:* Action, Manifestation, Passion, Banishment, Protection, Love, Health, and Motivation.

Base 1st Chakra: Survival, Family, Belonging, Connects the Witch to Mother Earth.

Orange: Energy, Luck, Creativity, Joy, and Vitality.

Sacral 2nd Chakra: Creativity, Sexuality, Well-Being, Pleasure.

Yellow: *Air Element:* The Mind, Inspiration, Direction, Travel, and Self-Esteem.

Solar Plexus 3rd Chakra: Self-Worth, Confidence, Discipline, Attainment.

Green: *Earth Element:* Healing, Grounding, Prosperity, Faery Magick.

Heart 4th Chakra: Feelings, Love, Serenity, Peace, Connection.

Pink: Romance, Friendship, and Forgiveness.

Heart 4th Chakra: Feelings, Love, Serenity, Peace, Connection.

Blue: *Water Element:* Emotions, Intuition, Dreams, Cleansing, and Rejuvenation.

Throat 5th Chakra: Truth, Communication, and Expression.

Indigo: Tranquillity, Intuition, Mysticism, and Psychic Vision.

Brow 6th Chakra: Psychic Ability, Imagination, Awareness, and Choice.

White: Peace, Beginnings, Spirituality, and Innocence.

Crown 7th Chakra: Spirituality, Divinity, Connection to the Universe.

Violet/ Purple: Divine Energy, the Ethereal, and Transcendence.

Crown 7th Chakra: Spirituality, Divinity, Connection to the Universe.

Black: Banishing, Courage, the Underworld, Mysteries, Unknown, and the Void.

Brown: Animal Magick, Tree Magick, Nature, Earth Magick, and Grounding.

Silver: Moon Magick, Goddess Magick, and Hope.

Gold: Solar and God Magick, Power and Enlightenment, Happiness, and Success.

Crown 7th Chakra: Spirituality, Divinity, Connection to the Universe.

The Magick of Numbers

Numerology is a fascinating study, complex with knowledge. The foundations of numerology were created by Pythagoras, a Greek philosopher born 570 BC.[319] The interest in the meaning, themes, and mysticism of numbers has been studied ever since.

Numbers, like all things, resonate an energetic vibration. Numbers are used in spells for knot magick, say tying eight knots on a cord for strength. For incantations, repeat words three times for a wish. The number of ingredients, including the number of candles chosen, say two for a love-binding spell. The number of amulets chosen, say four coins for a prosperity spell; or for an action, say moving a charm through incense smoke seven times for spirituality. The written number also vibrates a magickal energy so you can write numbers in written spells according to your purpose. The mystical power of numbers is encapsulated into geom-

---

319. Schimmel, *The Mystery of Numbers*, 11.

etry and magickal shapes as seen in chapter 11. This is a very basic list, including only numbers one to ten. May it inspire further discovery of the mysticism of numbers.

1. Beginning, Creation, Action, Independence, Personal Power, Determination, Creativity.
2. Romance, Relationships, Cooperation, Friendship, Community, Diplomacy, Choice, Opposites.
3. Manifestation, Wishes, Aspirations, Insight, Creative Expression, Innovation, Art, Vision.
4. Foundation, Prosperity, Money, Structure, Practicality, Systems, Logic, Concentration, Methods.
5. Freedom, Wildness, Sensuality, Adventure, Protection, Faith, Blessings, Life, Fifth Element, Spirit.
6. Family, Ideals, Harmony, Peace, Goodwill, Sacrifice, the Home.
7. Unites Physical and Spiritual Realms, Spirituality, Intuition, Wisdom, Meaning, Purpose.
8. Luck, Success, Business, Strength, Endurance, Balance, Organization, Justice.
9. Intellect, Completion, Attainment, Compassion, Empathy, Powerful in Spells as 3x3=9 (amplifies manifestation).
10. Wholeness, Potential, Exploration, Perfection, Confidence.

Days and Metals of the 7 Ancient Planets

The days of the week were first devised by the ancient Babylonians and named after the seven known heavenly bodies. Metals and characteristics became associated with the planets in ritual traditions. The creation of talismans and astrology are part of the witch's knowledge today.

Sun	Moon	Mars	Mercury	Jupiter	Venus	Saturn
☉	☾	♂	☿	♃	♀	♄
Sunday	Monday	Tuesday	Wednesday	Thursday	Friday	Saturday

Figure 10: Planetary Symbols

Sunday

"Day of the Sun": Old English, Latin, Greek, and Germanic origins.
Planet: The Sun
Metal: Gold

The precious metal gold is thought to have arrived on Earth in asteroids created during the explosions of supernovas. It has always been associated with beauty and divinity and defined the enlightenment that alchemists strived to create by changing lead into dazzling gold.

Gold is of the Sun, so is often associated with the gods. It is protective and enhances power, luck, and wisdom. Gold is the ultimate alchemical metal depicting illumination and oneness with the divine. It is associated with the gnomes and their cleverness, with money, and is the treasure everyone hopes to find both symbolically and literally.

Crowns are often made from gold to denote rulership and spiritual knowledge and jewellery made of gold in many traditions holds the quality of magick and guards the wearer.

The Sun in astrology encompasses what drives your life, your creativity, and lifeforce. The Sun rules the conscious mind, confidence, and will. The Sun is what you are, your identity, and how you shine. It is the "light" of your natal chart, the central force of the planets that revolve around the solar system. It is Father, male energy, and active. The Sun's energy inspires happiness and brings illumination.

For success: Write your name on paper with gold ink. Draw a circle around it and then imagine your spirit, heart, mind, and body imbued with gold as you burn the paper on a candle flame.

Monday

"Day of the Moon": Old English, Latin, Greek, and Germanic origins.
Planet: The Moon
Metal: Silver

Silver is found in the Earth's crust and more rarely in rivers. Like gold, it is thought to have been formed by supernovas. Silver is the best conductor of heat as well as electricity and can reflect light, hence its association with the moon.

Silver is the metal of the Goddess and chalices are often silver. It enhances psychic insight and balances the heart. Silver coins represent the moon and are placed in water to scry. Witches often wear silver to connect with the sacred feminine.

In astrology, the moon is also Mother and the unconscious. It rules your inner world and the unknown, your secrets and dreams. It is reactive, protective, as well as open. The moon is imagination, intuition, and harbours the wild and untamed within you.

To merge with the Goddess: Imagine a silver chalice filling with moonlight. The cup overflows with light; it reaches your hand and fills your entire being with brightness.

Tuesday

"Tiw's Day": Old English
"Day of Mars": Latin
"Day of Ares": Greek
Planet: Mars
Metal: Iron

Iron was known as the "metal from the heavens" because it came from the stars in the form of meteorites. Iron is found in the earth mixed with other types of rock.

Iron is protective and was once used for weapons. Iron nails are used in witch's bottles and other charms to ward off negative energy. It is a magnetic metal and is said to absorb any other energy, rendering that energy ineffective. Horseshoes were originally made from iron and have always been considered lucky, a talisman in alliance with divine forces. Ritual and religious objects were often made from iron and the ancient Egyptians called the crashing rocks from the sky "the gift of Seth."

In astrology, Mars rules our energy and desire, our passion and inner warrior. Mars is raw energy, sexuality, the fighter, and the adventurer within us. Named after the god of war, Mars fires us up, fuelling our aggression as well as our determination.

To banish fear: Imagine forging an iron sword and shield. Take up these magickal weapons and ask your fears to rise before you. Then transform your fears through the blade of the sword. As the blade touches them, see what they become.

Wednesday

"Day of Woden": Old English
"Day of Hermes": Greek
"Day of Mercury": Latin
Planet: Mercury
Metal: Quicksilver

Quicksilver is also called mercury and is highly poisonous, so should never be handled or used in a spell. Because of its mobility it was named after the fastest-moving planet, hence the winged-footed god Mercury.

Mercury rules messages and communication. It is the planet of ideas, the written word, and speech. Ruled by air, Mercury is of the intellect and mind. By nature quicksilver is toxic and harmful, so should only be used in the imagination.

For new direction: Imagine a liquid silver river. Mercury himself awaits you at its edge. He hands you wings for your feet and a winged hat. Together you glide through the silver river. Allow it to take you somewhere new.

Thursday

"Thor's Day": Norse
"Thunder's Day": Old English
"Day of Jupiter": Latin
"Day of Zeus": Greek
Planet: Jupiter
Metal: Tin

Jupiter holds the moist and warm characteristics of the element air and tin is also associated with this element. The fifteenth-century occultist Agrippa describes the metal's association with the planet due to the ease with which the metal can be worked with. Jupiter's magick creates growth and expansion in your life. The ability to preserve food in containers of tin may also be a reason for the partnership as Jupiter is associated with preservation, particularly with youth. A sheet of shaken tin makes a thunder-like sound that calls to the realm of the thunder gods Jupiter and Zeus.

In astrology, Jupiter is the planet of abundance and good fortune. The planet's energy seeks insight and knowledge and assists you to reach purpose and consider possibilities. It is the planet of optimism, humour, and good will.

To invoke luck: In your imagination, take a shiny piece of reflective tin and fashion a bottle from it. Go under the night sky and hold the bottle towards Jupiter, the gigantic orb of white, orange, red, and brown. Imagine the essence of luck flowing from the planet into the bottle. Each day imagine taking a sip of the "essence of luck."

Friday

"Freya's Day": Norse
"Venus's Day": Latin
"Day of Aphrodite": Greek
Planet: Venus
Metal: Copper

Copper was one of the earliest metals used. Decorative items were fashioned from it in Mesopotamia and the ancient Egyptians used it for mirrors, instruments, and adornments. The mining of copper in Cyprus, the home of Venus, may have associated the metal with the goddess of love and therefore her planet. A temple dedicated to Hathor was constructed in Egypt at copper mines in ancient Timna. The beautiful ornaments and personal adornments created with copper may have called the energy of attraction to mind and therefore the marriage of the metal to a planet associated with beauty and pleasure.

Copper is conductive so is often used for wands to draw. A wand of copper calls energy in and holds it in the grasp of your will.

Copper is also essential for the health of the body, enabling it to form red blood cells associating the metal with the youth and vitality of Venus. In astrology, Venus rules love and relationships. The planet's astrological influence embodies values, ascetics, and pleasures. Through Venus we learn about art, true beauty, and happiness. Grace, charm, and sensuality unfold in the arms of Venus and therefore her precious metal.

For truth: Imagine the goddess of love, Venus, handing you a piece of glowing copper. The material is soft and it is easy for you to create a spectacular mirror out of it. Imagine gazing into its surface every day to see what is truly valuable in your life.

Saturday
"Saturn's Day": Old English and Latin
"Day of Cronus": Greek
Planet: Saturn
Metal: Lead

Lead is a heavy metal that reflects the fatherly wrath of Saturn's energy as well as the planet's slow rotation around the Sun of approximately twenty-eight years. At the same time, it is soft and malleable with a low melting point. The ancient alchemist quest was to change lead into gold. This was symbolic of the quest to transform consciousness into divine enlightenment symbolised by the sun's own metal.

The classical Greeks associated lead with Cronus, Father Time. His emblem was the sickle or scythe, a symbol that speaks of death and his planet was Saturn.

Lead is found in the Earth's crust and is toxic, so its magickal uses should remain in the imagination.

In astrology, Saturn is the teacher and father figure. He reveals our limitations as well as our responsibilities, so the planet represents authority, structure, and self-control. The lessons of Saturn are difficult, but you transform through them.

For transformation: Imagine a dull, grey piece of lead; it represents your pain and fears and has been handed to you by Saturn. Hold a vessel towards the sun and fill it with light. Now pour this onto the lead and watch as it gradually changes to gold.

Bibliography

Agrippa, Henry Cornelius. *Three Books of Occult Philosophy*. Edited and Annotated by Donald Tyson, Translated by James Freake. St. Paul MN: Llewellyn Publications, 1998.

Andrews, Ted. *Animal Speak: The Spiritual and Magical Powers of Creatures Great and Small*. St. Paul, MN: Llewellyn Publications, 1998.

Baring, Anne, and Jules Cashford. *The Myth of the Goddess: Evolution of an Image*. London: Penguin Books Ltd, 1993.

Becker, Udo, ed. *The Element Encyclopedia of Symbols*. Trans. Lance W. Garmer. New York: The Continuum Publishing Company, 1996.

Beyerl, Paul. *The Master Book of Herbalism*. Washington: Phoenix Publishing Co., 1984.

Briggs, Katharine. *An Encyclopedia of Fairies: Hobgoblins, Brownies, Bogies, and Other Supernatural Creatures*. London: Penguin Books, 1977.

Buckland, Raymond. *The Witch Book: The Encyclopedia of Witchcraft, Wicca, and Neopaganism*. Canton, MI: Visible Ink Press, 2002.

Bulfinch, Thomas. *Bulfinch's Complete Mythology*. London: Hamlyn Publishing Group Limited, 1989.

Burland, C. A. *Myths of Life and Death*. London: Macmillan, 1974.

Cambell, Joseph. *Goddesses: Mysteries of the Feminine Divine*, edited by Safron Rossi. Novato California: New World Library, 2013.

Chevalier, Jean, and Alain Gheerbrant. *The Penguin Dictionary of Symbols*. Trans. John Buchanan-Brown. London: Penguin Press, 1996.

Conway, D. J. *Magical Mythical Mystical Beasts: How to Invite Them into Your Life*. St. Paul, MN: Llewellyn Publications, 1996.

Cooper, J. C. *An Illustrated Encyclopedia of Traditional Symbols*. London: Thames and Hudson, 1978.

Cotterell, Arthur, and Rachel Storm. *The Ultimate Encyclopedia of Mythology*. London: Anness Publishing Ltd, 1999.

Cunningham, Scott. *Cunningham's Encyclopedia of Magical Herbs*. St. Paul, MN: Llewellyn Publications, 2000.

Cunningham, Scott. *The Complete Book of Incense, Oils and Brews*. St. Paul, MN: Llewellyn Publications, 1991.

Cusack, Carole M. *The Sacred Tree: Ancient and Medieval Manifestations*. Newcastle Upon Tyne: Cambridge Scholars Publishing, 2011.

Davies, Owen. *Grimoires: A History of Magic Books*. New York: Oxford University Press, 2009.

De Cleene, Marcel, and Marie Claire Lejeune. *Compendium of Symbolic and Ritual Plants in Europe*. Ghent, Belgium: Man and Culture Publishers, 2003.

Drury, Nevill. *The Watkins Dictionary of Magic*. London: Watkins Publishing, 2005.

Evans-Wentz, W. Y. *The Fairy Faith in Celtic Countries*. Library of the Mystic Arts Edition. New York: Citadel Press, 1994.

Farrar, Janet, and Stewart Farrar. *The Witches' God*. Blaine, WA, Phoenix Publishing Inc., 2008.

Farrar, Janet, and Stewart Farrar. *The Witches' Goddess*. Blaine, WA, Phoenix Publishing Inc., 1987.

Flowers, Stephen E. *The Galdrabók: An Icelandic Book of Magic*. Second, Revised Edition. Smithville, TX: Rûna-Raven Press, 2005.

Franklin, Anna. *Working With Fairies: Magick, Spells, Potions, and Recipes to Attract and See Them*. New Jersey: Career Press, 2006.

Frazer, J. G. *The Golden Bough: A Study in Magic and Religion*. London: Papermac, 1994.

González-Wippler, Migene. *The Complete Book of Amulets and Talismans*. St. Paul, MN: Llewellyn Publications, 1991.

Grimassi, Raven. *Italian Witchcraft: The Old Religion of Southern Europe*. St. Paul, MN: Llewellyn Publications, 2000.

Grimassi, Raven. *The Witch's Craft: The Roots of Witchcraft and Magical Transformation*. St. Paul, MN: Llewellyn Publications, 2002.

Grimassi, Raven. *Encyclopedia of Wicca and Witchcraft*. St. Paul, MN: Llewellyn Publications, 2000.

Gundarsson, Kveldulf. *Teutonic Magic: The Magical and Spiritual Practices of the Germanic Peoples*. St. Paul, MN: Llewellyn Publications, 1990.

Guiley, Rosemary Ellen. *The Encyclopedia of Witches and Witchcraft*. New York: Facts on File, Inc., 1989.

Hall, Manly P. *The Secret Teachings of All Ages*. New York: Jeremy P. Tarcher/Penguin, 2003.

Hoffman, John George. *Pow-Wows: Or, Long Lost Friend*. Middletown, DE: Forgotten Books, 2007.

Huxley, Francis. *The Eye: The Seer and the Seen*. London: Thames and Hudson, 1990.

Jung, Carl. *Man and His Symbols*. London: Picador, 1978.

Lecouteux, Claude. *Encyclopedia of Norse and Germanic Folklore, Mythology and Magic*. Translated by Jon E. Graham. Rochester, VT: Inner Traditions International, 2016.

Leitch, Aaron. *Secrets of the Magickal Grimoires: The Classical Texts of Magick Deciphered*. Woodbury, MN: Llewellyn Publications, 2016.

Leland, Charles G. *Aradia: Gospel of the Witches*. Washington: Pheonix Publishing, Inc., 1996.

Le Strange, Richard. *A History of Herbal Plants*. London: Angus and Robertson, 1977.

Lethbridge, T. C. *Witches: Investigating an Ancient Religion*. 6th Edition. New York: Routledge, 1962.

Lurker, Manfred. *An Illustrated Dictionary of the Gods and Symbols of Ancient Egypt*. English Language Edition. London: Thames and Hudson Ltd, 1995.

Mankey, Jason, and Laura Tempest Zakroff. *The Witch's Altar: The Craft, Lore and Magick of Sacred Space*. Woodbury, MN: Llewellyn Publications, 2019.

Markale, Jean. *The Great Goddess: Reverence of the Divine Feminine from the Paleolithic to the Present*. Translated by Jody Gladding. Rochester, Vermont: Inner Traditions International, 1999.

Mathers, S. Liddell MacGregor, tr. and ed. *The Key of Solomon the King*. Maine: Samuel Weiser, Inc., 1989.

McCoy, Daniel. *The Viking Spirit: An Introduction to Norse Mythology and Religion*. Kentucky: CreateSpace Independent Publishing Platform, 2016.

McCoy, Edain. *Sabbats: A Witch's Approach to Living the Old Ways*. St. Paul, MN: Llewellyn Publications, 2003.

Monaghan, Patricia. *The New Book of Goddesses and Heroines*. St. Paul, MN: Llewellyn Publications, 1997.

Murray, Alexander S. *Who's Who in Mythology: A Classic Guide to the Ancient World*. London: Bracken Books, 1994.

Nozedar, Adele. *The Illustrated Signs and Symbols Sourcebook: An A to Z Compendium of Over 1000 Designs*. London: HarperCollins, 2010.

Paracelsus. *Selected Writings*. Edited by Jolande Jacobi. New Jersey: Princeton University Press, 1988.

Pickering, David. *Dictionary of Witchcraft*. London: Cassell, 1996.

Potter, Carole. *A–Z of Superstitions*. London: Chancellor Press, 1993.

Roob, Alexander. *Alchemy and Mysticism*. Translated by Shaun Whiteside. Koln: Taschen GmbH, 2005.

Ronnberg, Ami, and Kathleen Martin, eds. *The Book of Symbols: Reflections on Archetypal Images*. Cologne, Germany: Taschen GMBH, 2010.

Russell, Jeffrey B., and Brooks Alexander. *A History of Witchcraft: Sorcerers, Heretics, and Pagans*. London: Thames and Hudson Ltd, 2007.

Schimmel, Annemarie. *The Mystery of Numbers*. New York: Oxford University Press, 1993.

Sjöö, Monica, and Barbara Mor. *The Great Cosmic Mother: Rediscovering the Religion of the Earth*. New York: HarperCollins Publishers. Reprint with new introduction, 1987.

Stone, Merlin. *Ancient Mirrors of Womanhood: A Treasury of Goddess and Heroine Lore from Around the World*. Boston: Beacon Press, 1990.

Trismegistus, Hermes. *The Emerald Tablet of Hermes*. Dublin: Merchant Books, 2013.

Walker, Barbara G. *The Woman's Dictionary of Symbols and Sacred Objects*. London: HarperCollins, 1995.

Walker, Barbara G. *The Woman's Encyclopedia of Myths and Secrets*. San Francisco: HarperCollins, 1985.

Willis, Roy, ed. *World Mythology: The Illustrated Guide*. London: Duncan Baird Publishers, 1996.

Yeats, William Butler. *Fairy and Folk Tales of the Irish Peasantry*. New York: Dover Publications Inc., 2014.

Online References

"350,000 types of plants." B10NUMB3R5. The Database of Useful Biological Numbers. Accessed December 28, 2020. https://bionumbers.hms.harvard.edu/bionumber.aspx?id=113395&ver=0&trm=plant&org=.

"Athame." Liquisearch.com. Accessed August 21, 2020, http://www.liquisearch.com/athame/etymology.

Beech, E., M. Rivers, S. Oldfield, and P. P. Smith. "GlobalTreeSearch: The first complete global database of tree species and country distributions." *Journal of Sustainable Forestry*. 36:5 (2017): 454–489, doi: 10.1080/10549811.2017.1310049.

English–Latin translation of "Witch," Glosbe.com. Accessed August 21, 2020. https://glosbe.com/en/la/witch.

"Familiar." Online Etymology Dictionary. Accessed August 21, 2020. https://www.etymonline.com/word/familiar.

"Fascinate." Online Etymology Dictionary. Accessed August 21, 2020. https://www.etymonline.com/word/fascinate.

"Genius." Encyclopedia Mythica, Roman Mythology. Accessed August 21, 2020. Page created Monday March 3, 1997. https://pantheon.org/articles/g/genius.html.

"Grimnismál - The Ballad of Grimnir." Stanza 5, Völuspá.org. Accessed August 21, 2020. http://www.voluspa.org/grimnismal.htm.

"History." National Candle Association. Accessed August 20, 2020. https://candles.org/history/.

"Pharmakis." Online Etymology Dictionary. Accessed August 21, 2020. https://www.etymonline.com/word/pharmacy.

"Spell." Online Etymology Dictionary. Accessed August 21, 2020. https://www.etymonline.com/word/spell.

"Vahana." The Editors of Encyclopedia Britannica. Accessed August 23, 2020. https://www.britannica.com/topic/vahana.

"Wand." Online Etymology Dictionary. Accessed August 21, 2020. https://www.etymonline.com/word/wand#etymonline_v_4817.

To Write to the Author

If you wish to contact the author or would like more information about this book, please write to the author in care of Llewellyn Worldwide Ltd. and we will forward your request. Both the author and the publisher appreciate hearing from you and learning of your enjoyment of this book and how it has helped you. Llewellyn Worldwide Ltd. cannot guarantee that every letter written to the author can be answered, but all will be forwarded. Please write to:

Danae Moon Thorp
℅ Llewellyn Worldwide
2143 Wooddale Drive
Woodbury, MN 55125-2989
Please enclose a self-addressed stamped envelope for reply,
or $1.00 to cover costs. If outside the U.S.A., enclose
an international postal reply coupon.

Many of Llewellyn's authors have websites with additional
information and resources. For more information,
please visit our website at http://www.llewellyn.com.